YOU STILL CALL YOUR PARENTS MOMMY AND DADDY?
O-OLD HABITS DIE HARD, OKAY?
カァ…
BLUSH

Four Knights of [the Apoc]alypse

8

Nakaba Suzuki Presents

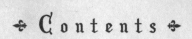

❖ Contents ❖

Four Knights
Of The Apocalypse

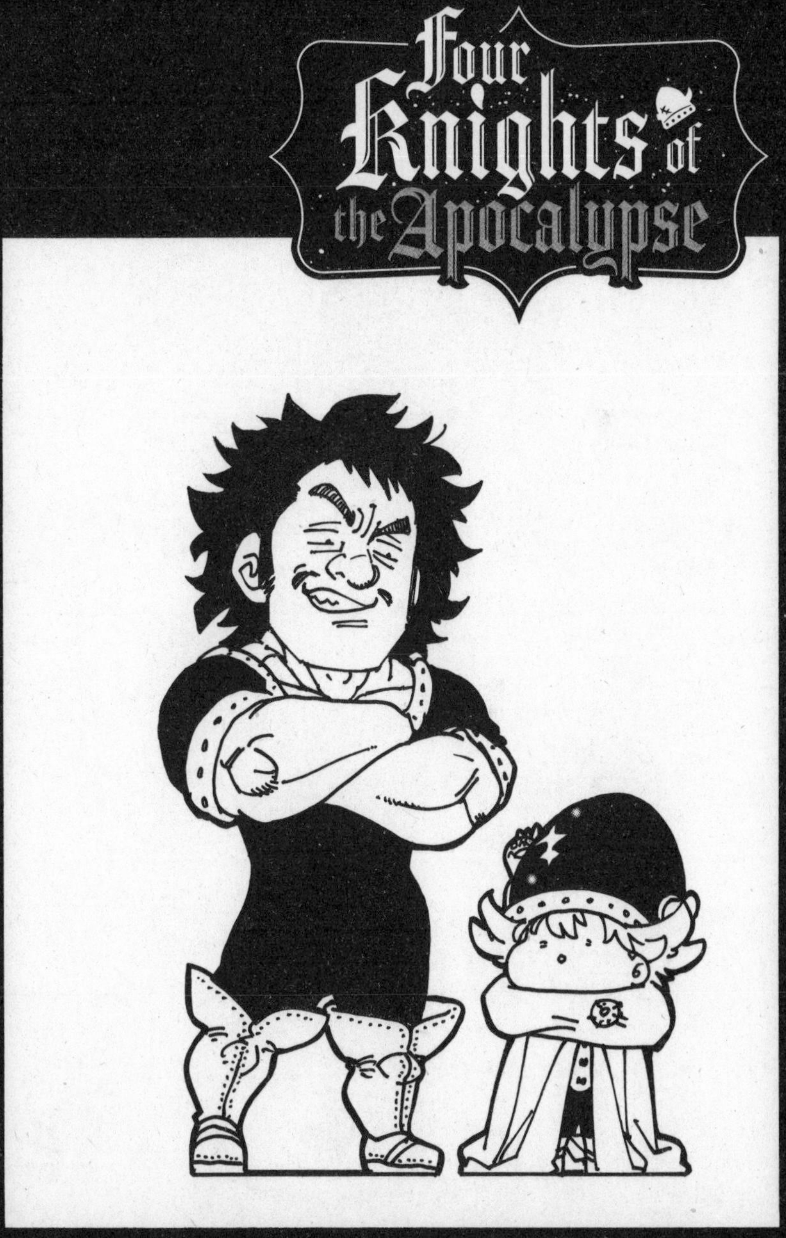
Four Knights of the Apocalypse

CHAPTER 60: LIONES IN FLAMES

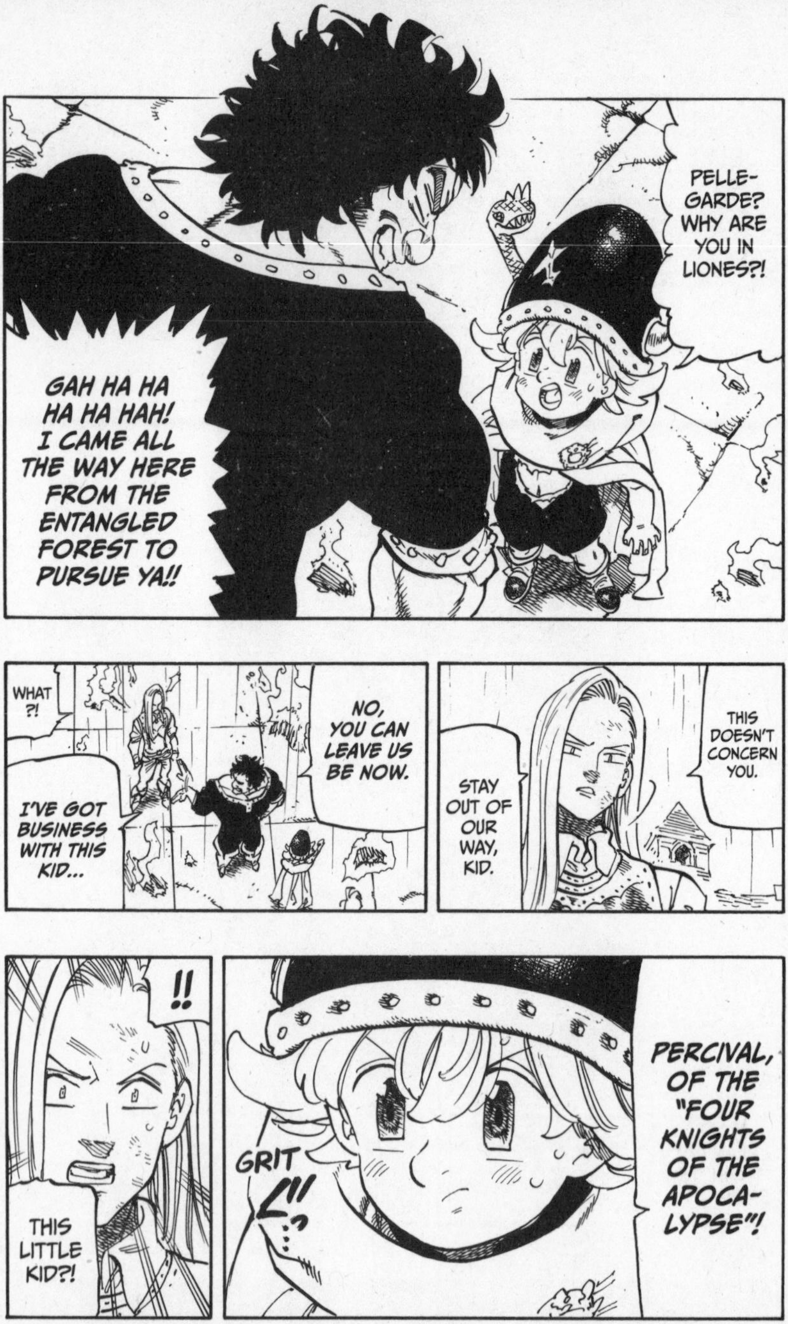
PELLE-GARDE? WHY ARE YOU IN LIONES?!
GAH HA HA HA HA HAH! I CAME ALL THE WAY HERE FROM THE ENTANGLED FOREST TO PURSUE YA!!
THIS DOESN'T CONCERN YOU.
STAY OUT OF OUR WAY, KID.
NO, YOU CAN LEAVE US BE NOW.
WHAT ?!
I'VE GOT BUSINESS WITH THIS KID...
PERCIVAL, OF THE "FOUR KNIGHTS OF THE APOCA-LYPSE"!
GRIT
!!
THIS LITTLE KID?!

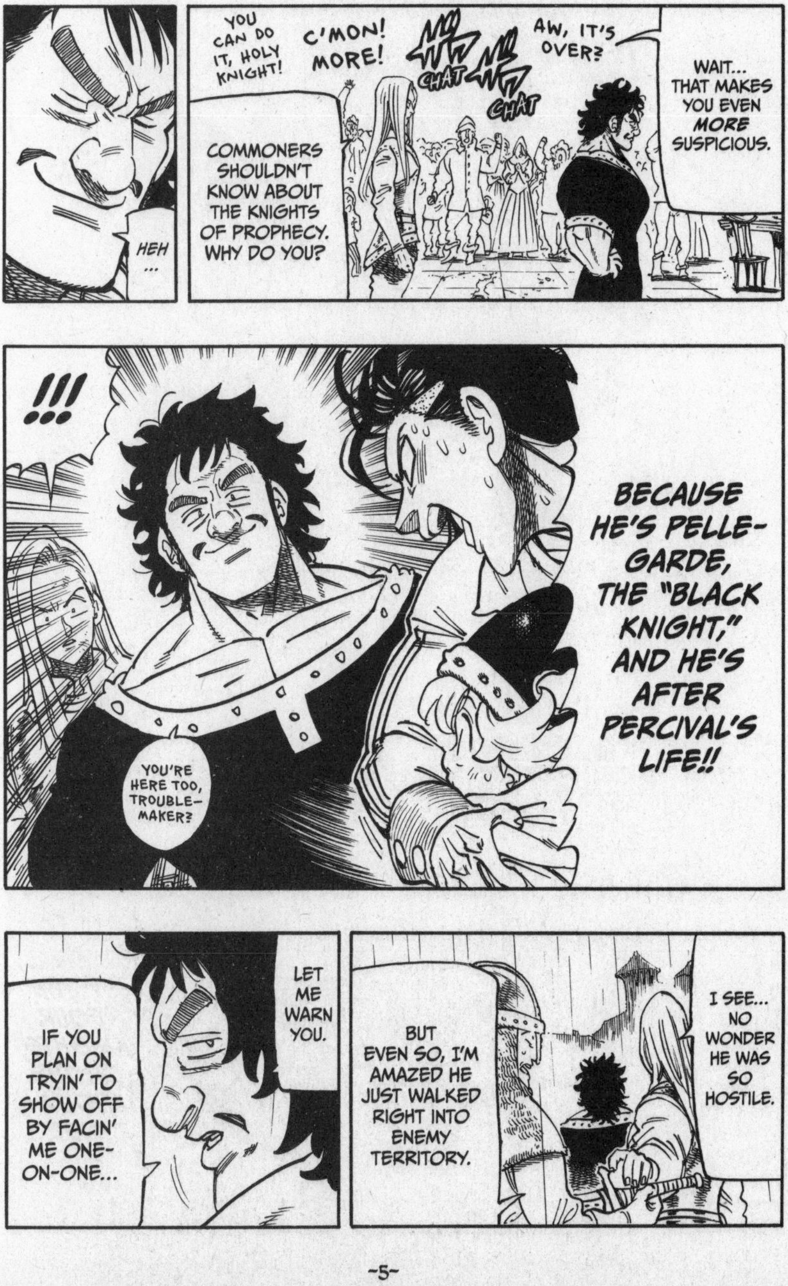
WAIT... THAT MAKES YOU EVEN MORE SUSPICIOUS.
AW, IT'S OVER?
CHAT
CHAT
C'MON! MORE!
YOU CAN DO IT, HOLY KNIGHT!
COMMONERS SHOULDN'T KNOW ABOUT THE KNIGHTS OF PROPHECY. WHY DO YOU?
HEH...
BECAUSE HE'S PELLEGARDE, THE "BLACK KNIGHT," AND HE'S AFTER PERCIVAL'S LIFE!!
!!!
YOU'RE HERE TOO, TROUBLEMAKER?
I SEE... NO WONDER HE WAS SO HOSTILE.
BUT EVEN SO, I'M AMAZED HE JUST WALKED RIGHT INTO ENEMY TERRITORY.
LET ME WARN YOU.
IF YOU PLAN ON TRYIN' TO SHOW OFF BY FACIN' ME ONE-ON-ONE...

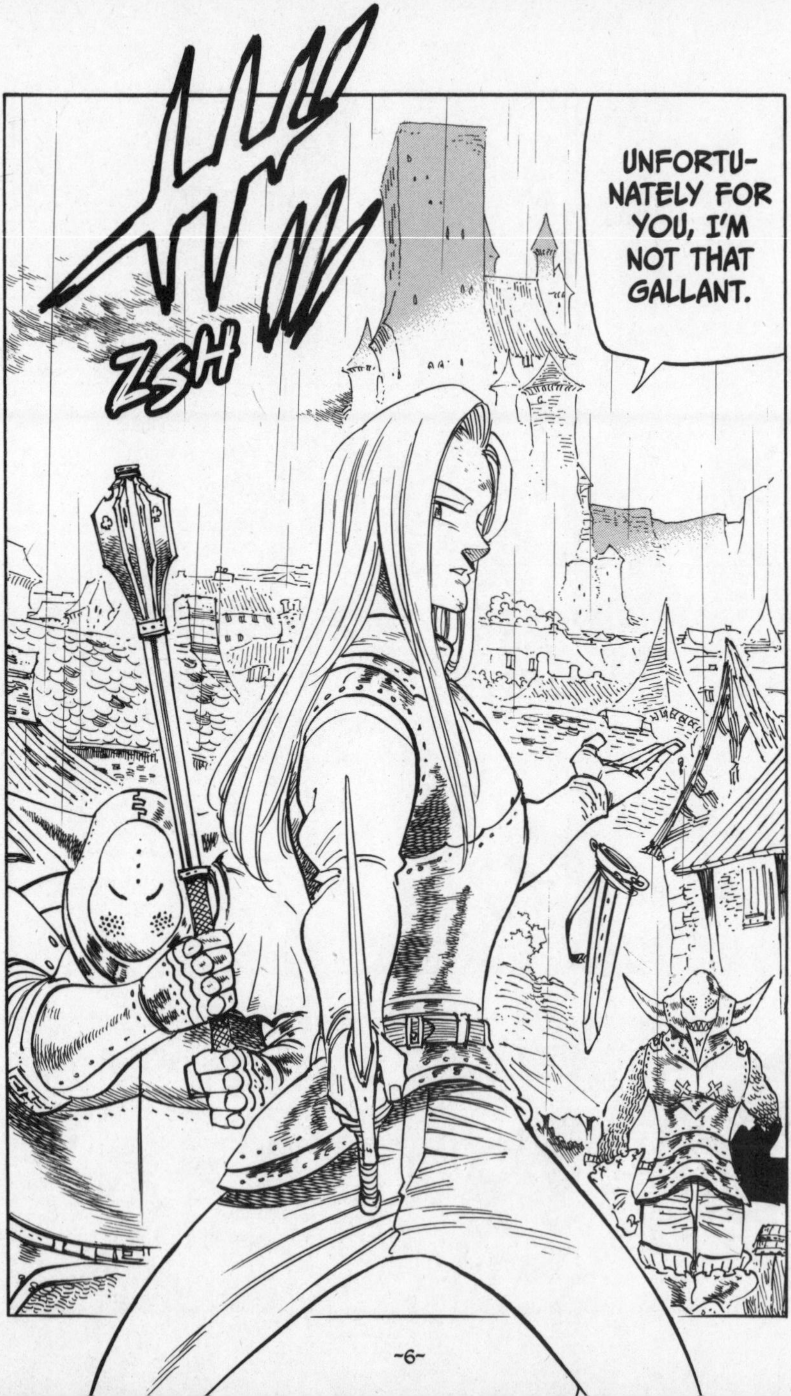

UNFORTU-NATELY FOR YOU, I'M NOT THAT GALLANT.
ZSH

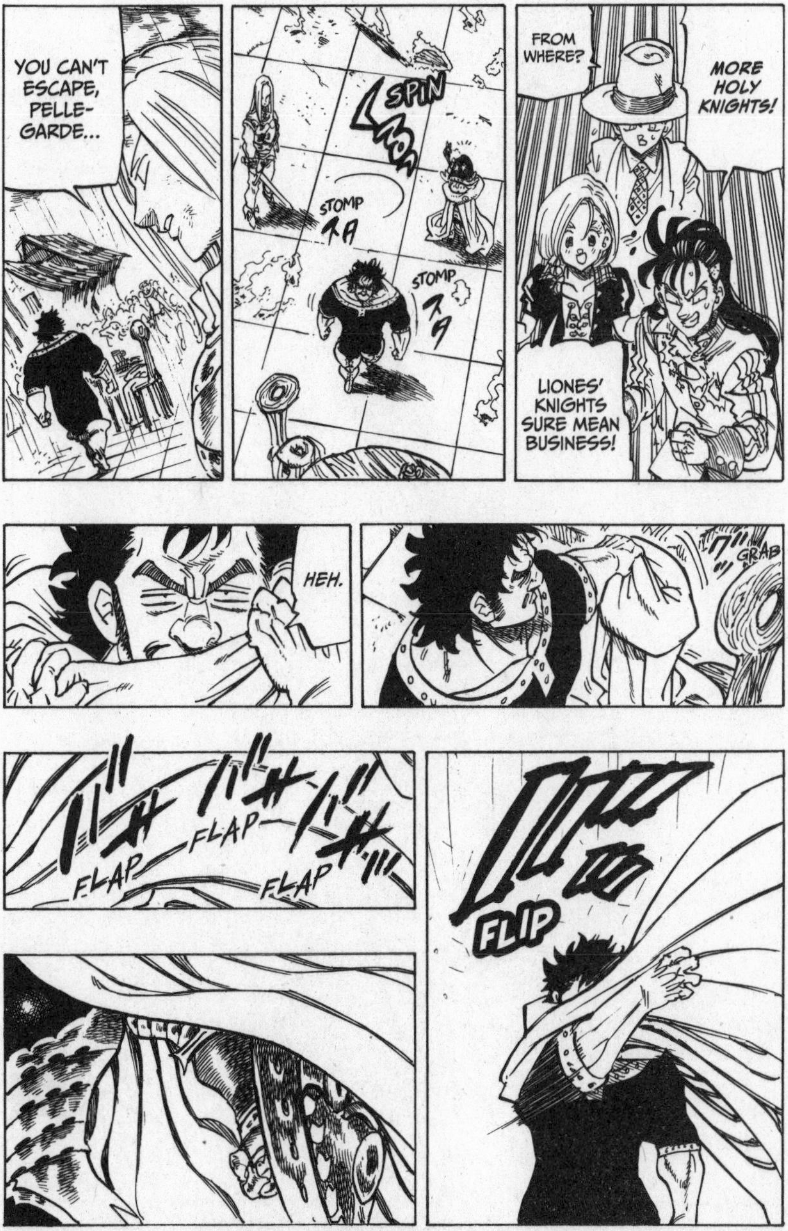
MORE HOLY KNIGHTS!
FROM WHERE?
LIONES' KNIGHTS SURE MEAN BUSINESS!
SPIN
STOMP
STOMP
YOU CAN'T ESCAPE, PELLE-GARDE...
GRAB
HEH.
FLIP
FLAP
FLAP
FLAP
FLAP

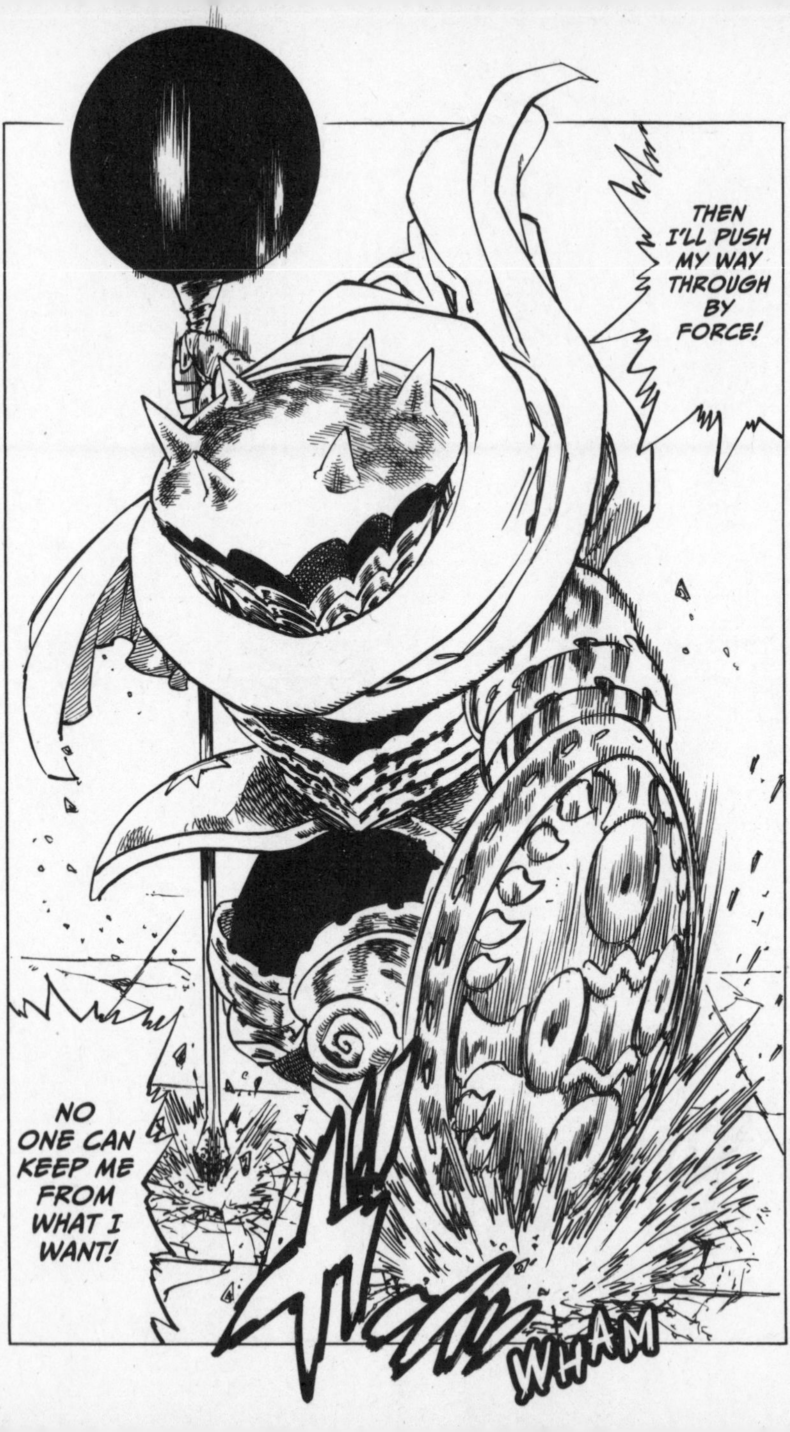
THEN I'LL PUSH MY WAY THROUGH BY FORCE!
NO ONE CAN KEEP ME FROM WHAT I WANT!
WHAM

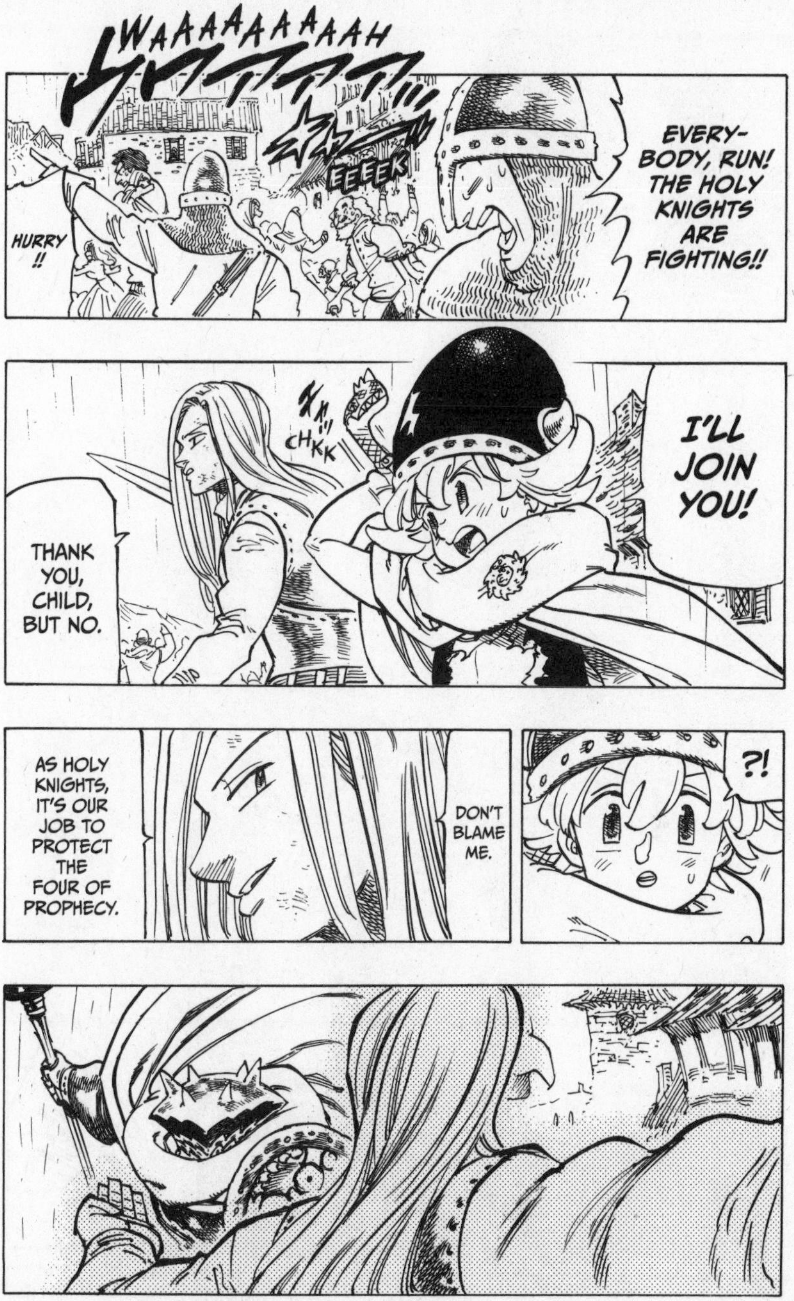
WAAAAAAAAAH
EVERY-BODY, RUN! THE HOLY KNIGHTS ARE FIGHTING!!
EEEEK
HURRY !!
I'LL JOIN YOU!
CHKK
THANK YOU, CHILD, BUT NO.
?!
DON'T BLAME ME.
AS HOLY KNIGHTS, IT'S OUR JOB TO PROTECT THE FOUR OF PROPHECY.

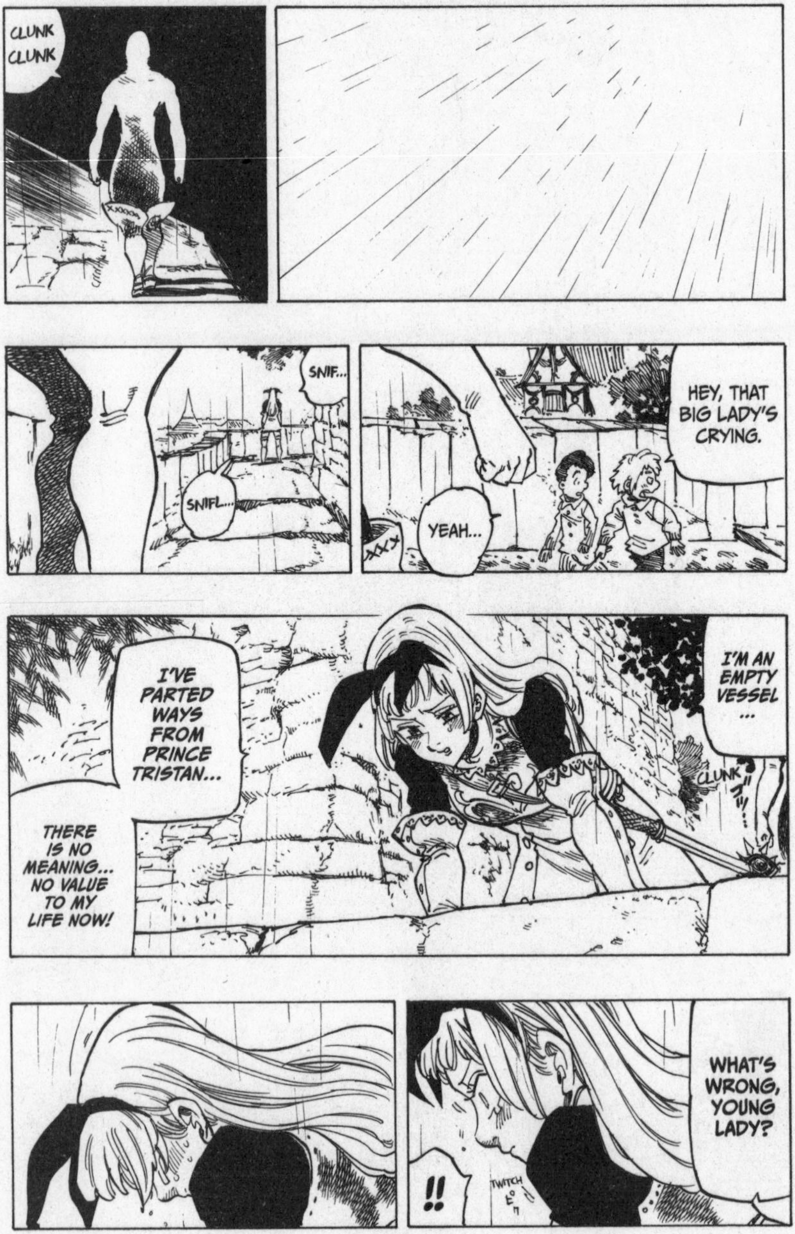
CLUNK CLUNK
HEY, THAT BIG LADY'S CRYING.
YEAH...
SNIF...
SNIFL...
I'M AN EMPTY VESSEL...
CLUNK
I'VE PARTED WAYS FROM PRINCE TRISTAN...
THERE IS NO MEANING... NO VALUE TO MY LIFE NOW!
WHAT'S WRONG, YOUNG LADY?
TWITCH
!!

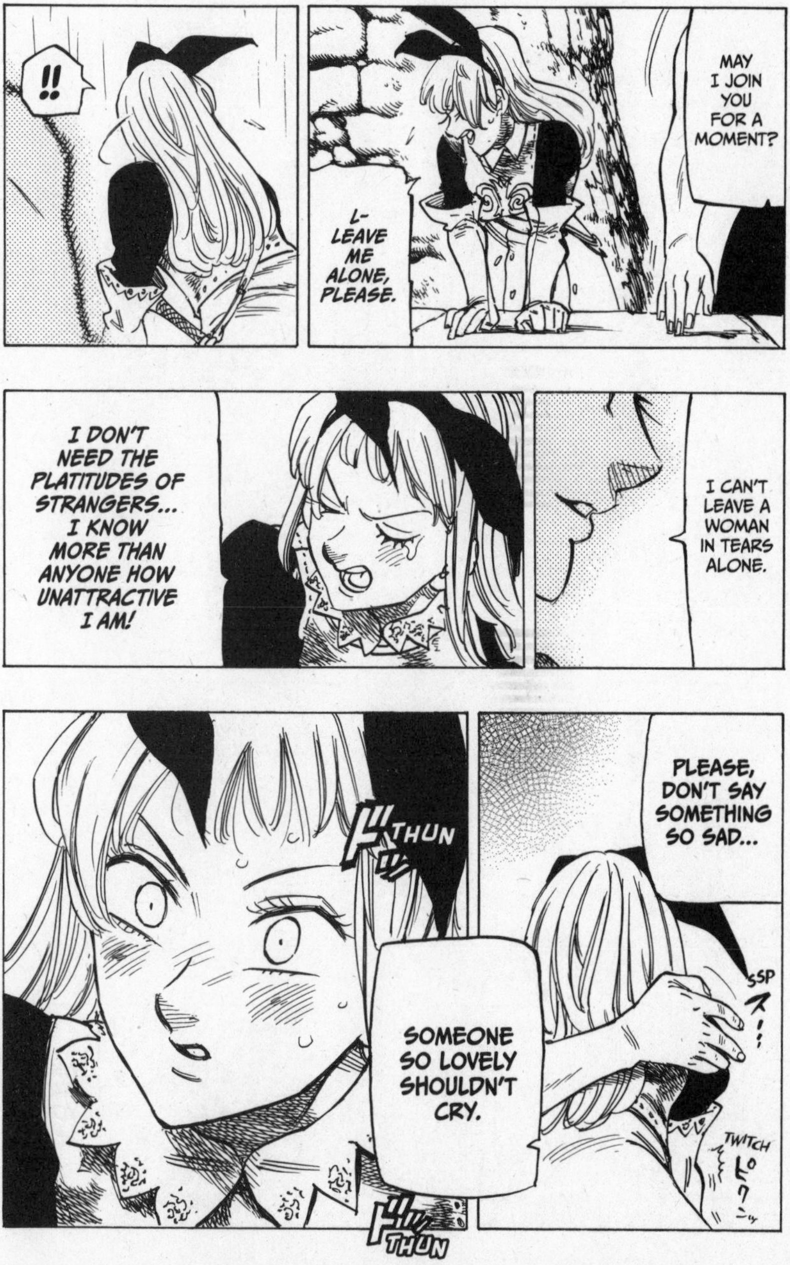
MAY I JOIN YOU FOR A MOMENT?
L-LEAVE ME ALONE, PLEASE.
!!
I CAN'T LEAVE A WOMAN IN TEARS ALONE.
I DON'T NEED THE PLATITUDES OF STRANGERS... I KNOW MORE THAN ANYONE HOW UNATTRACTIVE I AM!
PLEASE, DON'T SAY SOMETHING SO SAD...
SSP
TWITCH
THUN
SOMEONE SO LOVELY SHOULDN'T CRY.
THUN

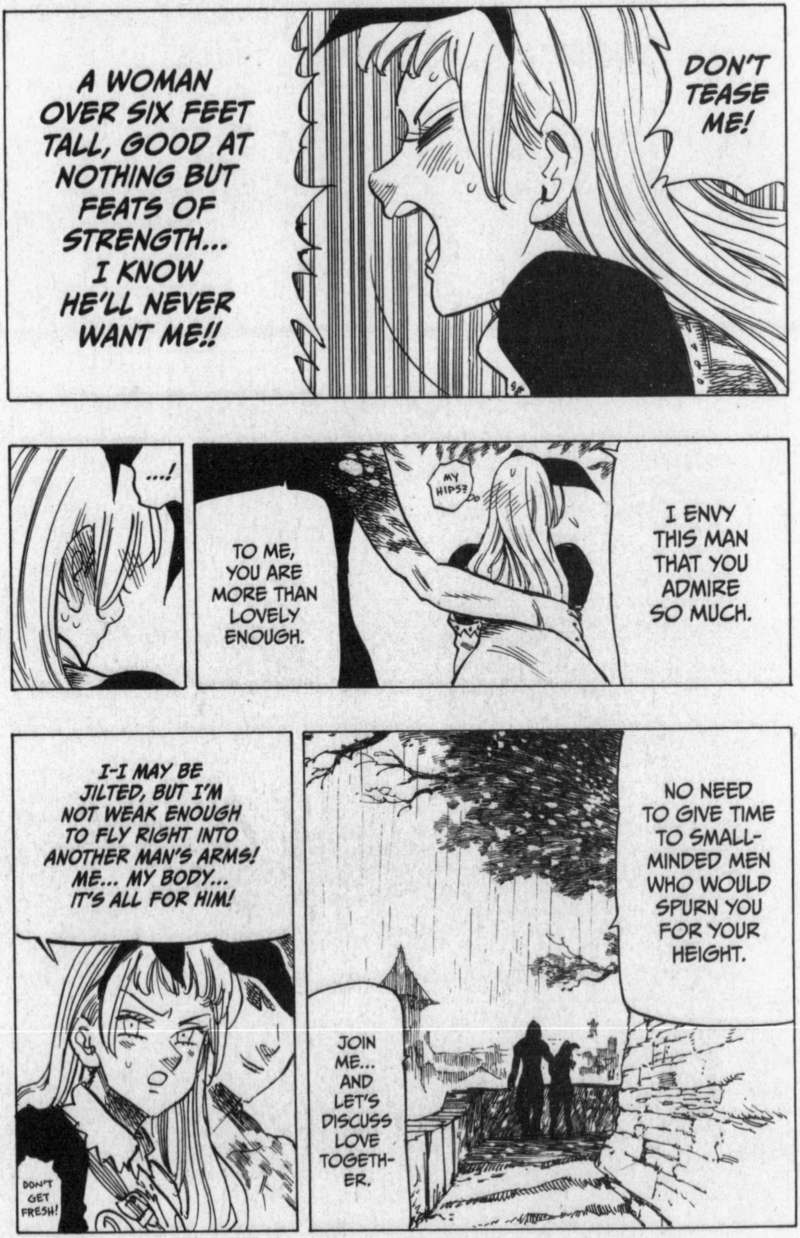
DON'T TEASE ME!
A WOMAN OVER SIX FEET TALL, GOOD AT NOTHING BUT FEATS OF STRENGTH... I KNOW HE'LL NEVER WANT ME!!
I ENVY THIS MAN THAT YOU ADMIRE SO MUCH.
MY HIPS?
TO ME, YOU ARE MORE THAN LOVELY ENOUGH.
...!
NO NEED TO GIVE TIME TO SMALL-MINDED MEN WHO WOULD SPURN YOU FOR YOUR HEIGHT.
JOIN ME... AND LET'S DISCUSS LOVE TOGETH-ER.
I-I MAY BE JILTED, BUT I'M NOT WEAK ENOUGH TO FLY RIGHT INTO ANOTHER MAN'S ARMS! ME... MY BODY... IT'S ALL FOR HIM!
DON'T GET FRESH!

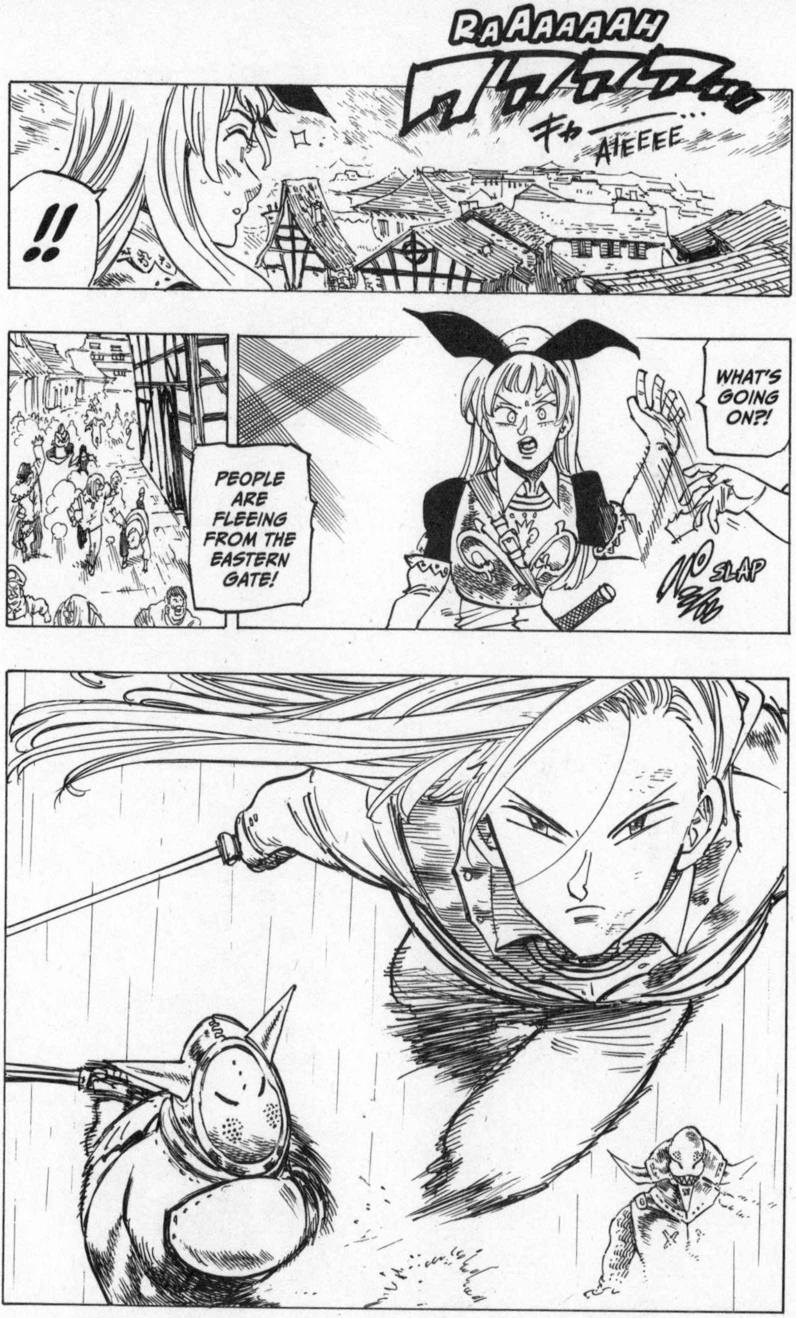
RAAAAAAH
AIEEEE
!!
WHAT'S GOING ON?!
SLAP
PEOPLE ARE FLEEING FROM THE EASTERN GATE!

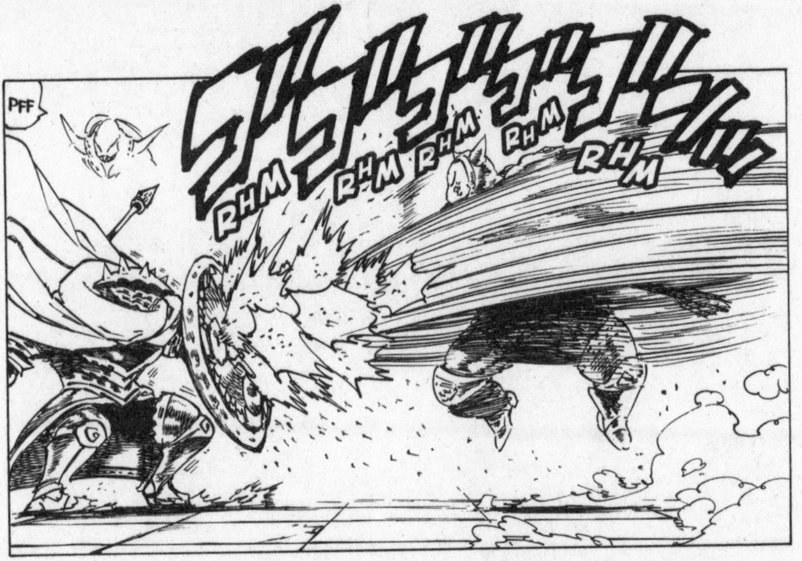
PFF
RHM RHM RHM RHM RHM
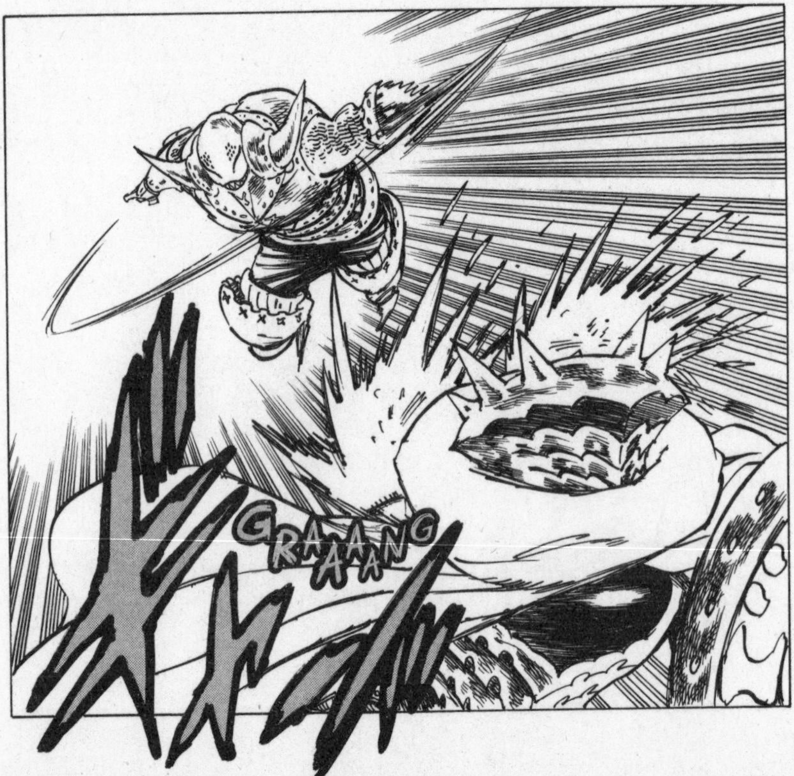
GRAAAANG

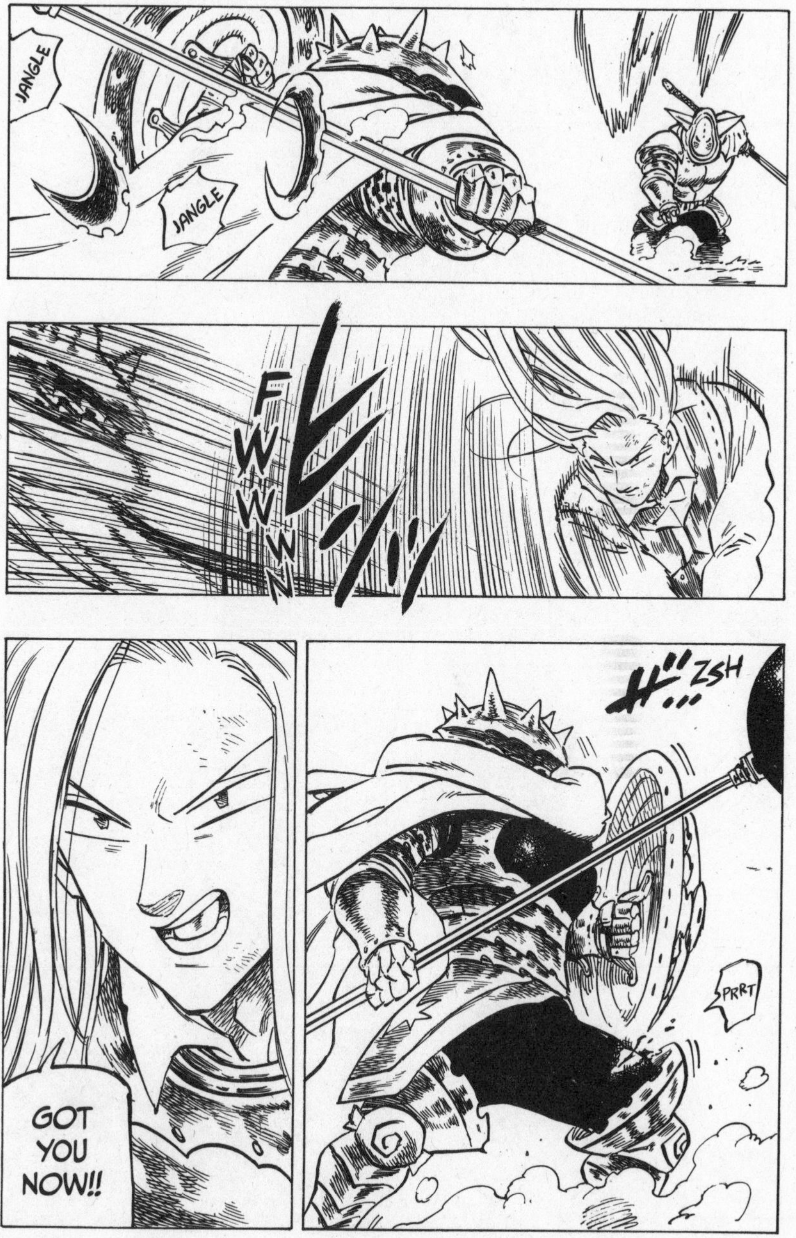
JANGLE
JANGLE
FWWWWN
ZSH
PRRT
GOT YOU NOW!!

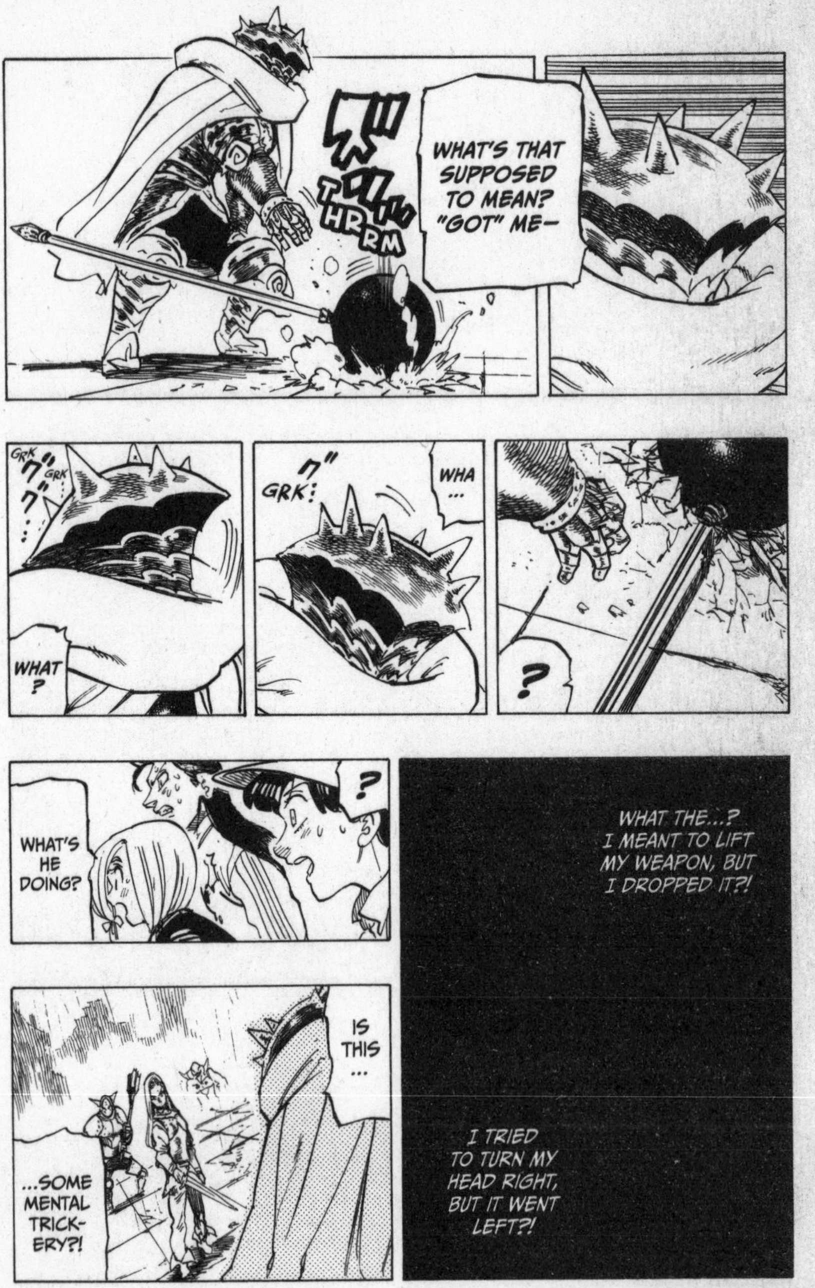
WHAT'S THAT SUPPOSED TO MEAN? "GOT" ME—
THRRM
?
WHA ...
GRK!
GRK GRK
WHAT?
WHAT THE...? I MEANT TO LIFT MY WEAPON, BUT I DROPPED IT?!
I TRIED TO TURN MY HEAD RIGHT, BUT IT WENT LEFT?!
?
WHAT'S HE DOING?
IS THIS ...
...SOME MENTAL TRICK-ERY?!

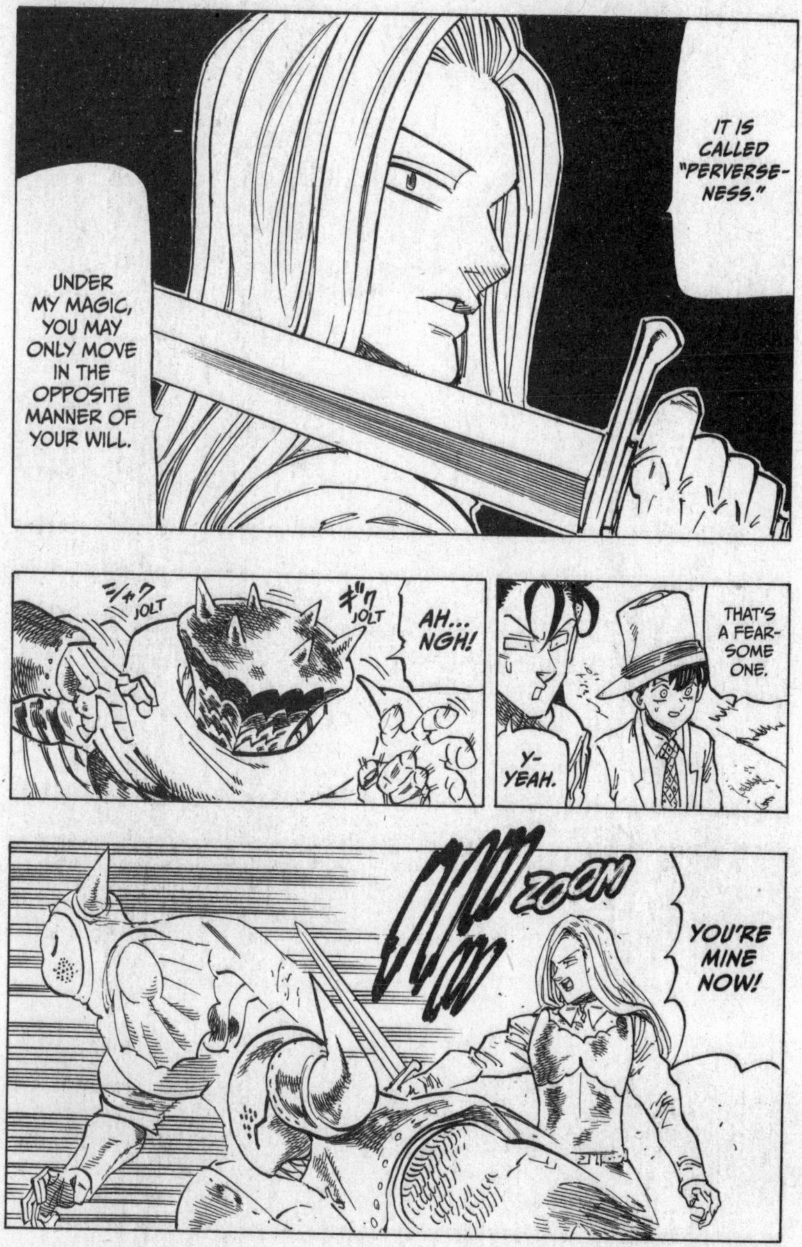
IT IS CALLED "PERVERSE-NESS."
UNDER MY MAGIC, YOU MAY ONLY MOVE IN THE OPPOSITE MANNER OF YOUR WILL.
THAT'S A FEAR-SOME ONE.
Y-YEAH.
AH... NGH!
ギク JOLT
シャク JOLT
ZOOM
YOU'RE MINE NOW!

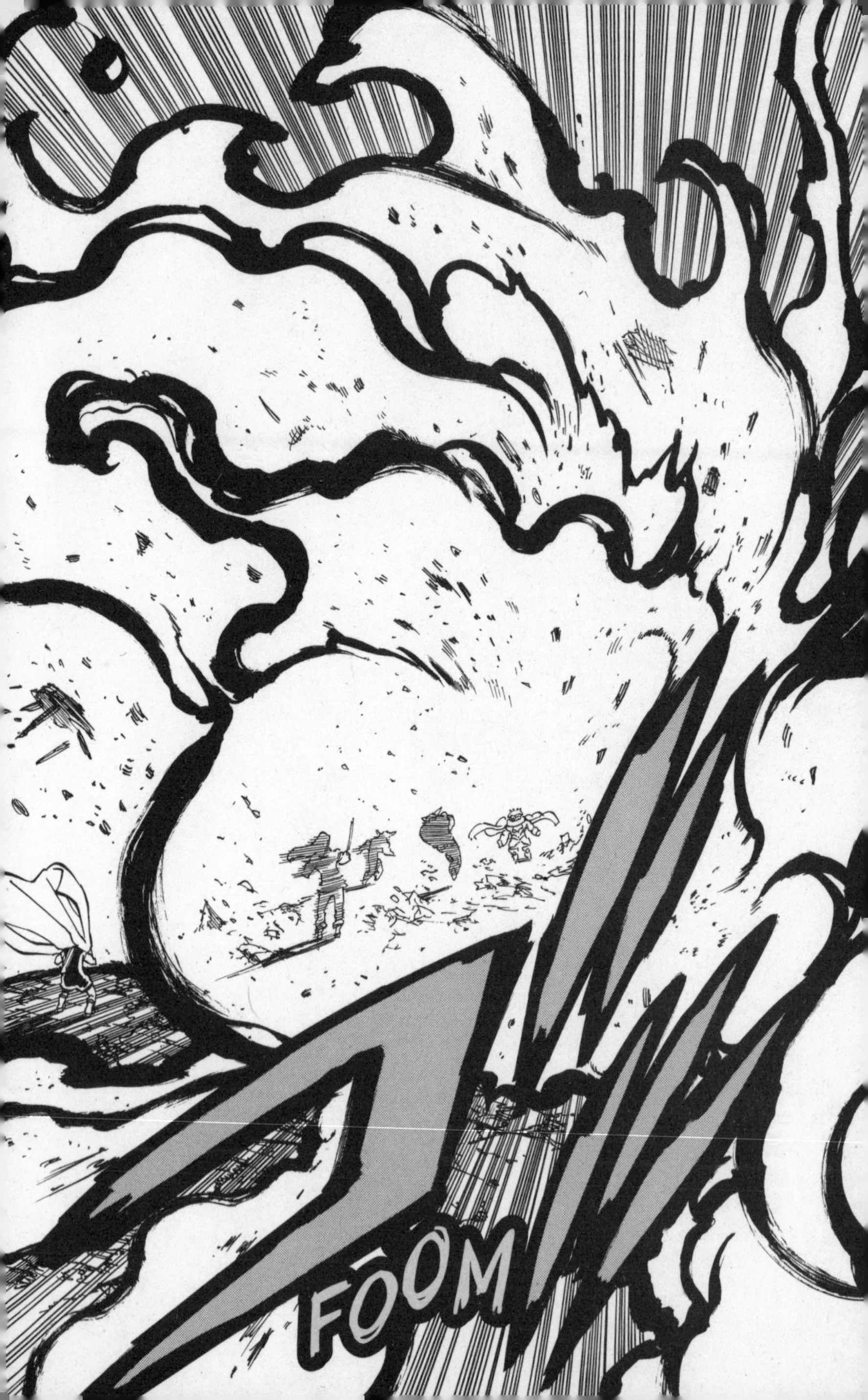
FOOM

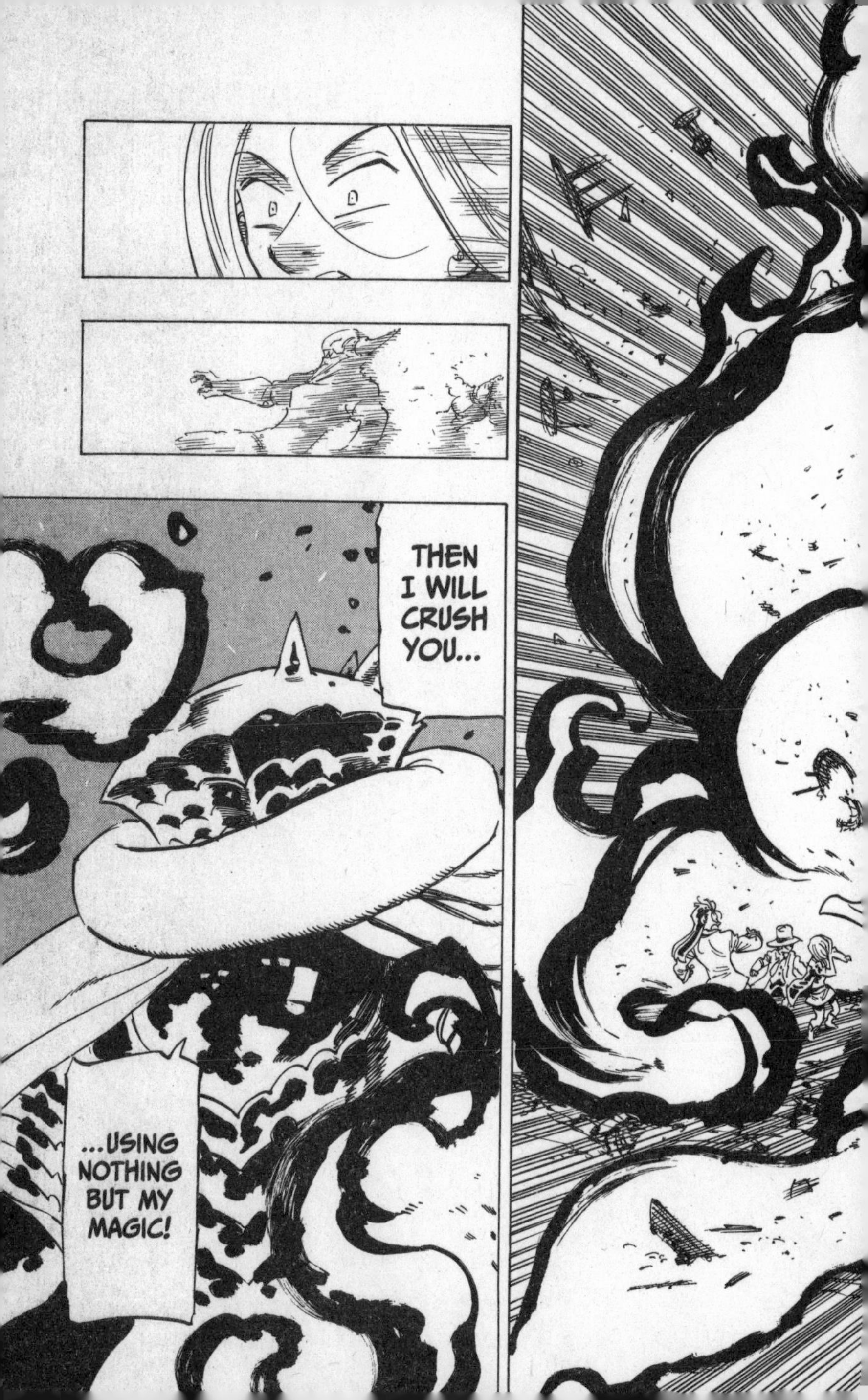
THEN I WILL CRUSH YOU...
...USING NOTHING BUT MY MAGIC!

WHAT ON...?

SUCH MAGIC FORCE...!

KA BOOM!!

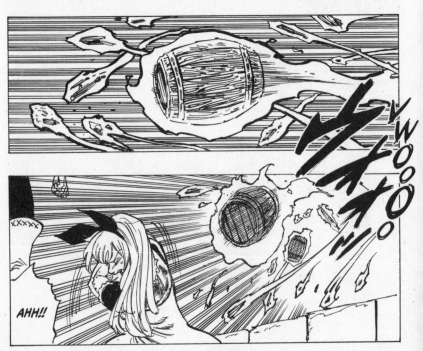

VWOOOO!!

AHH!!

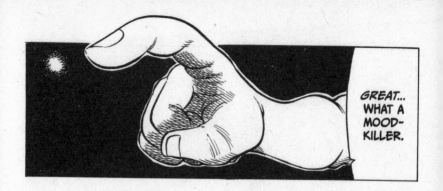

GREAT... WHAT A MOOD-KILLER.

BRRRSH

WHO ARE YOU?!

WHAT DID YOU JUST DO?

HUH?

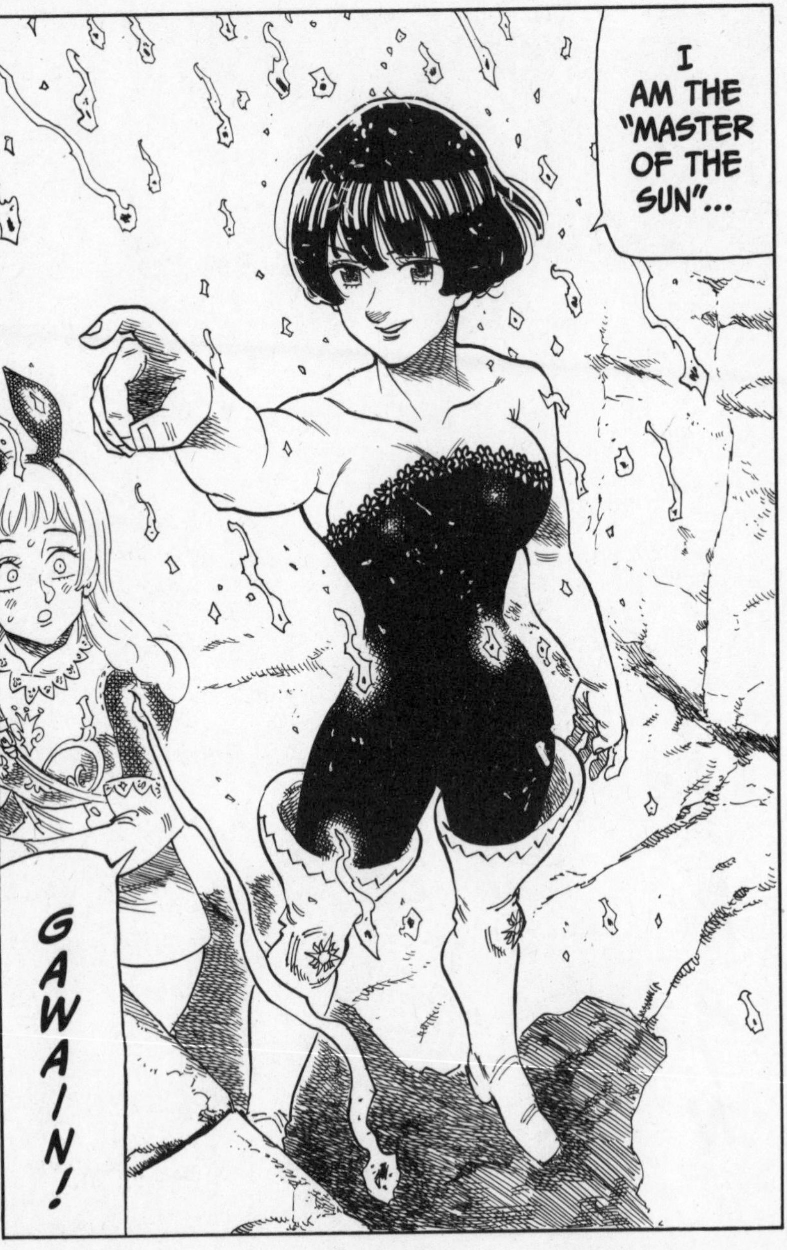
I AM THE "MASTER OF THE SUN"...
GAWAIN!

CHAPTER 61 | THE FOURTH ARRIVES

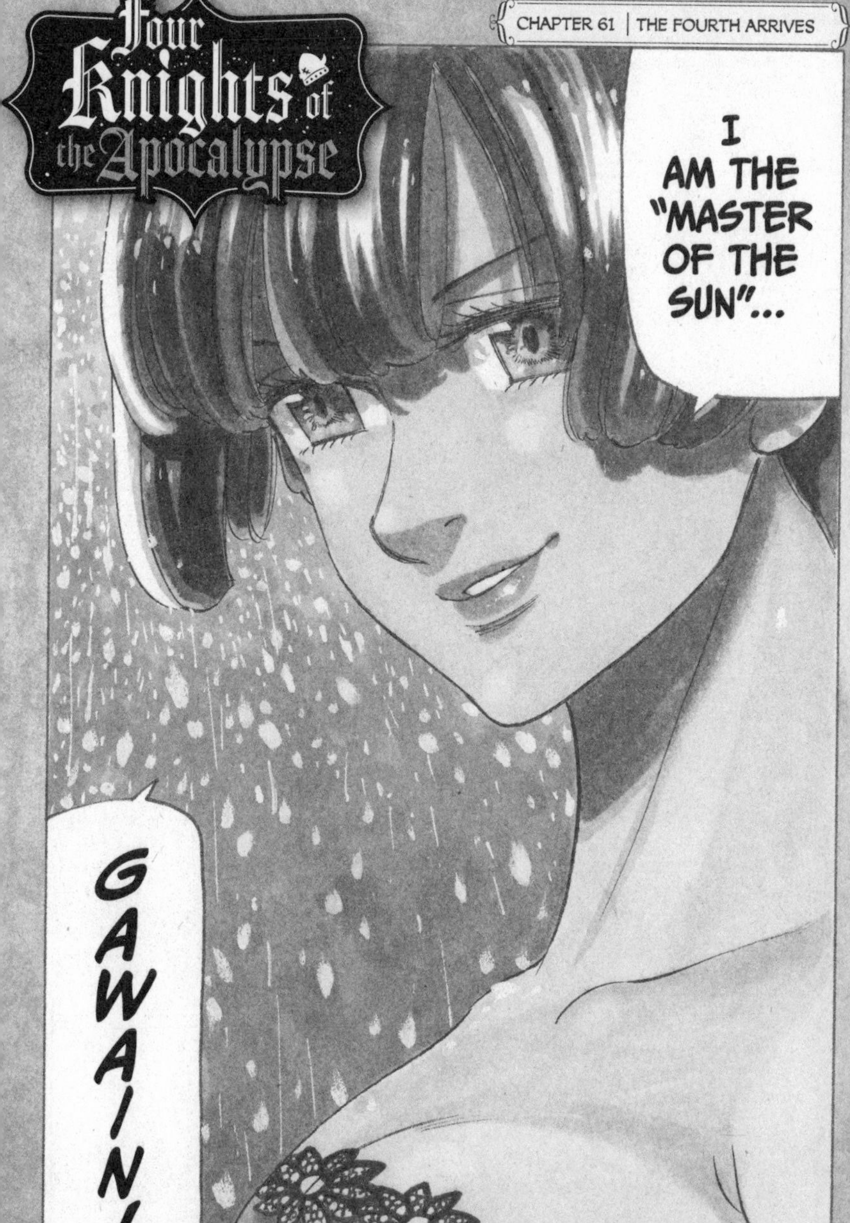

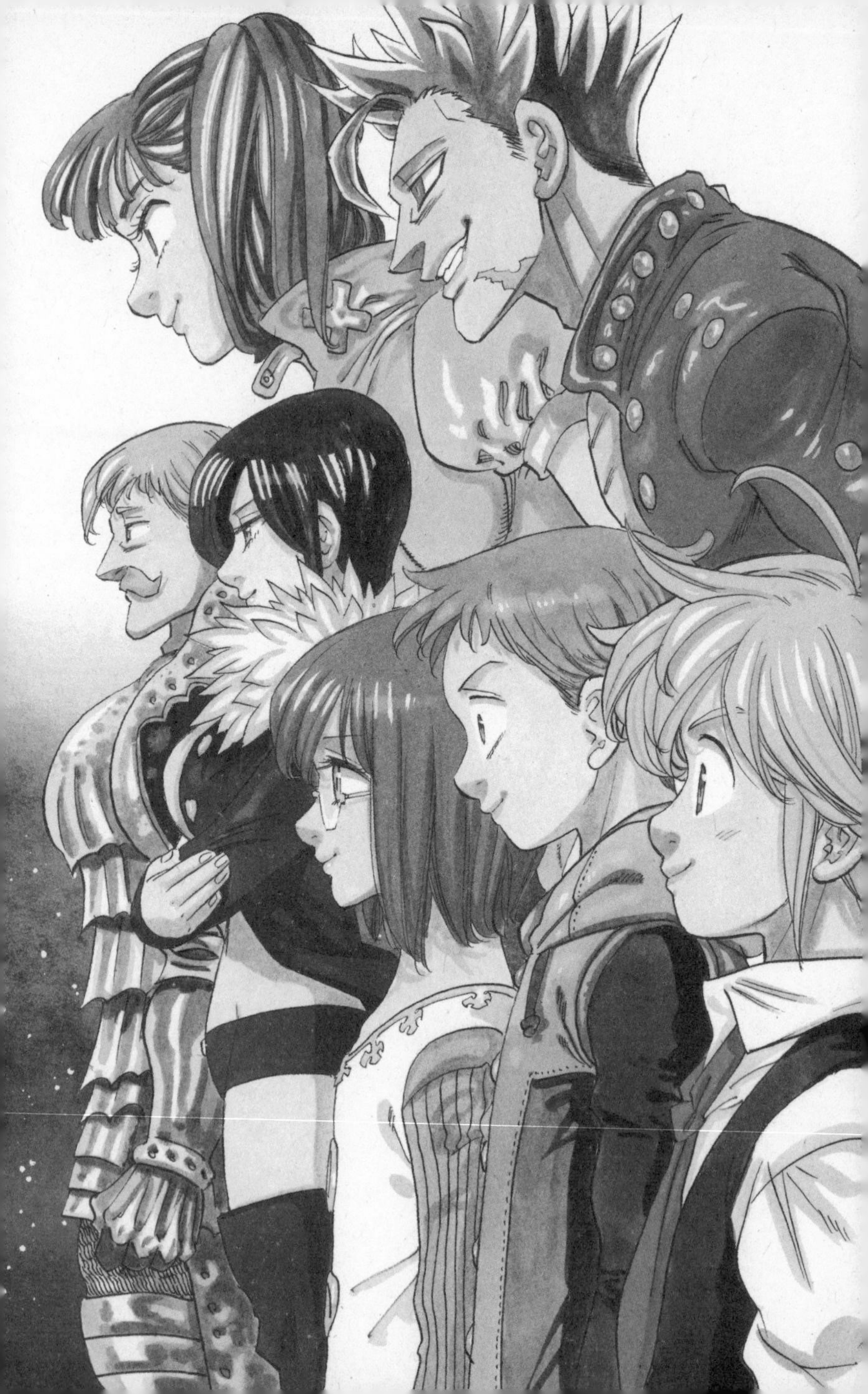

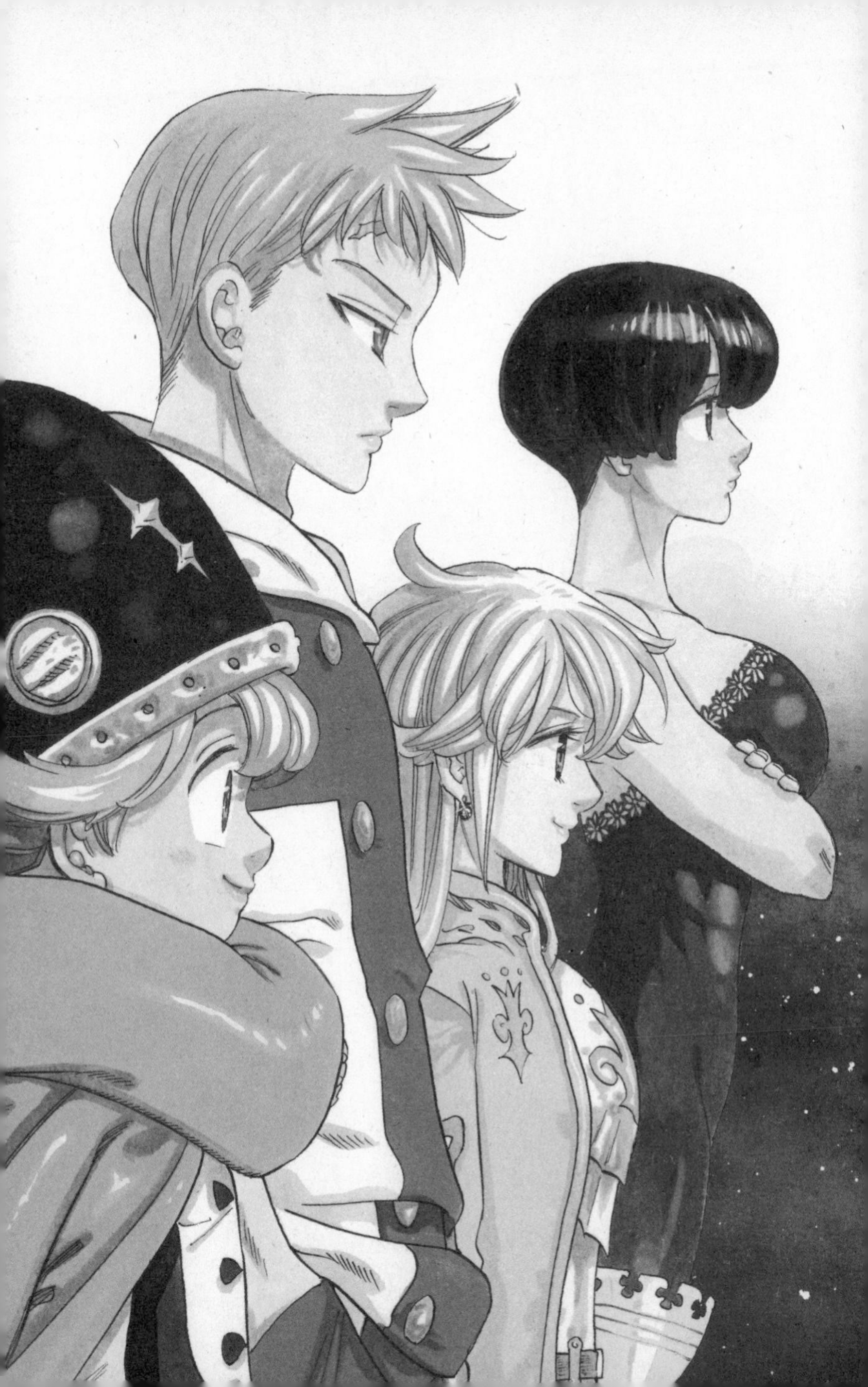

AT LIONES CASTLE

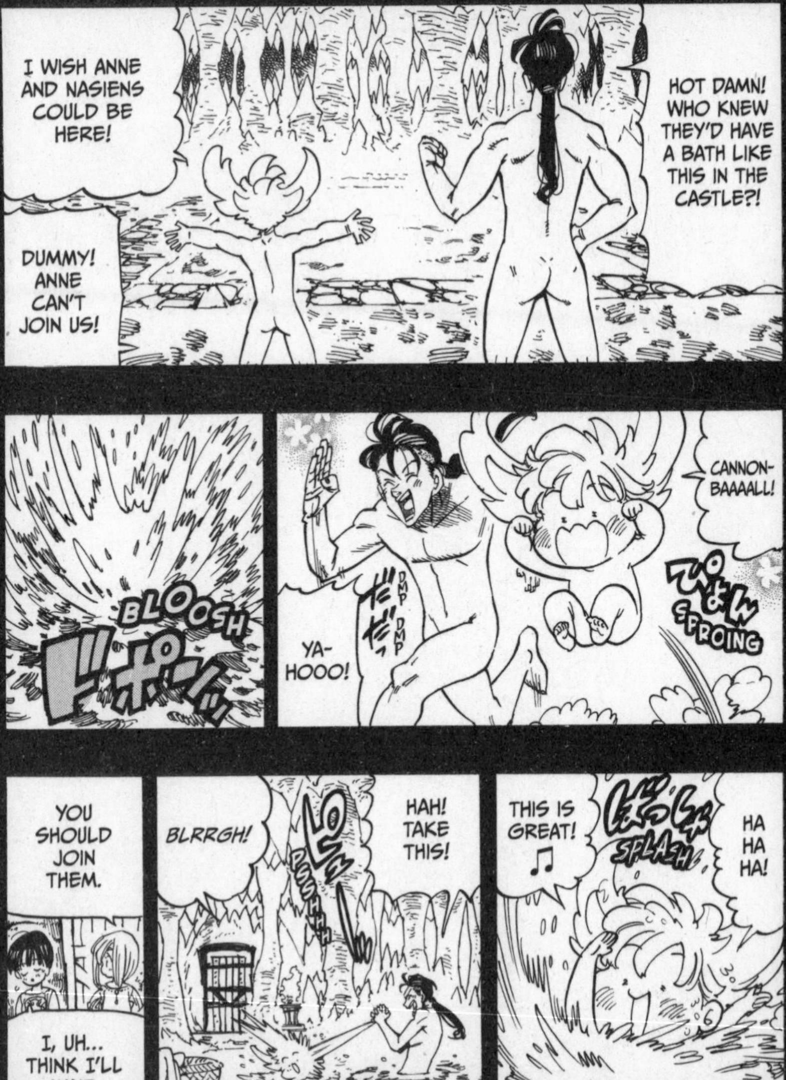

HOT DAMN! WHO KNEW THEY'D HAVE A BATH LIKE THIS IN THE CASTLE?!
I WISH ANNE AND NASIENS COULD BE HERE!
DUMMY! ANNE CAN'T JOIN US!
CANNON-BAAAALL!
SPROING
DMP DMP
YA-HOOO!
BLOOSH
HA HA HA!
SPLASH
THIS IS GREAT! ♫
HAH! TAKE THIS!
PSSHHH
BLRRGH!
YOU SHOULD JOIN THEM.
I, UH... THINK I'LL WAIT.

CONT'D ON P. 148

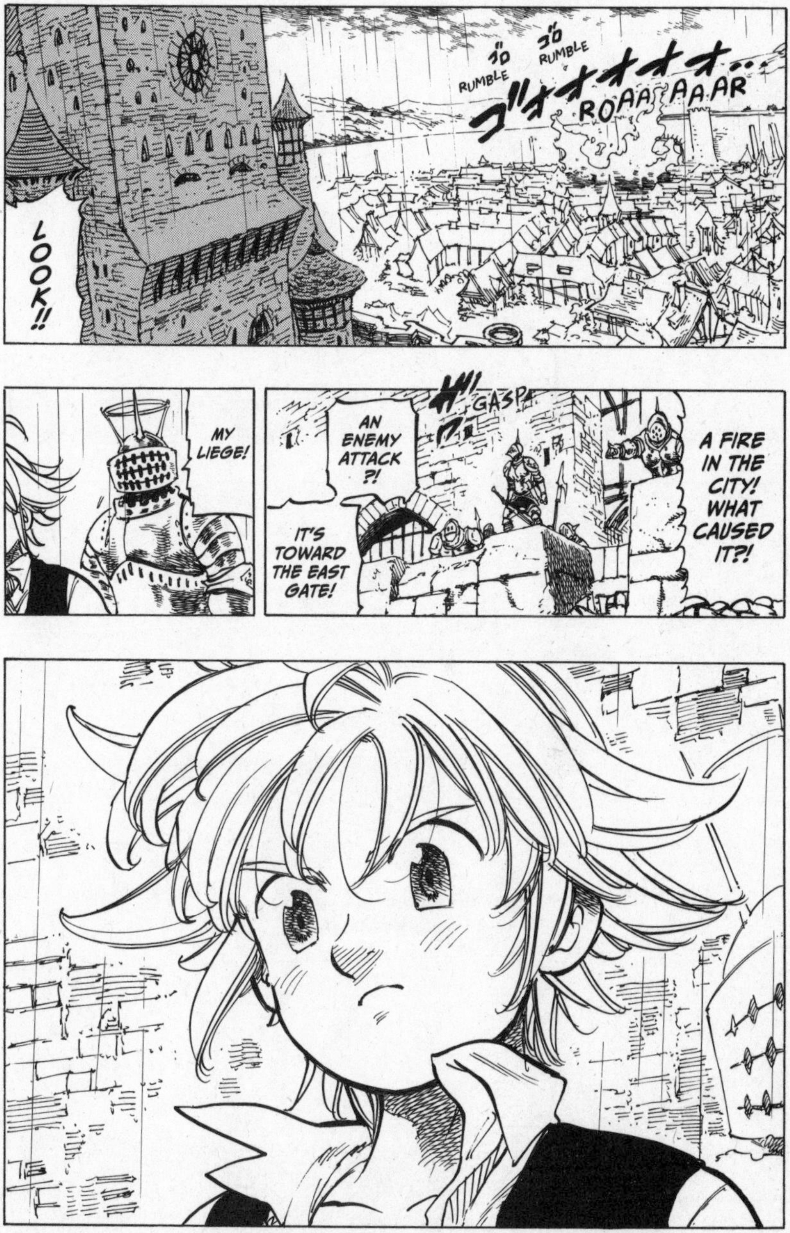

ゴロ RUMBLE
ゴロ RUMBLE
ゴオオオオオ… ROAAAAAAR
LOOK!!
A FIRE IN THE CITY! WHAT CAUSED IT?!
AN ENEMY ATTACK?!
ハッ GASP
IT'S TOWARD THE EAST GATE!
MY LIEGE!

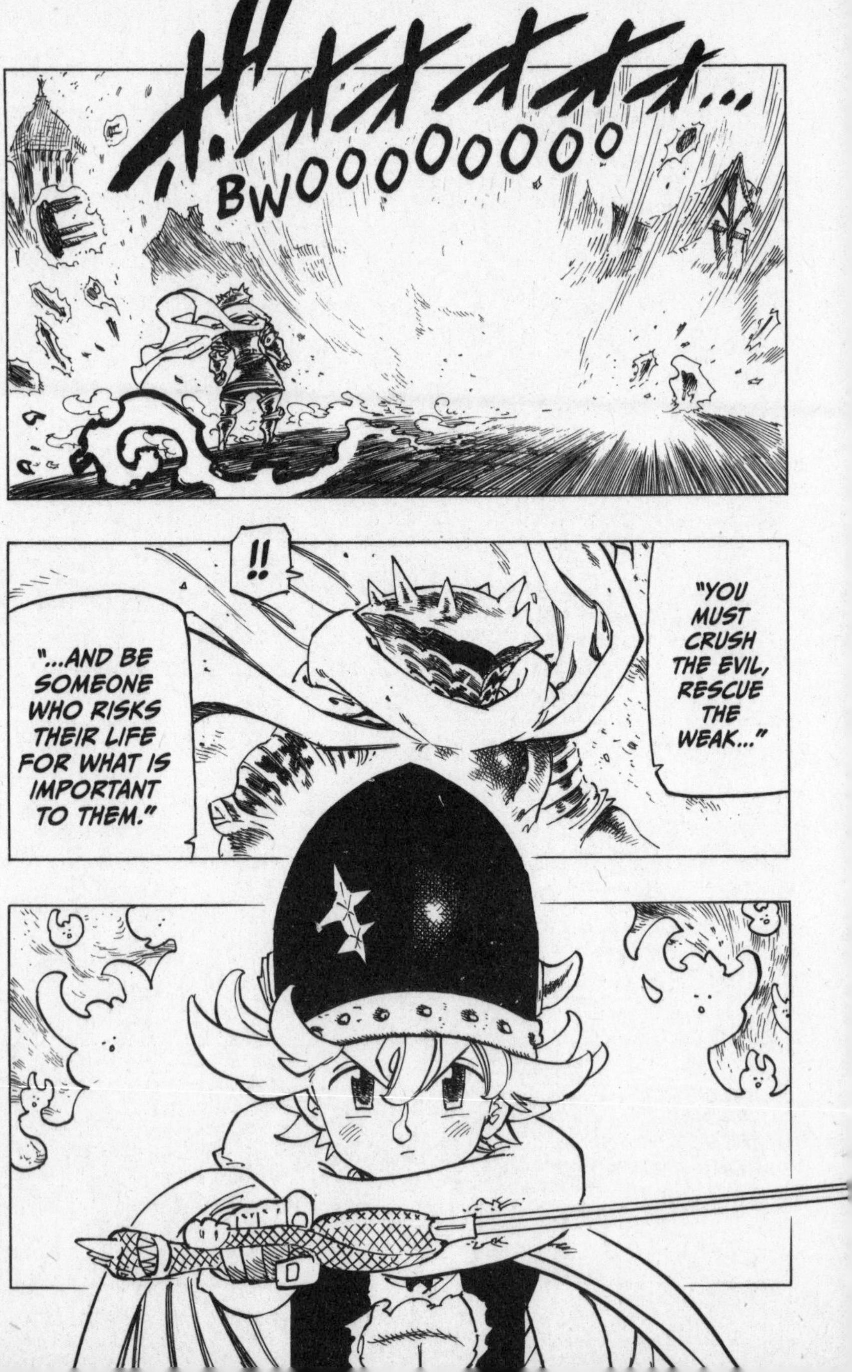
BWOOOOOOOO
"YOU MUST CRUSH THE EVIL, RESCUE THE WEAK..."
!!
"...AND BE SOMEONE WHO RISKS THEIR LIFE FOR WHAT IS IMPORTANT TO THEM."

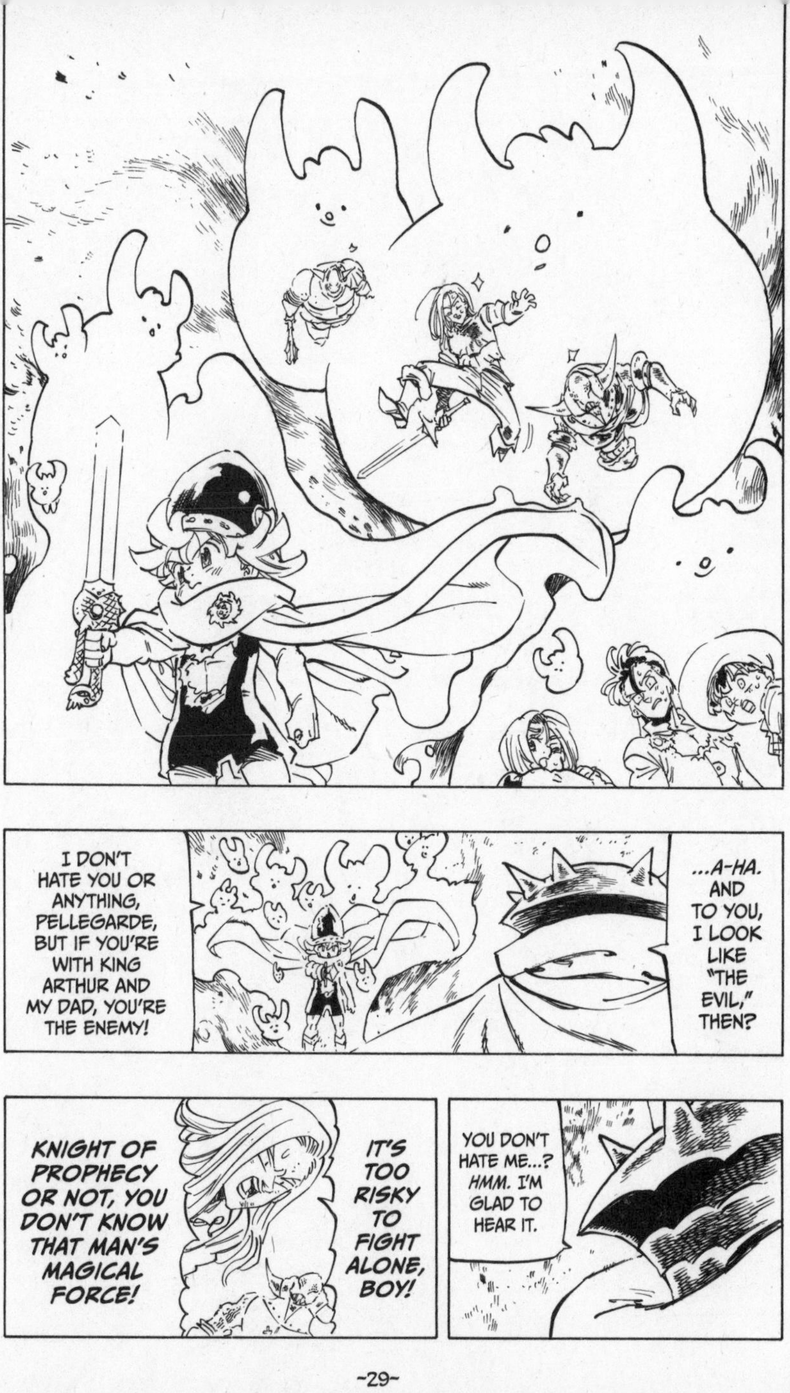
I DON'T HATE YOU OR ANYTHING, PELLEGARDE, BUT IF YOU'RE WITH KING ARTHUR AND MY DAD, YOU'RE THE ENEMY!
...A-HA. AND TO YOU, I LOOK LIKE "THE EVIL," THEN?
YOU DON'T HATE ME...? *HMM.* I'M GLAD TO HEAR IT.
IT'S TOO RISKY TO FIGHT ALONE, BOY!
KNIGHT OF PROPHECY OR NOT, YOU DON'T KNOW THAT MAN'S MAGICAL FORCE!

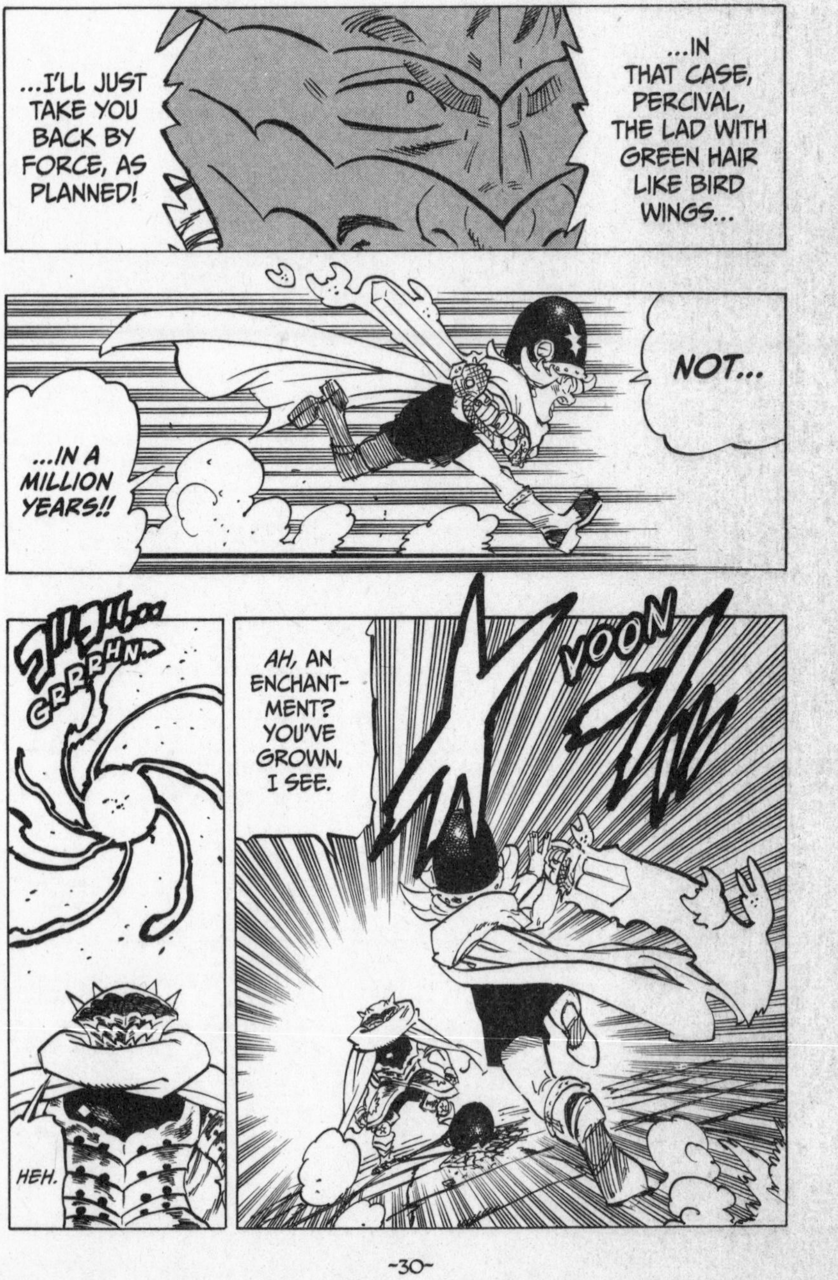
...IN THAT CASE, PERCIVAL, THE LAD WITH GREEN HAIR LIKE BIRD WINGS...
...I'LL JUST TAKE YOU BACK BY FORCE, AS PLANNED!
NOT...
...IN A MILLION YEARS!!
VOON
AH, AN ENCHANTMENT? YOU'VE GROWN, I SEE.
GRRRHN..
HEH.

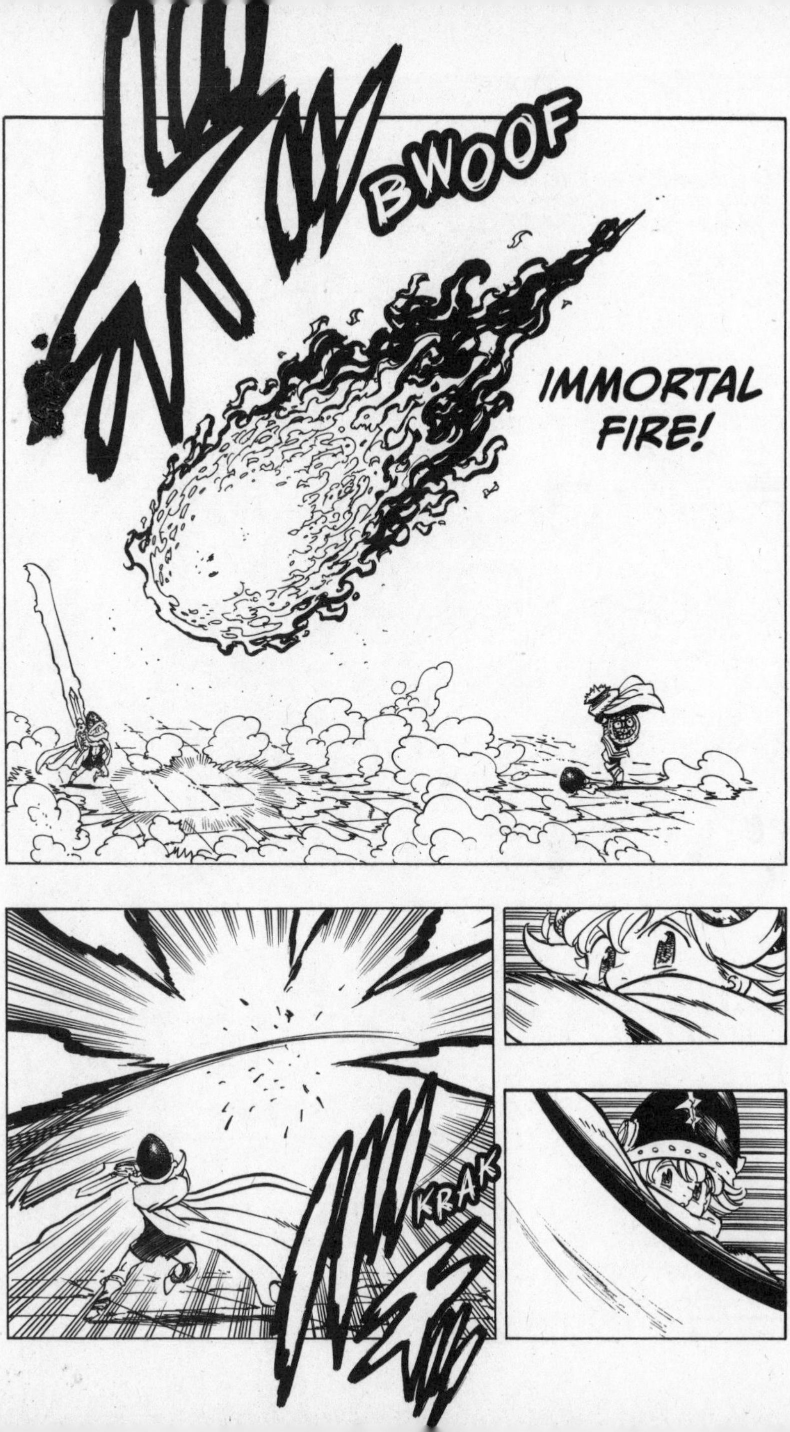
BWOOF
IMMORTAL FIRE!
KRAK

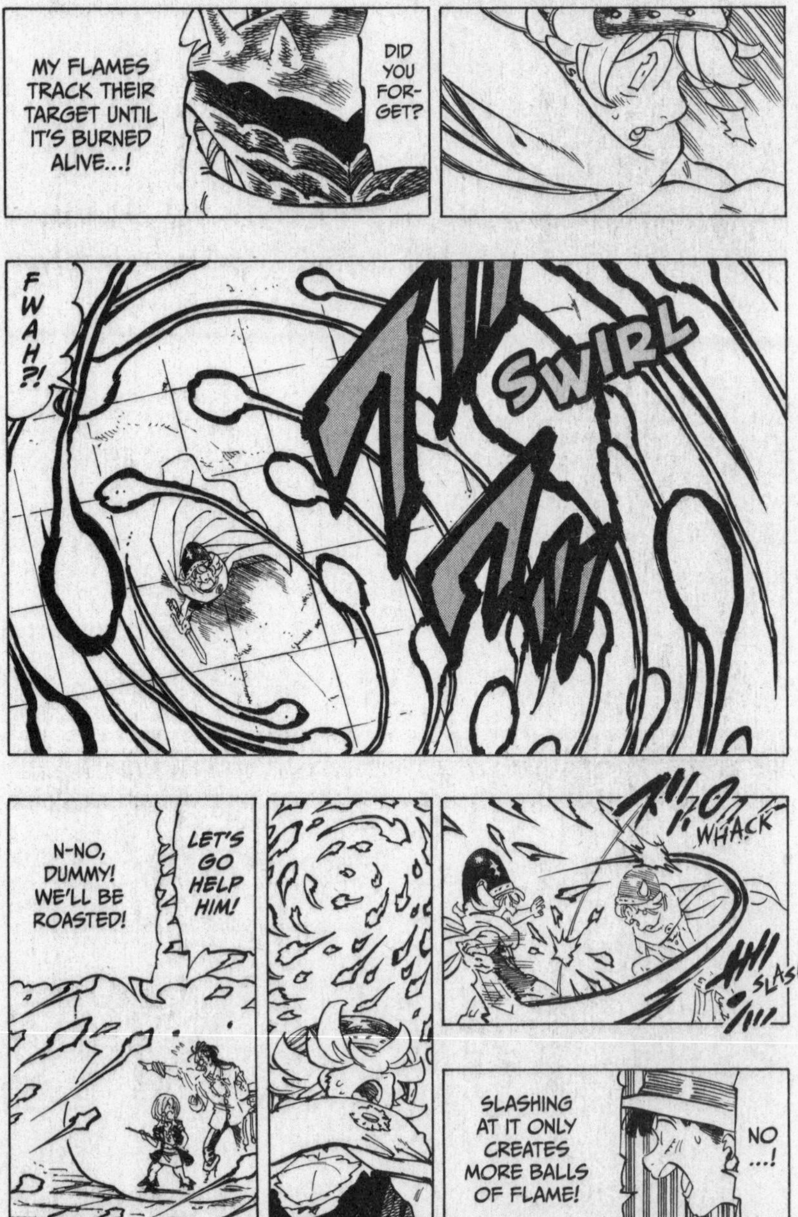
DID YOU FOR-GET?
MY FLAMES TRACK THEIR TARGET UNTIL IT'S BURNED ALIVE...!
SWIRL
FWAH?!
WHACK
SLASH
NO ...!
SLASHING AT IT ONLY CREATES MORE BALLS OF FLAME!
LET'S GO HELP HIM!
N-NO, DUMMY! WE'LL BE ROASTED!

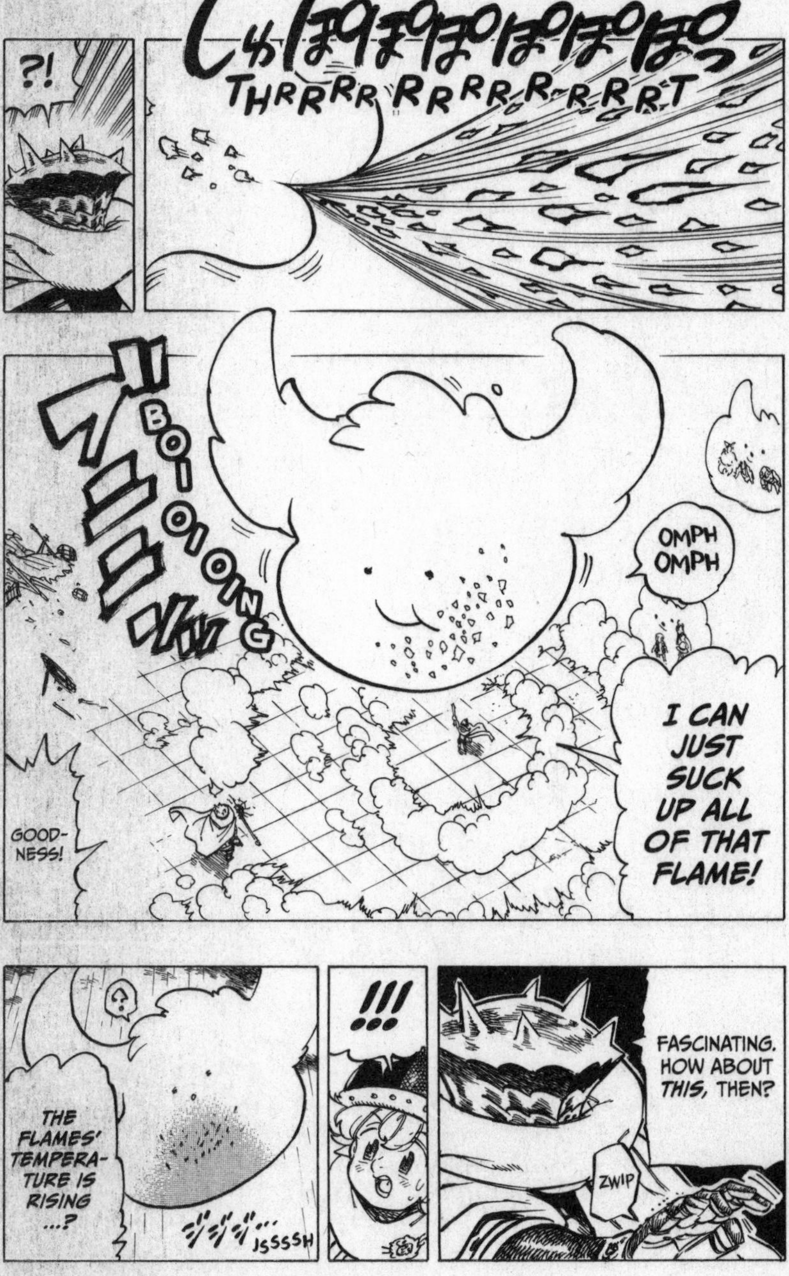
しゅぼぼぽぽぽぽっ
THRRRR RRRRR-R-RRRT
?!
OMPH OMPH
I CAN JUST SUCK UP ALL OF THAT FLAME!
BOI-OI-OING
GOOD-NESS!
FASCINATING. HOW ABOUT THIS, THEN?
ZWIP
!!!
THE FLAMES' TEMPERA-TURE IS RISING ...?
ジジジ...
JSSSSH

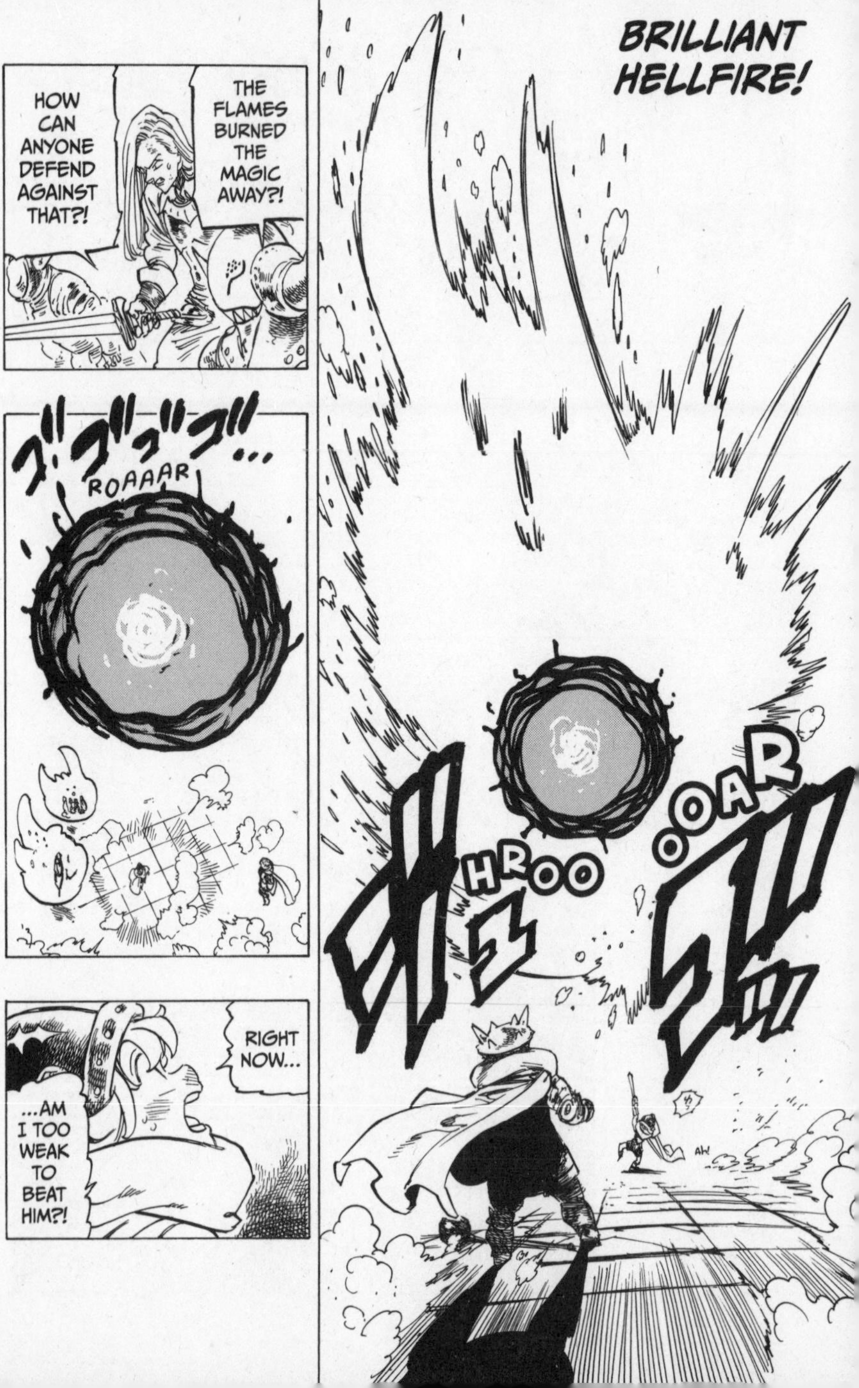
BRILLIANT HELLFIRE!
HROO..OAR
AH!
THE FLAMES BURNED THE MAGIC AWAY?!
HOW CAN ANYONE DEFEND AGAINST THAT?!
ROAAAR
RIGHT NOW...
...AM I TOO WEAK TO BEAT HIM?!

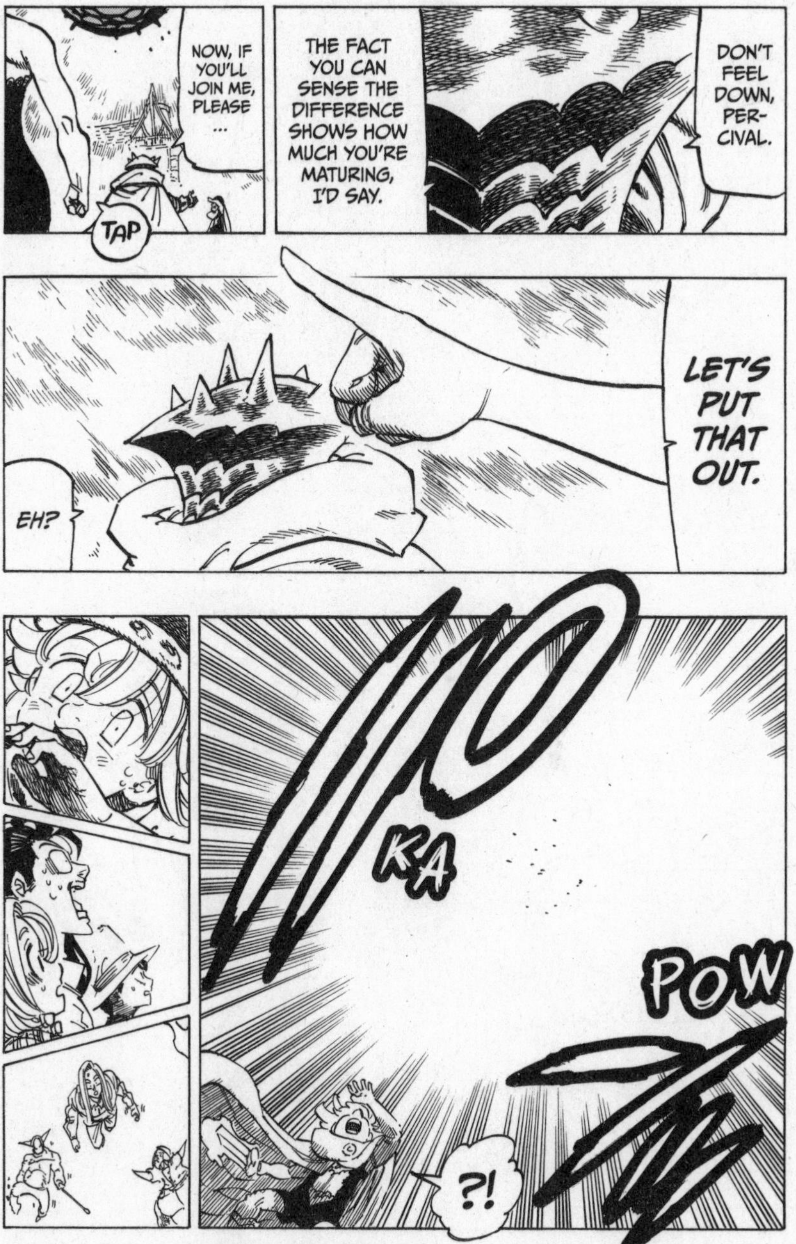
DON'T FEEL DOWN, PERCIVAL.
THE FACT YOU CAN SENSE THE DIFFERENCE SHOWS HOW MUCH YOU'RE MATURING, I'D SAY.
NOW, IF YOU'LL JOIN ME, PLEASE ...
TAP
LET'S PUT THAT OUT.
EH?
KA
POW
?!

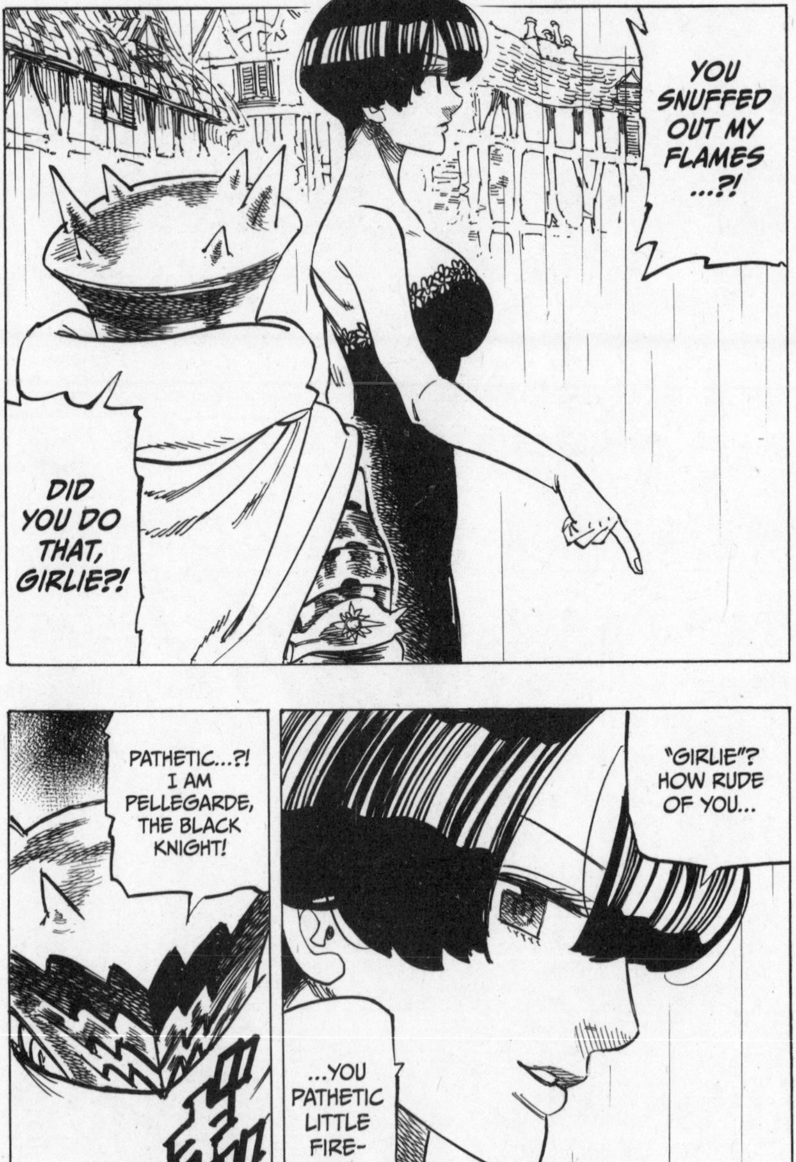
YOU SNUFFED OUT MY FLAMES ...?!
DID YOU DO THAT, GIRLIE?!
"GIRLIE"? HOW RUDE OF YOU...
...YOU PATHETIC LITTLE FIRE-BUG.
PATHETIC...?! I AM PELLEGARDE, THE BLACK KNIGHT!
GRIT

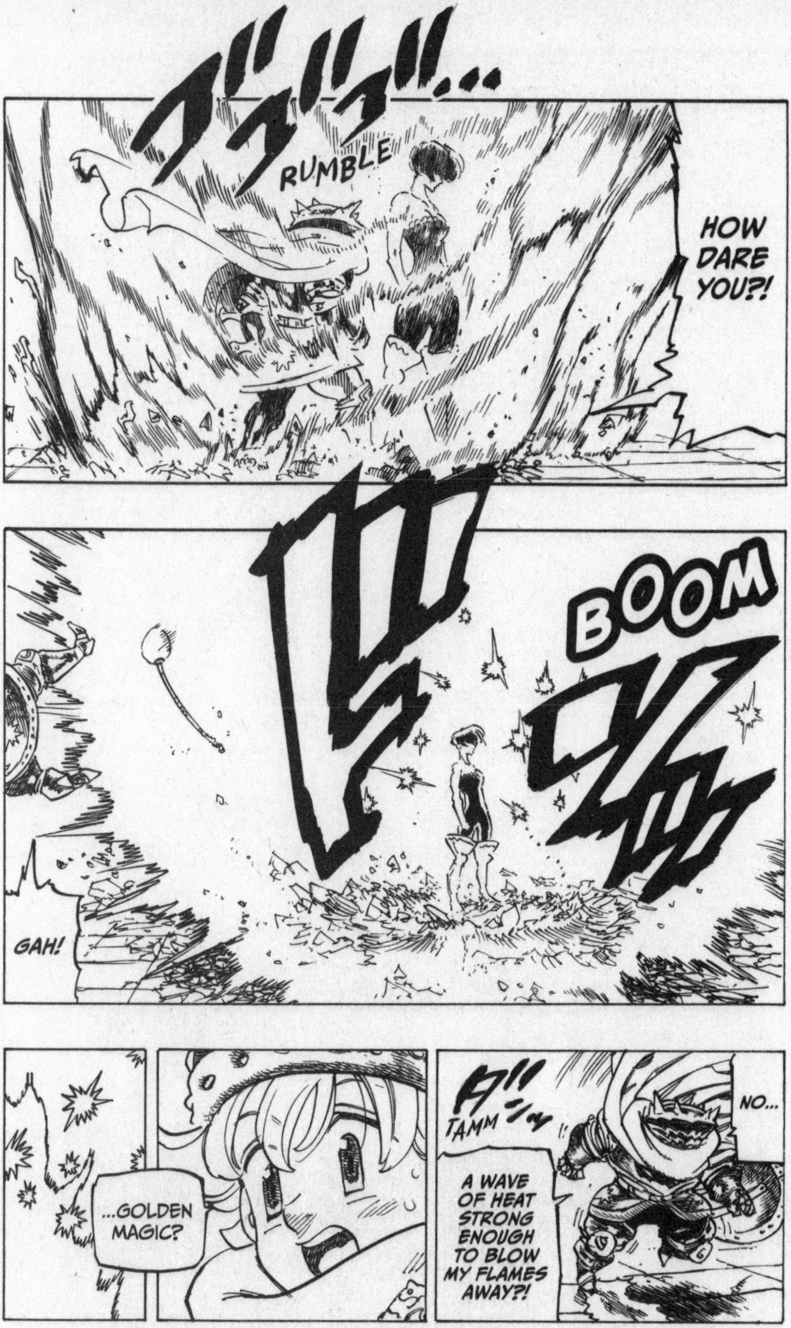
HOW DARE YOU?!
RUMBLE
BOOM
GAH!
NO...
TAMM
A WAVE OF HEAT STRONG ENOUGH TO BLOW MY FLAMES AWAY?!
...GOLDEN MAGIC?

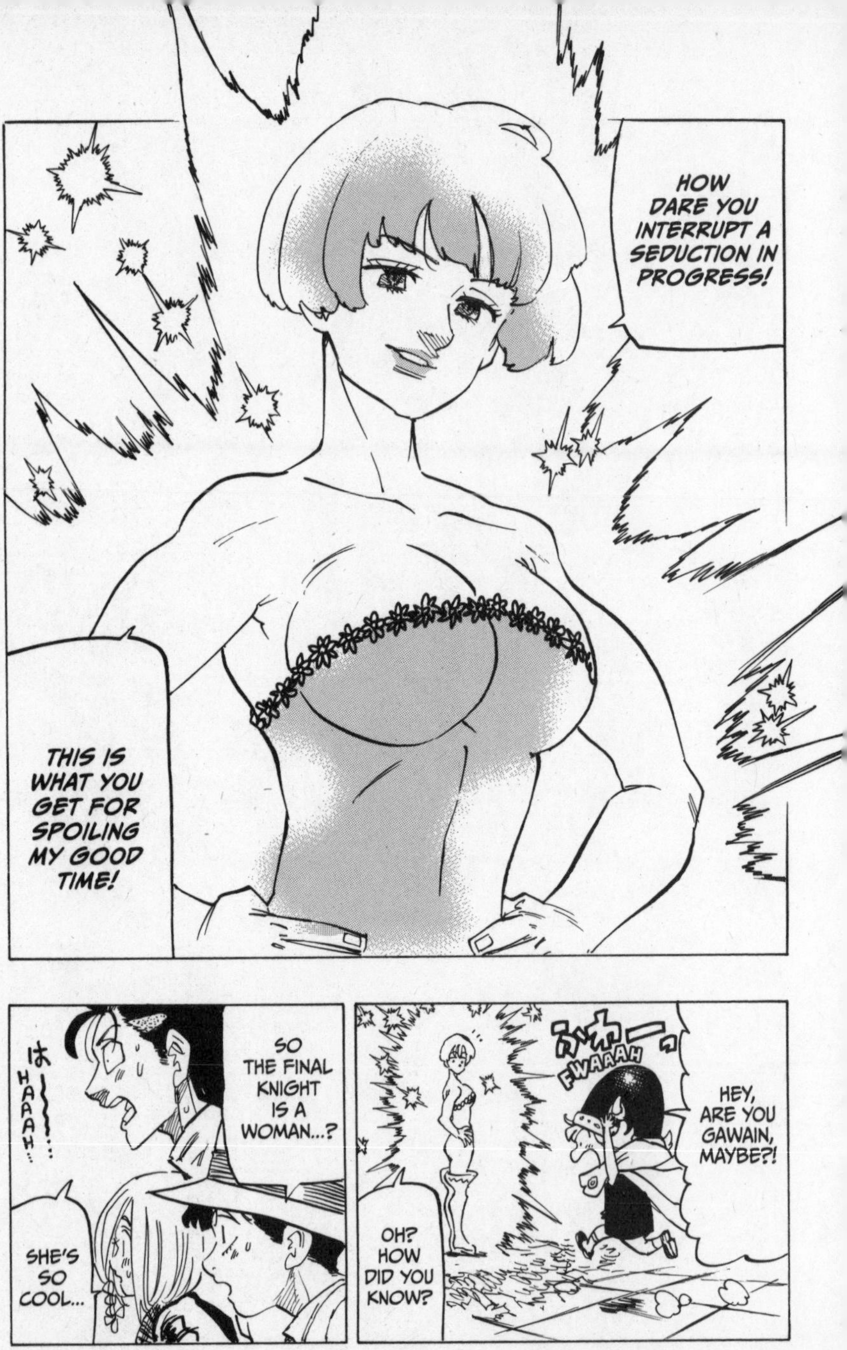
HOW DARE YOU INTERRUPT A SEDUCTION IN PROGRESS!
THIS IS WHAT YOU GET FOR SPOILING MY GOOD TIME!
ふわー
FWAAAH
HEY, ARE YOU GAWAIN, MAYBE?!
OH? HOW DID YOU KNOW?
SO THE FINAL KNIGHT IS A WOMAN...?
は～
HAAAAH...
SHE'S SO COOL...

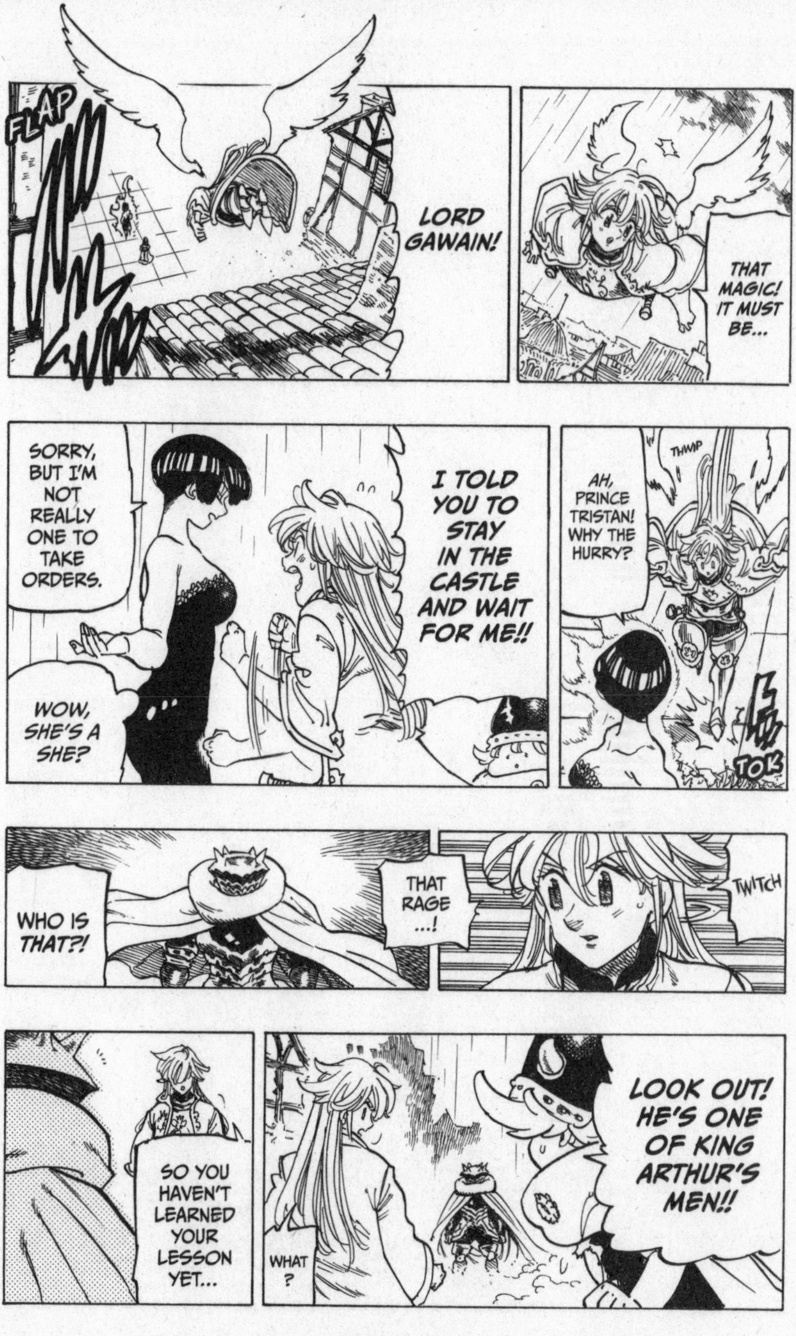
THAT MAGIC! IT MUST BE...
LORD GAWAIN!
FLAP
THWIP
AH, PRINCE TRISTAN! WHY THE HURRY?
TOK
I TOLD YOU TO STAY IN THE CASTLE AND WAIT FOR ME!!
SORRY, BUT I'M NOT REALLY ONE TO TAKE ORDERS.
WOW, SHE'S A SHE?
TWITCH
THAT RAGE ...!
WHO IS THAT?!
LOOK OUT! HE'S ONE OF KING ARTHUR'S MEN!!
WHAT ?
SO YOU HAVEN'T LEARNED YOUR LESSON YET...

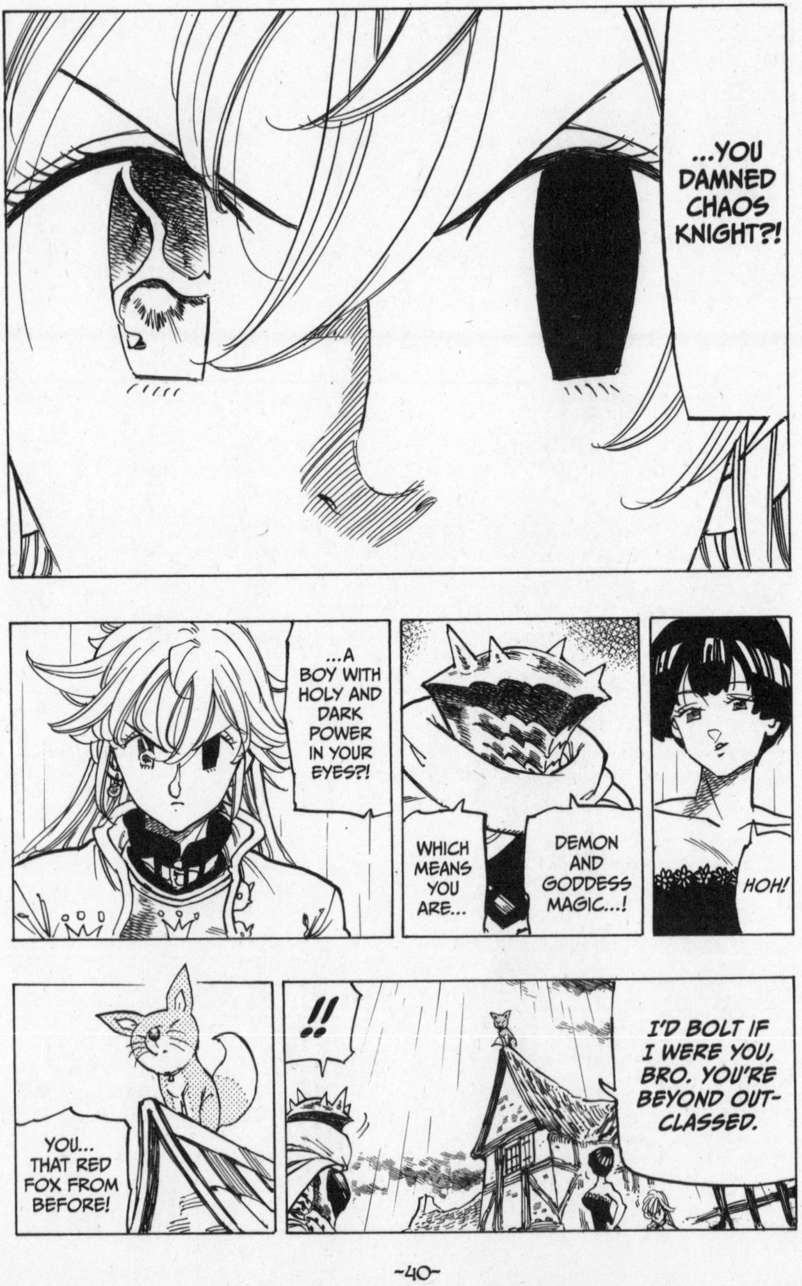

...YOU DAMNED CHAOS KNIGHT?!
HOH!
DEMON AND GODDESS MAGIC...!
WHICH MEANS YOU ARE...
...A BOY WITH HOLY AND DARK POWER IN YOUR EYES?!
I'D BOLT IF I WERE YOU, BRO. YOU'RE BEYOND OUT-CLASSED.
!!
YOU... THAT RED FOX FROM BEFORE!

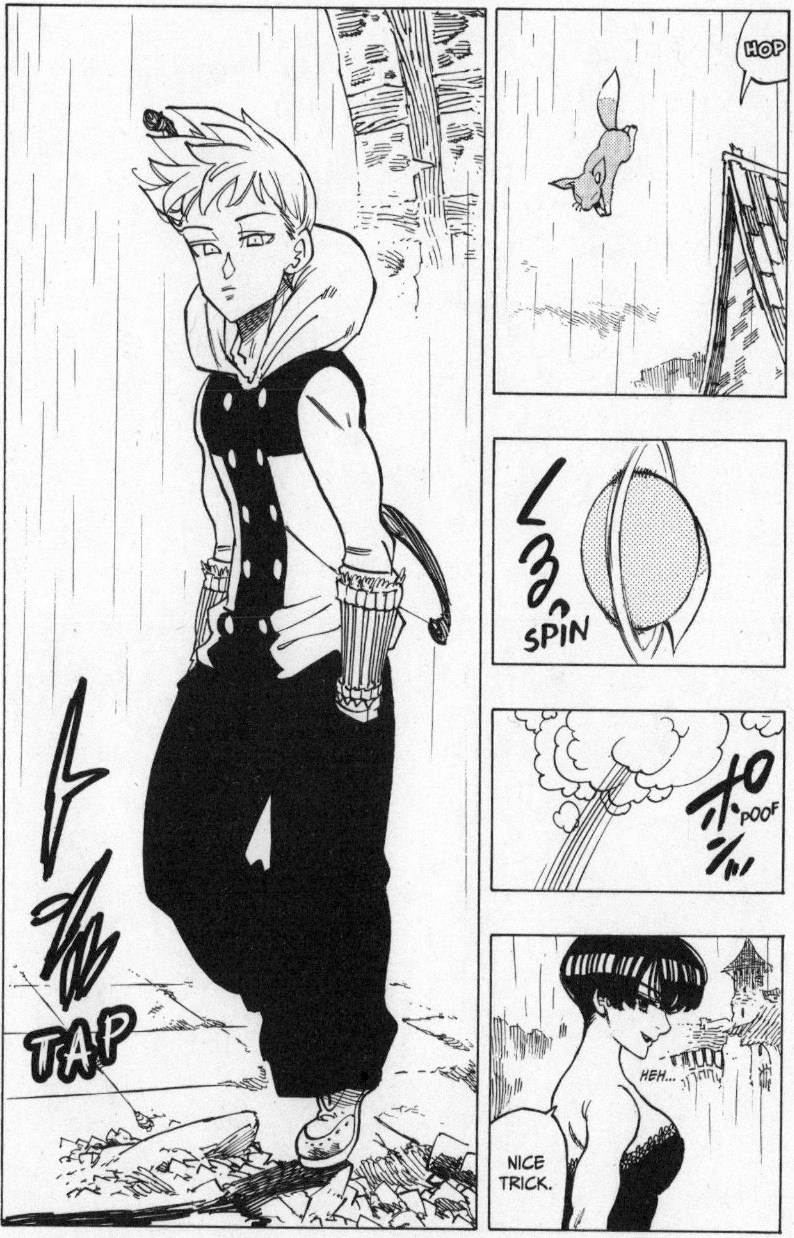
HOP
くる
SPIN
ポンッ
POOF
HEH...
NICE TRICK.
TAP

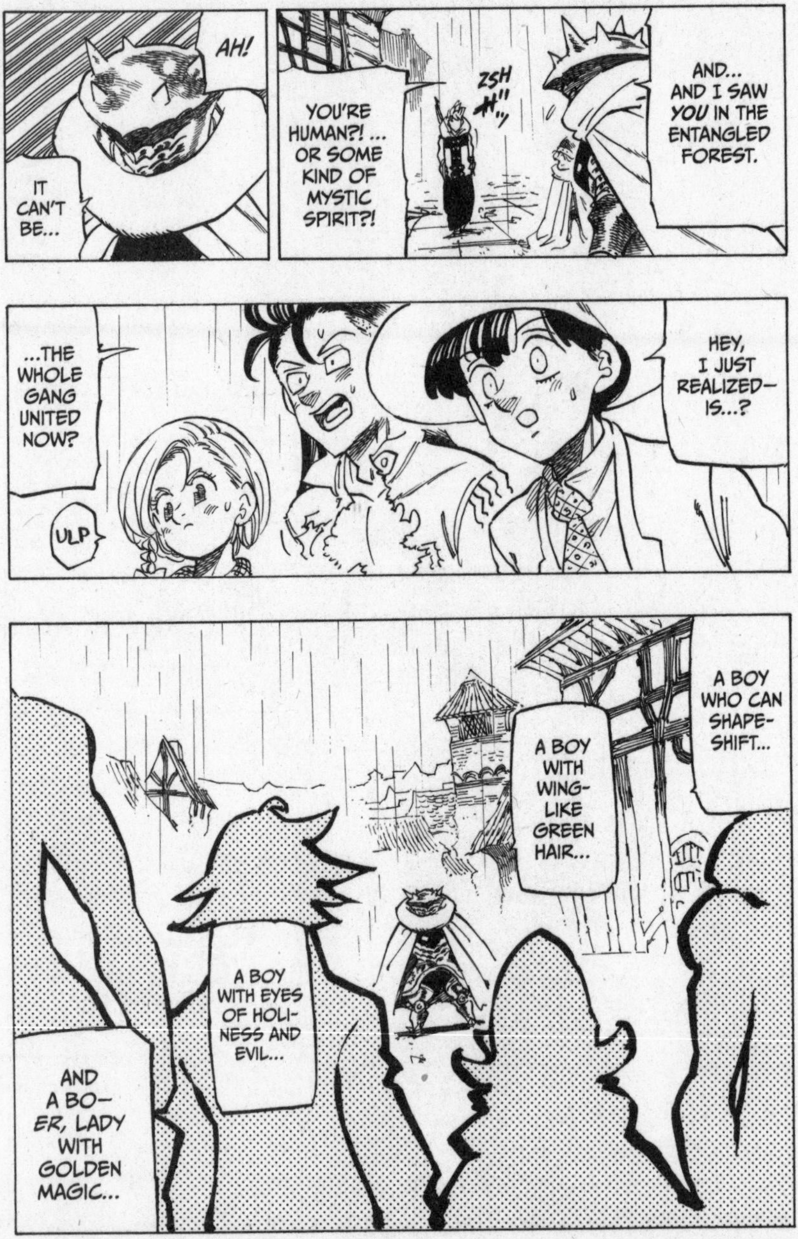
AND... AND I SAW *YOU* IN THE ENTANGLED FOREST.
ZSH HH
YOU'RE HUMAN?! ... OR SOME KIND OF MYSTIC SPIRIT?!
AH!
IT CAN'T BE...
HEY, I JUST REALIZED— IS...?
...THE WHOLE GANG UNITED NOW?
ULP
A BOY WHO CAN SHAPE-SHIFT...
A BOY WITH WING-LIKE GREEN HAIR...
A BOY WITH EYES OF HOLI-NESS AND EVIL...
AND A BO— *ER*, LADY WITH GOLDEN MAGIC...

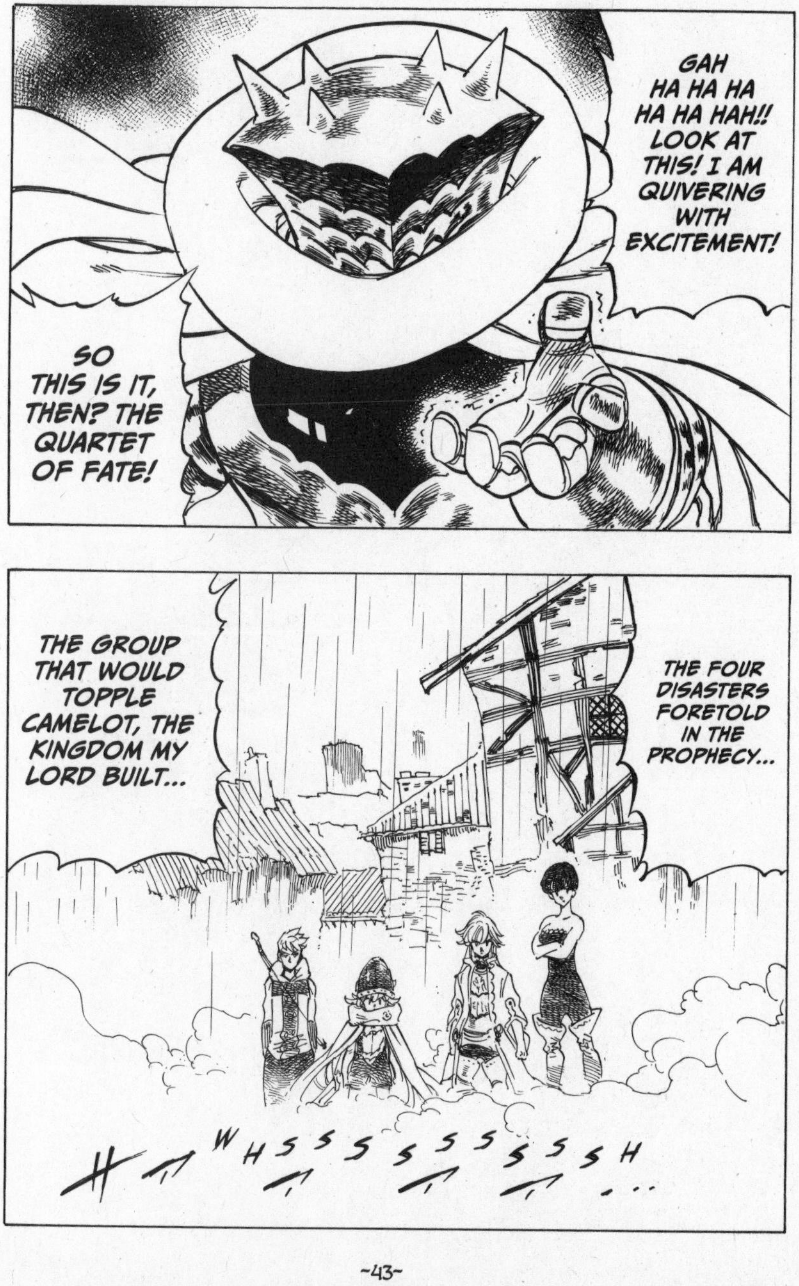
GAH HA HA HA HA HA HAH!! LOOK AT THIS! I AM QUIVERING WITH EXCITEMENT!
SO THIS IS IT, THEN? THE QUARTET OF FATE!
THE FOUR DISASTERS FORETOLD IN THE PROPHECY...
THE GROUP THAT WOULD TOPPLE CAMELOT, THE KINGDOM MY LORD BUILT...
WHSSSSSSSSSH

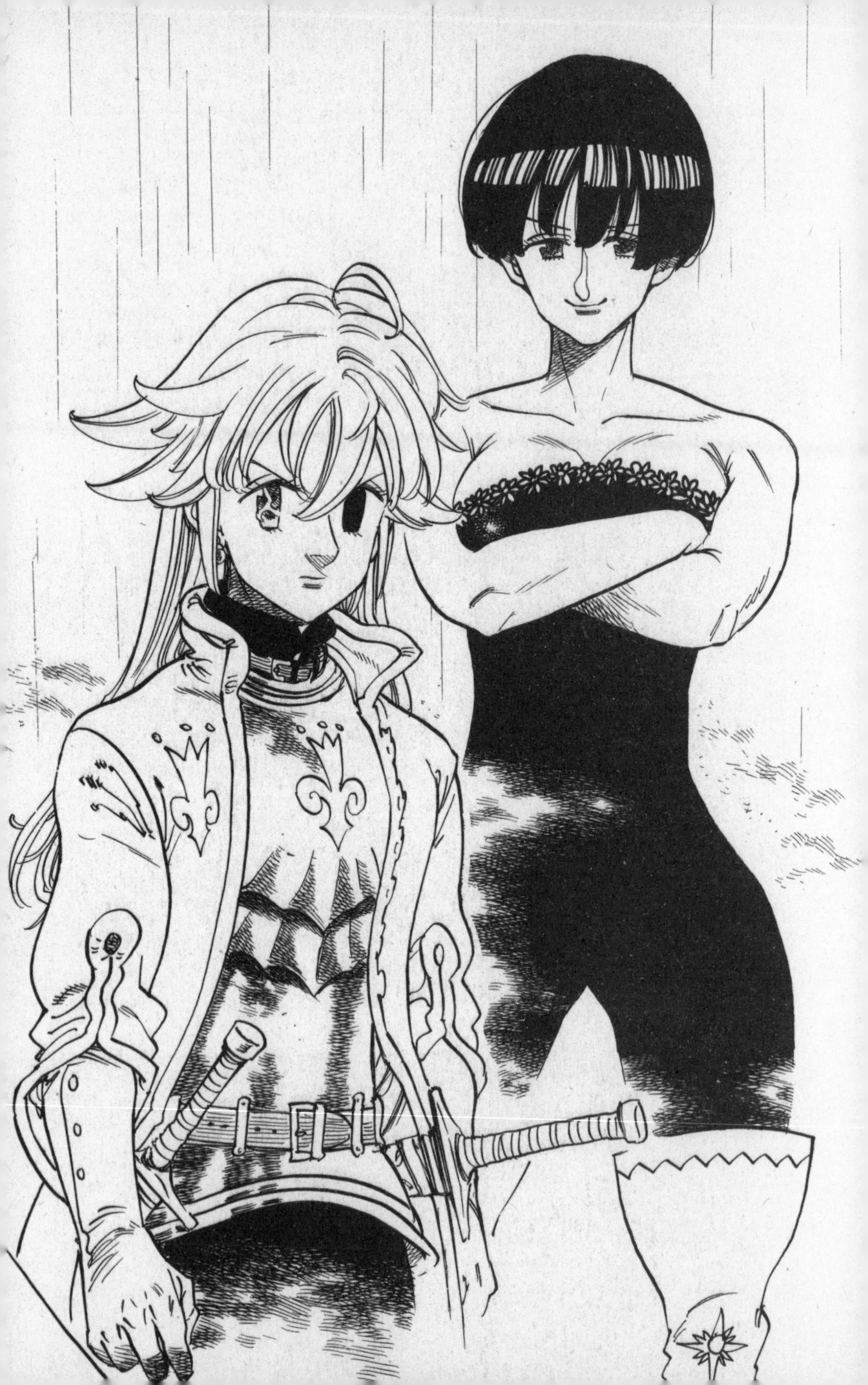

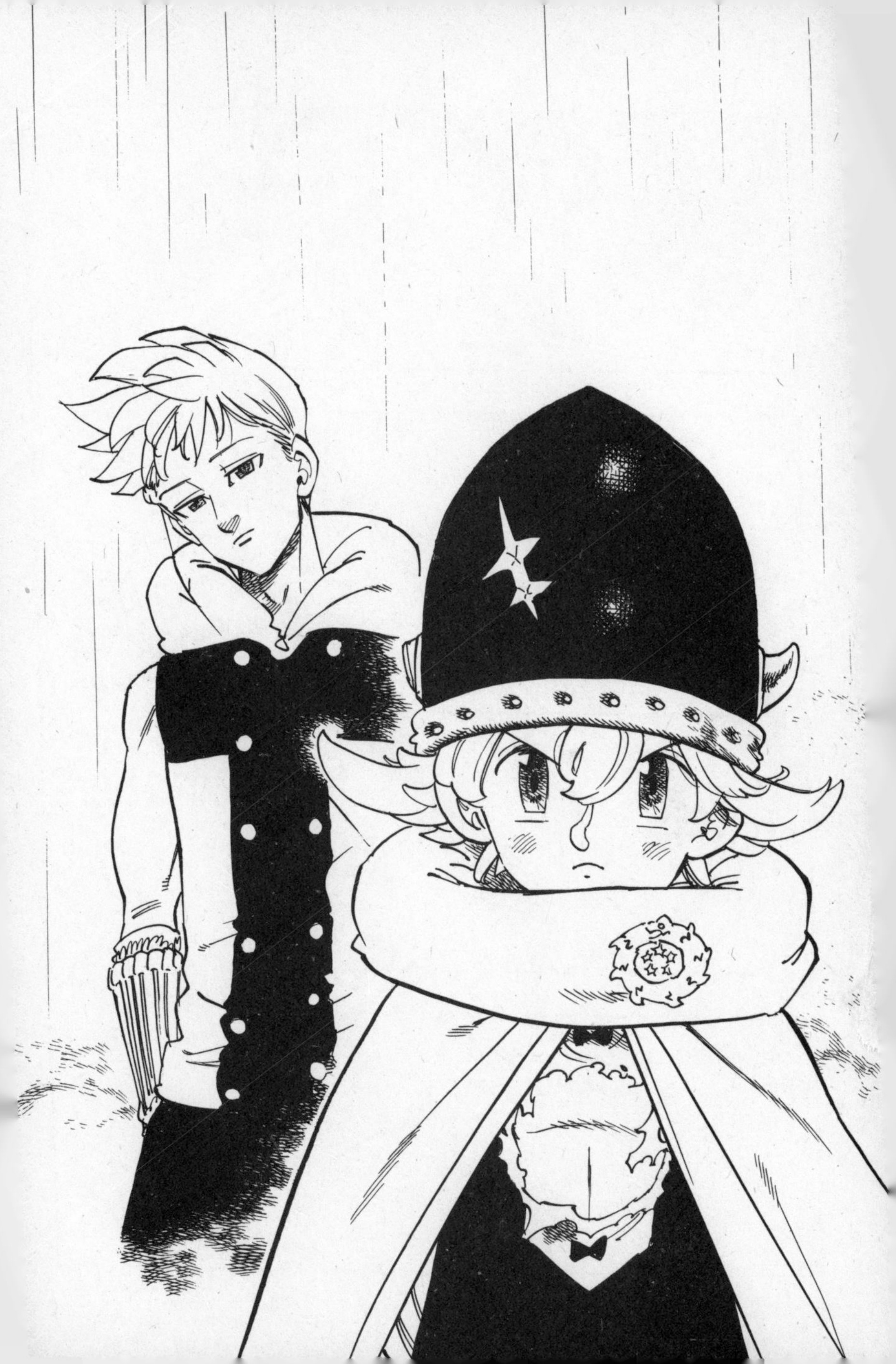

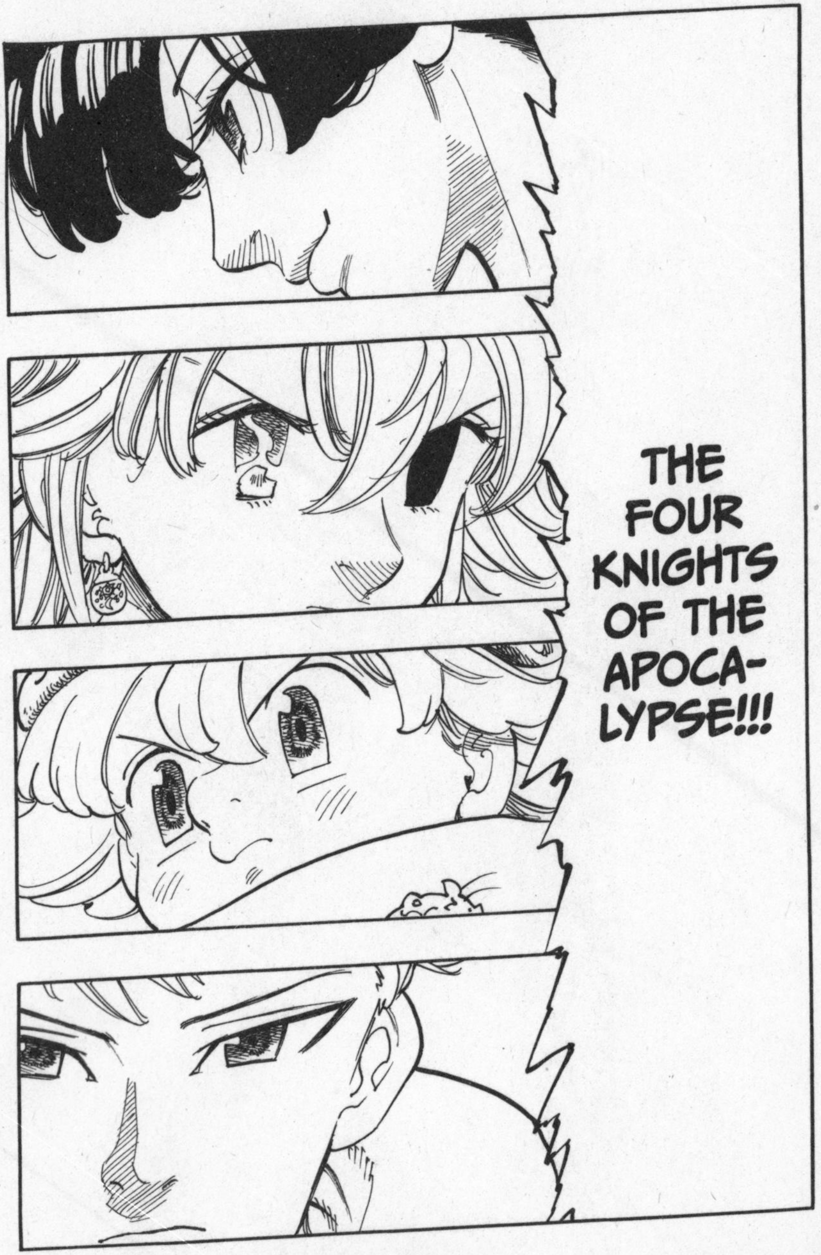
THE FOUR KNIGHTS OF THE APOCA-LYPSE!!!

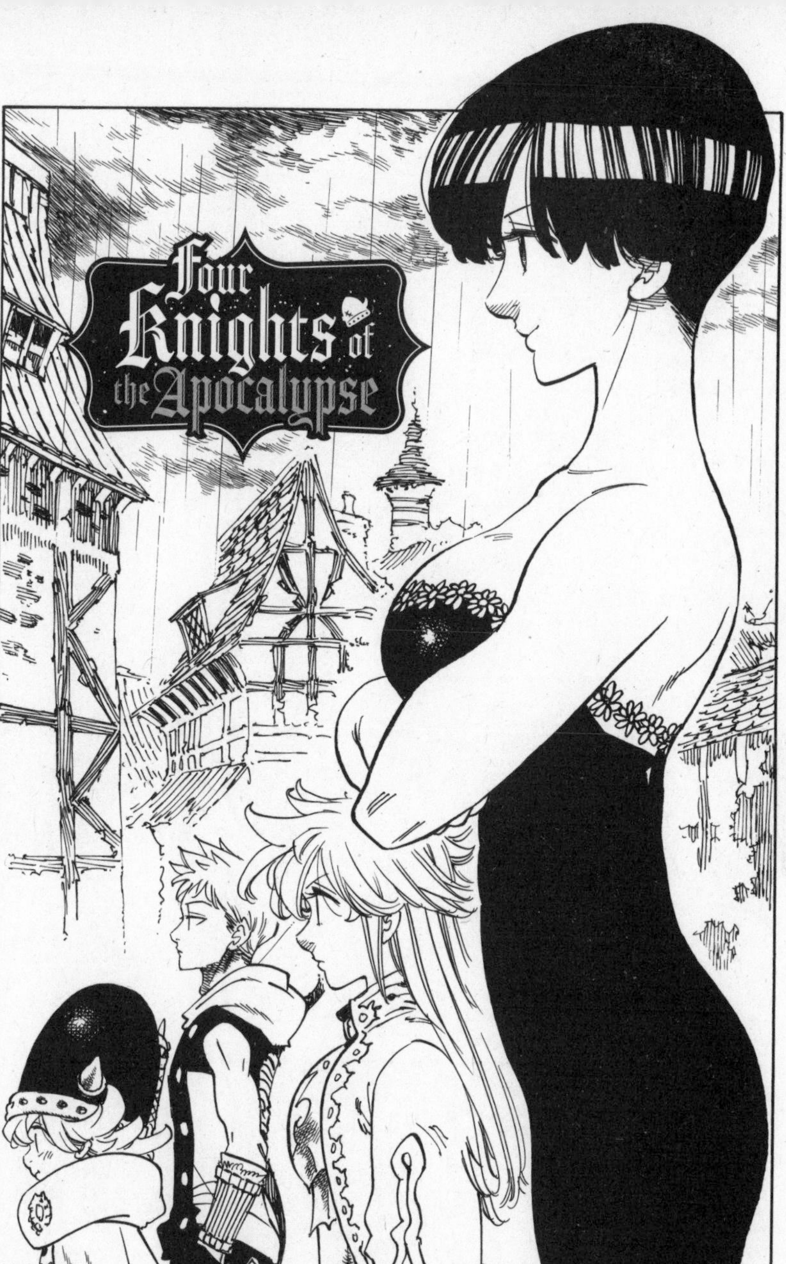
Four Knights of the Apocalypse

CHAPTER 62: THE START OF A NEW LEGEND

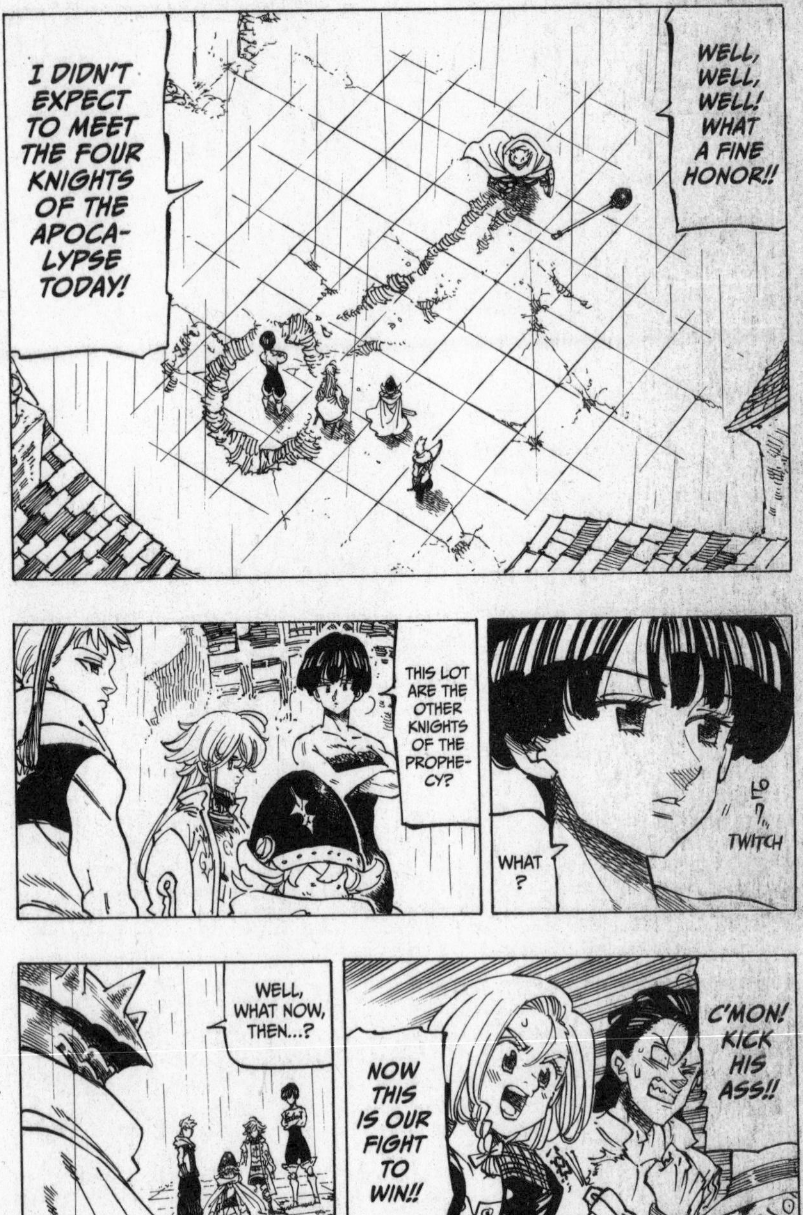
WELL, WELL, WELL! WHAT A FINE HONOR!!
I DIDN'T EXPECT TO MEET THE FOUR KNIGHTS OF THE APOCALYPSE TODAY!
TWITCH
WHAT ?
THIS LOT ARE THE OTHER KNIGHTS OF THE PROPHECY?
C'MON! KICK HIS ASS!!
NOW THIS IS OUR FIGHT TO WIN!!
WELL, WHAT NOW, THEN...?

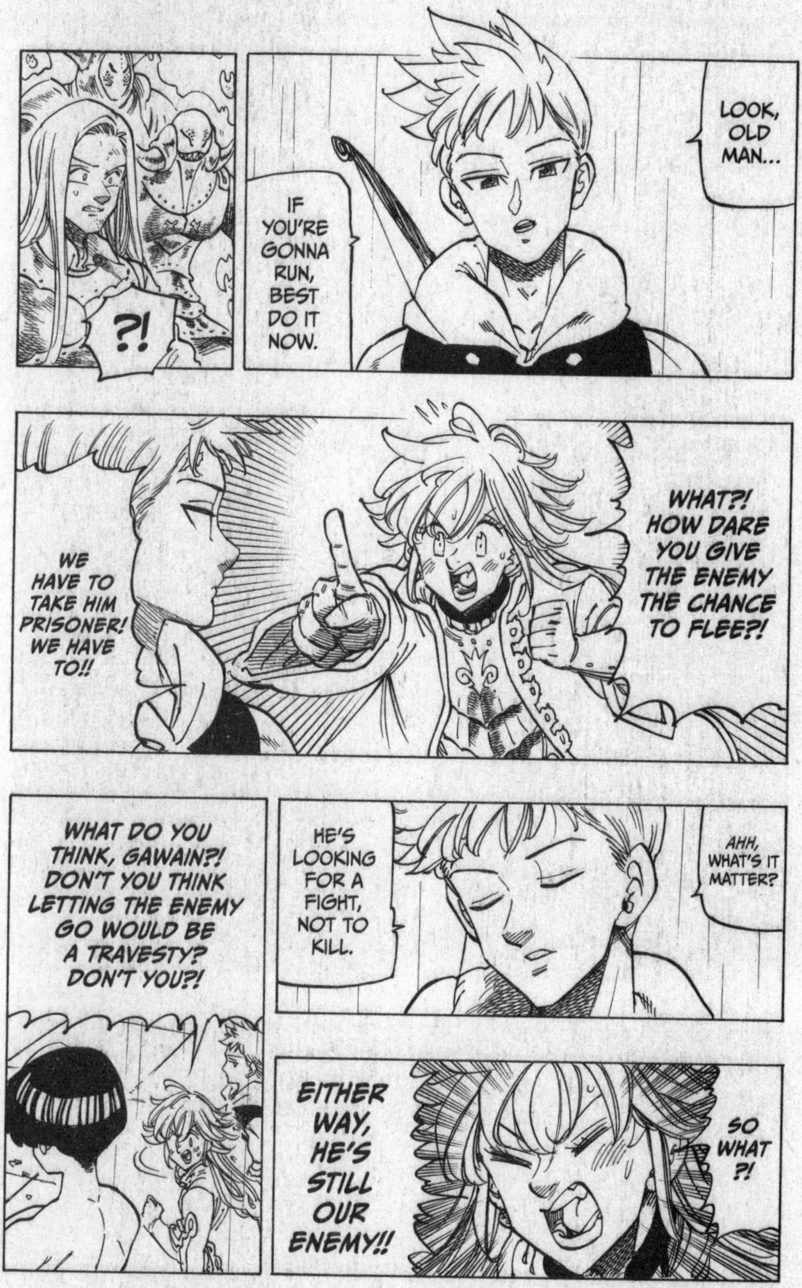
LOOK, OLD MAN...
IF YOU'RE GONNA RUN, BEST DO IT NOW.
?!
WHAT?! HOW DARE YOU GIVE THE ENEMY THE CHANCE TO FLEE?!
WE HAVE TO TAKE HIM PRISONER! WE HAVE TO!!
AHH, WHAT'S IT MATTER?
HE'S LOOKING FOR A FIGHT, NOT TO KILL.
SO WHAT ?!
EITHER WAY, HE'S STILL OUR ENEMY!!
WHAT DO YOU THINK, GAWAIN?! DON'T YOU THINK LETTING THE ENEMY GO WOULD BE A TRAVESTY? DON'T YOU?!

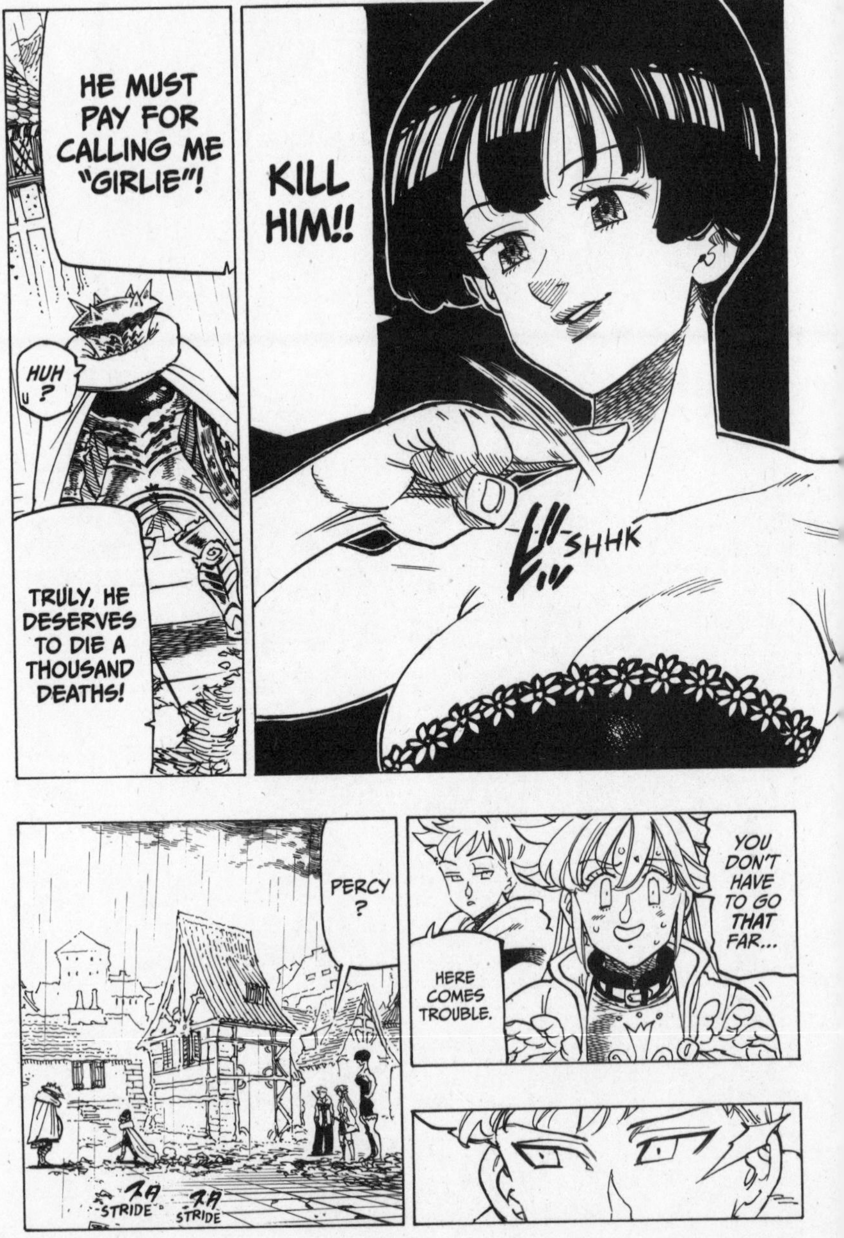
KILL HIM!!
SHHK
HE MUST PAY FOR CALLING ME "GIRLIE"!
HUH?
TRULY, HE DESERVES TO DIE A THOUSAND DEATHS!
YOU DON'T HAVE TO GO THAT FAR...
HERE COMES TROUBLE.
PERCY?
スタ STRIDE
スタ STRIDE

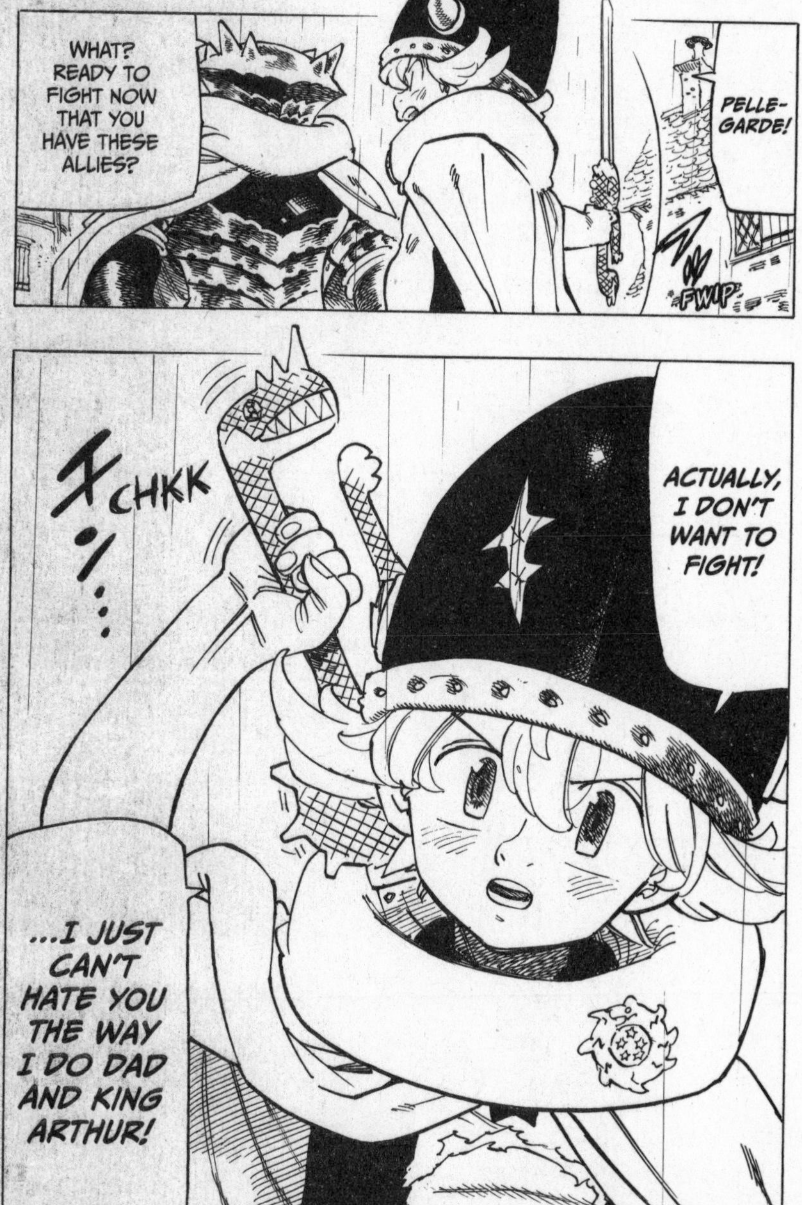
PELLE-GARDE!
FWIP
WHAT? READY TO FIGHT NOW THAT YOU HAVE THESE ALLIES?
ACTUALLY, I DON'T WANT TO FIGHT!
CHKK
...I JUST CAN'T HATE YOU THE WAY I DO DAD AND KING ARTHUR!

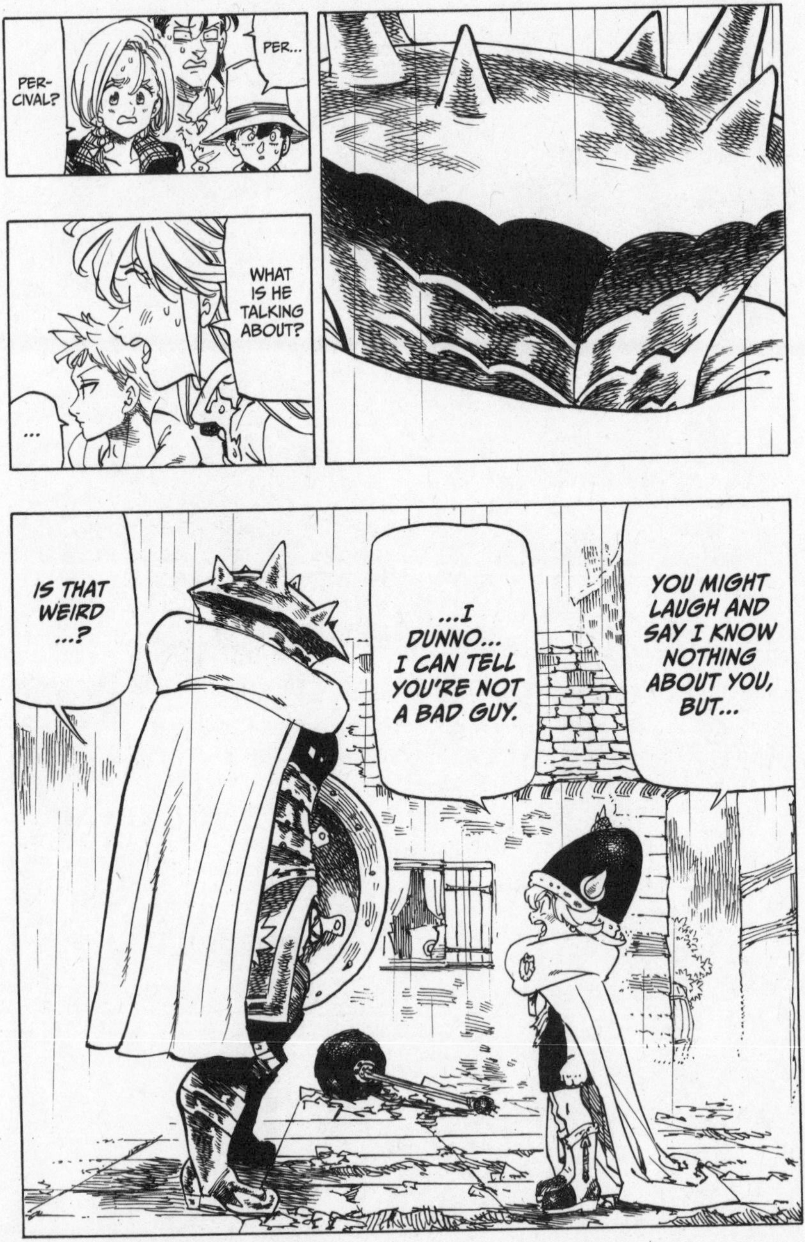
PER...
PER-CIVAL?
WHAT IS HE TALKING ABOUT?
...
YOU MIGHT LAUGH AND SAY I KNOW NOTHING ABOUT YOU, BUT...
...I DUNNO... I CAN TELL YOU'RE NOT A BAD GUY.
IS THAT WEIRD ...?

WELL...
YEAH!

PAT ♪
PAT ♪

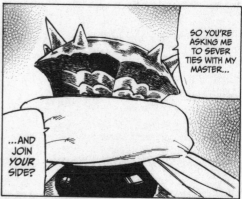

SO YOU'RE
ASKING ME
TO SEVER
TIES WITH MY
MASTER...

IS HE
FOR
REAL?

HUH
...?

...AND
JOIN
YOUR
SIDE?

FWIP

DANGLE

THAT'S
NOT
GONNA
HAPPEN.

SORRY,
KID.

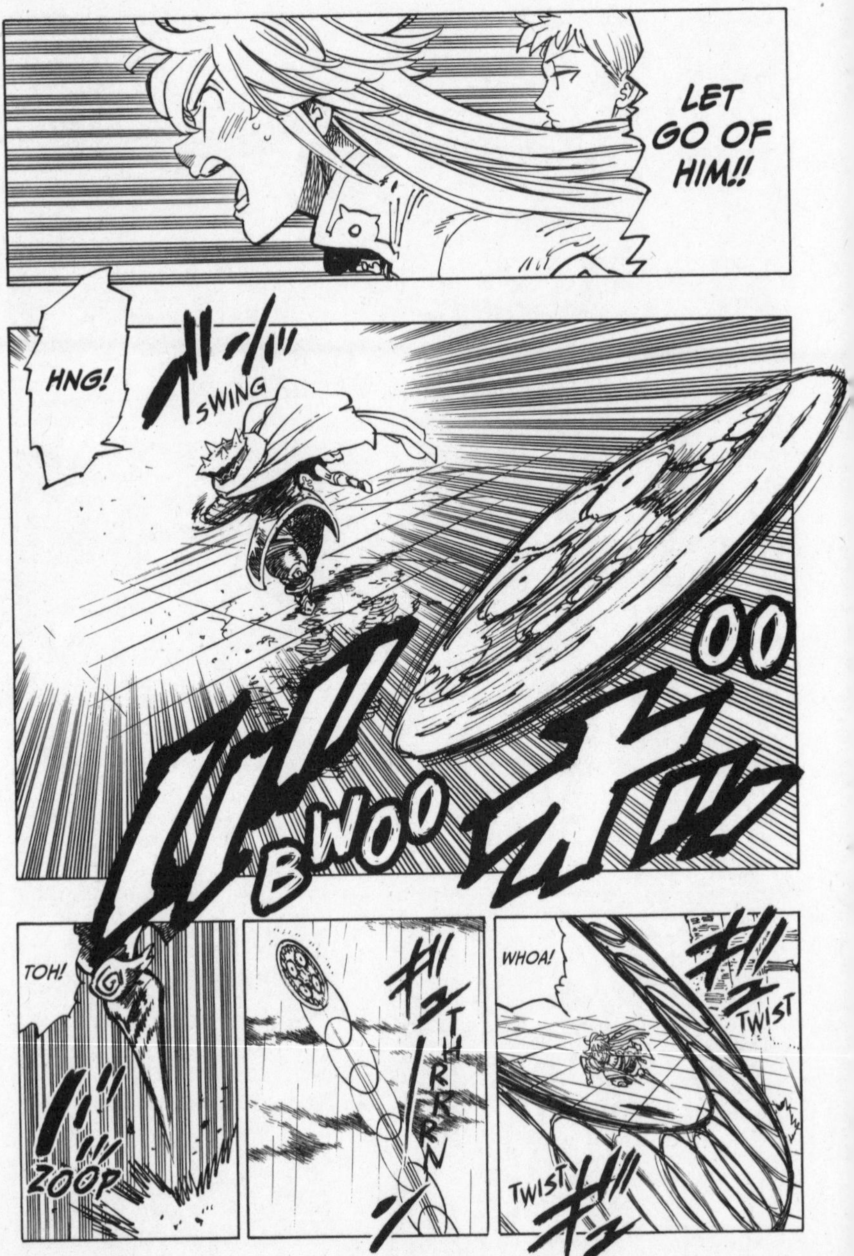
LET GO OF HIM!!
HNG!
SWING
BWOO
OO
WHOA!
TWIST
TWIST
THRRRRN
TOH!
ZOOP

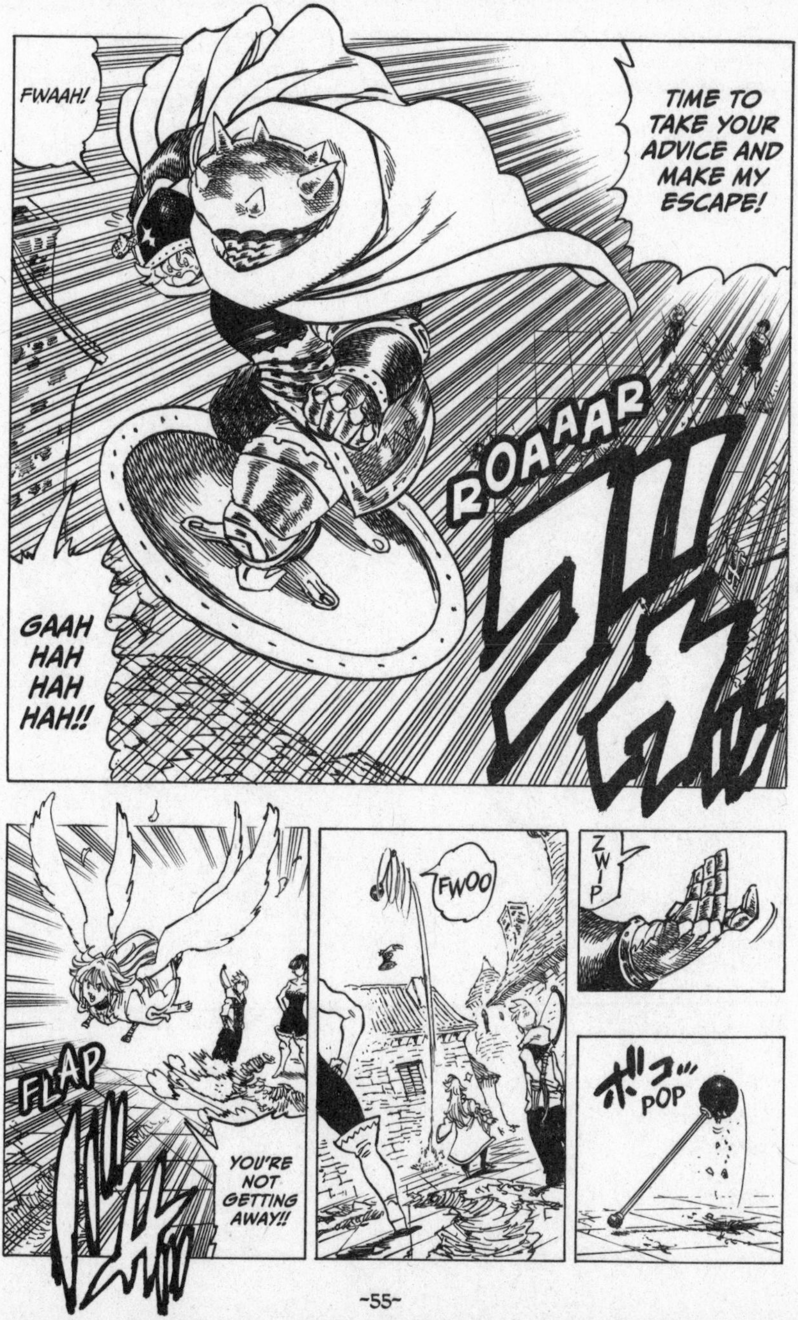

TIME TO TAKE YOUR ADVICE AND MAKE MY ESCAPE!
FWAAH!
ROAAAR
GAAH HAH HAH HAH!!
ZWIP
ボコッ
POP
FWOO
FLAP
YOU'RE NOT GETTING AWAY!!

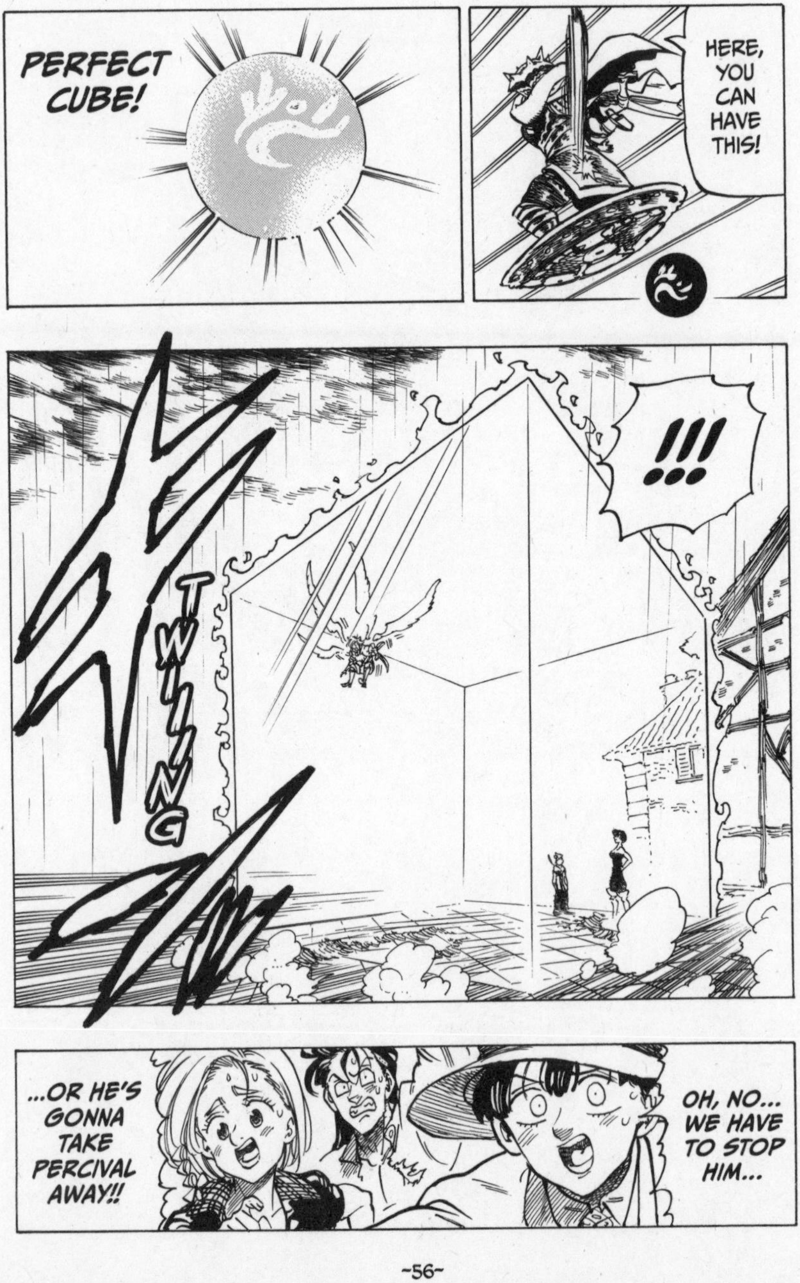
HERE, YOU CAN HAVE THIS!
PERFECT CUBE!
!!!
TWIING
OH, NO... WE HAVE TO STOP HIM...
...OR HE'S GONNA TAKE PERCIVAL AWAY!!

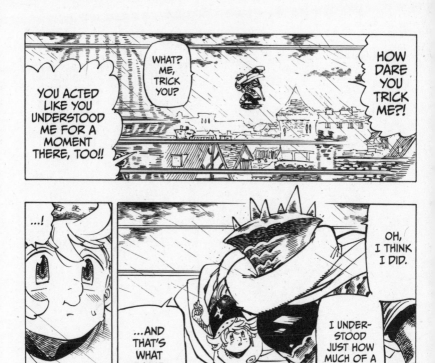

HOW DARE YOU TRICK ME?!

WHAT? ME, TRICK YOU?

YOU ACTED LIKE YOU UNDERSTOOD ME FOR A MOMENT THERE, TOO!!

...!

OH, I THINK I DID.

I UNDERSTOOD JUST HOW MUCH OF A PUSHOVER YOU ARE...

...AND THAT'S WHAT I LIKE ABOUT YOU.

JUST LET ME GOOOO!!

WHOA THERE! STOP STRUGGLING! JUST SIT TIGHT FOR ME!!

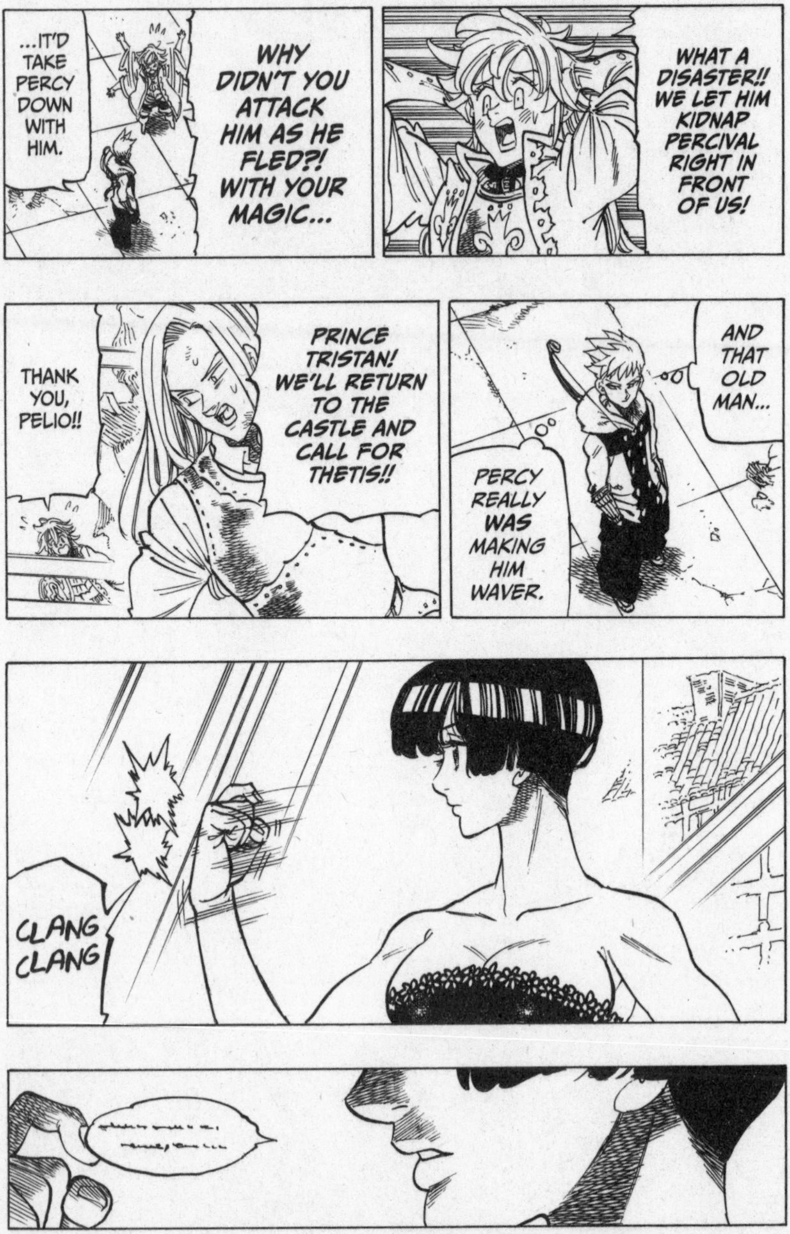
WHAT A DISASTER!! WE LET HIM KIDNAP PERCIVAL RIGHT IN FRONT OF US!
WHY DIDN'T YOU ATTACK HIM AS HE FLED?! WITH YOUR MAGIC...
...IT'D TAKE PERCY DOWN WITH HIM.
AND THAT OLD MAN...
PERCY REALLY WAS MAKING HIM WAVER.
PRINCE TRISTAN! WE'LL RETURN TO THE CASTLE AND CALL FOR THETIS!!
THANK YOU, PELIO!!
CLANG CLANG

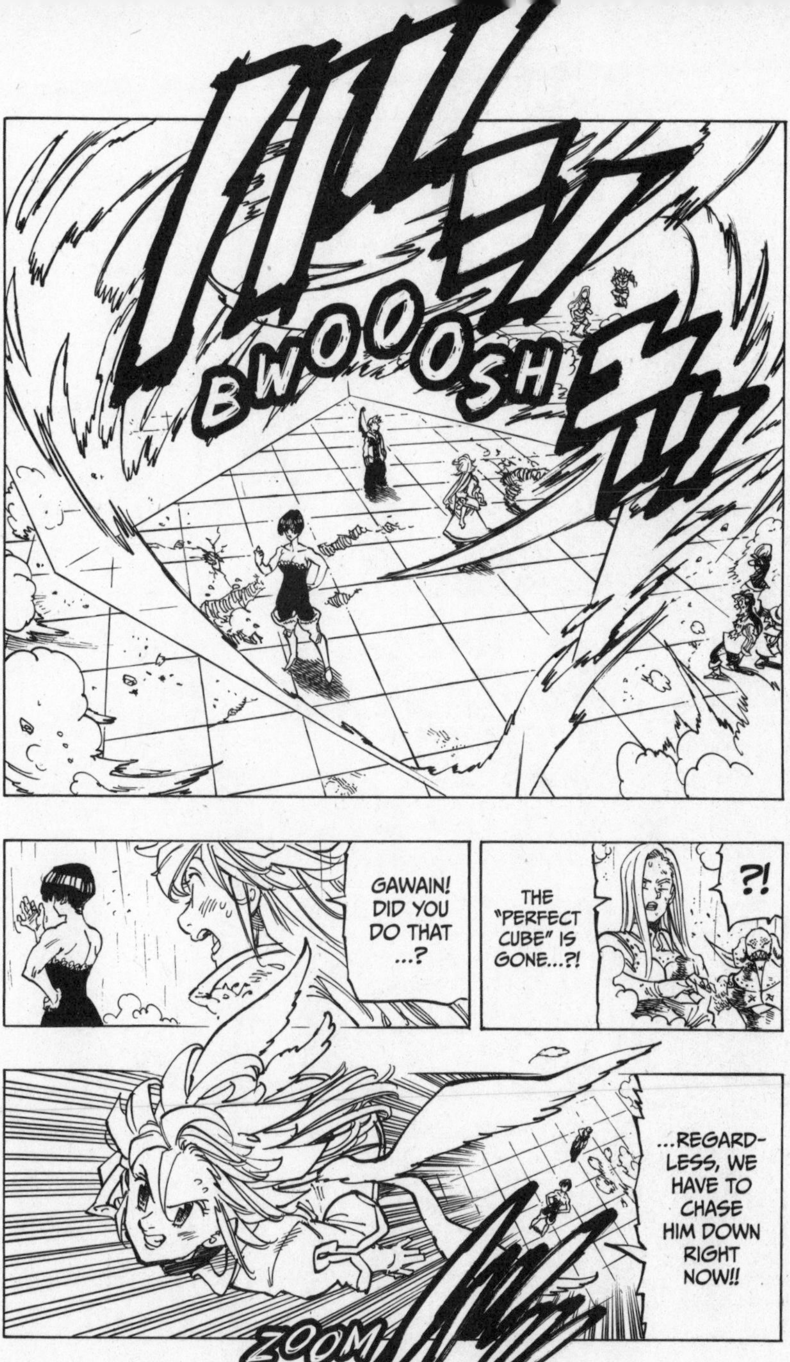
BWOOOSH
?!
THE "PERFECT CUBE" IS GONE...?!
GAWAIN! DID YOU DO THAT ...?
...REGARD-LESS, WE HAVE TO CHASE HIM DOWN RIGHT NOW!!
ZOOM

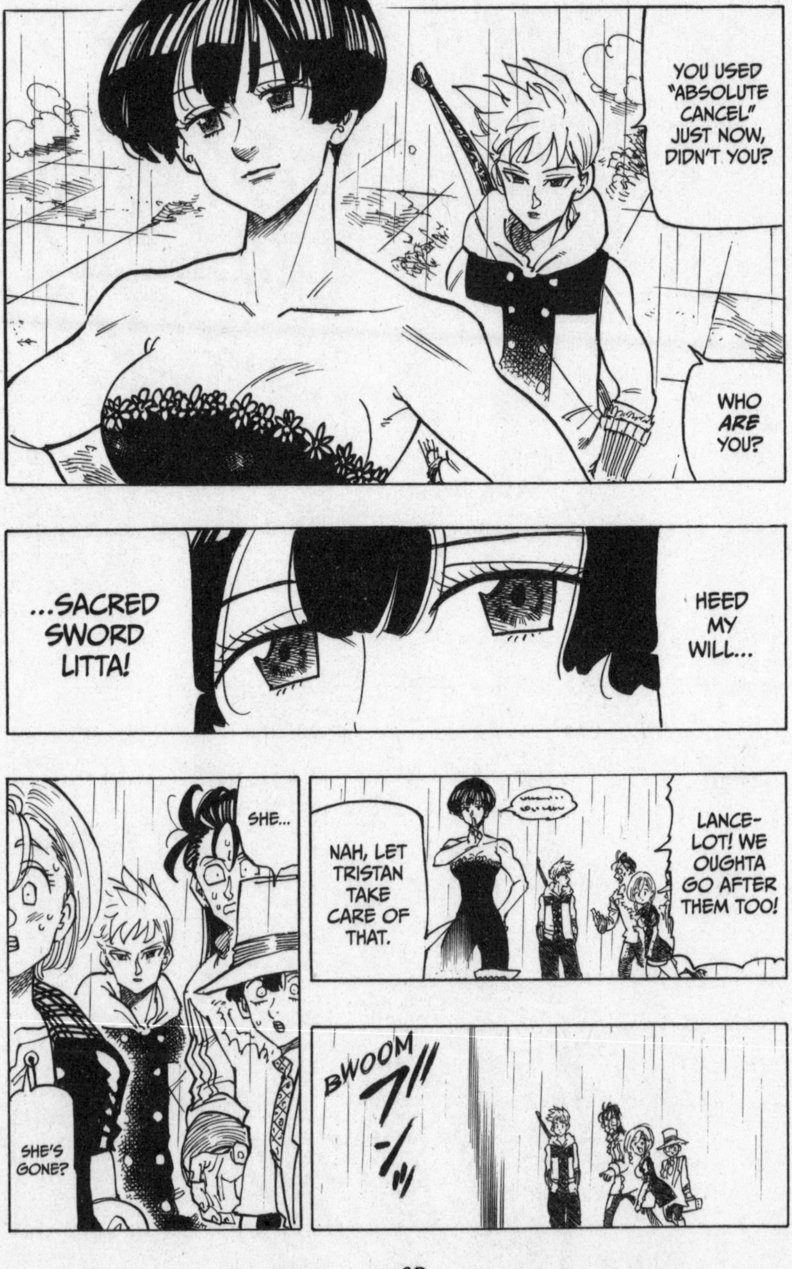
YOU USED "ABSOLUTE CANCEL" JUST NOW, DIDN'T YOU?
WHO ARE YOU?
HEED MY WILL...
...SACRED SWORD LITTA!
LANCE-LOT! WE OUGHTA GO AFTER THEM TOO!
NAH, LET TRISTAN TAKE CARE OF THAT.
BWOOM
SHE...
SHE'S GONE?

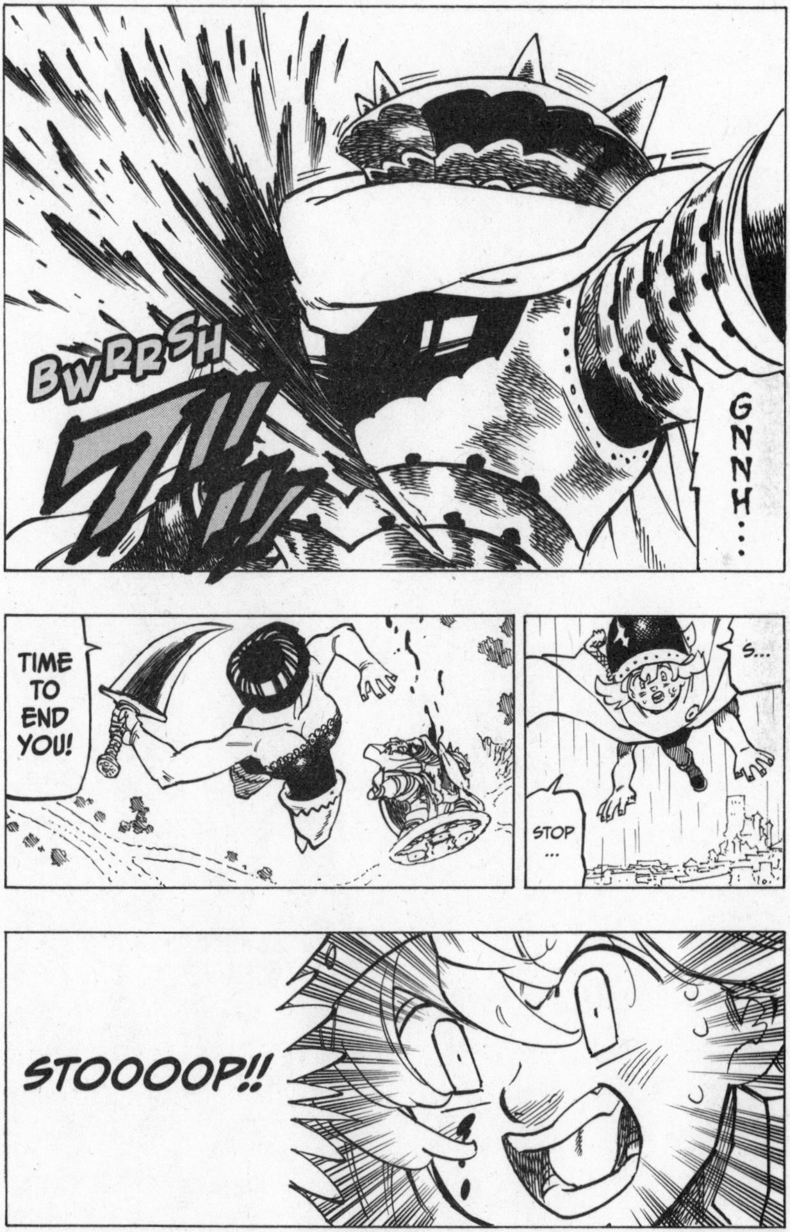
GNNH...
BWRRSH
S...
STOP ...
TIME TO END YOU!
STOOOOP!!

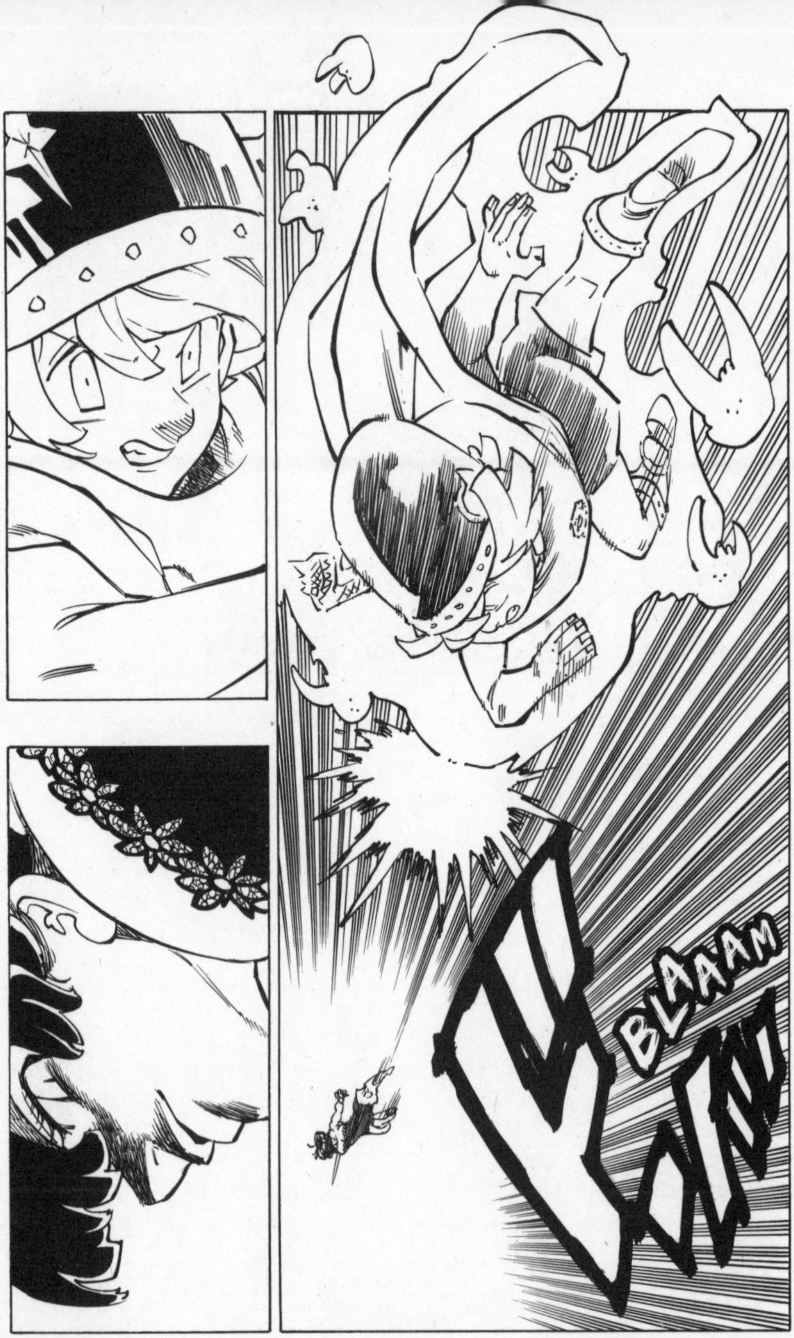
BLAAAM

Four Knights of the Apocalypse

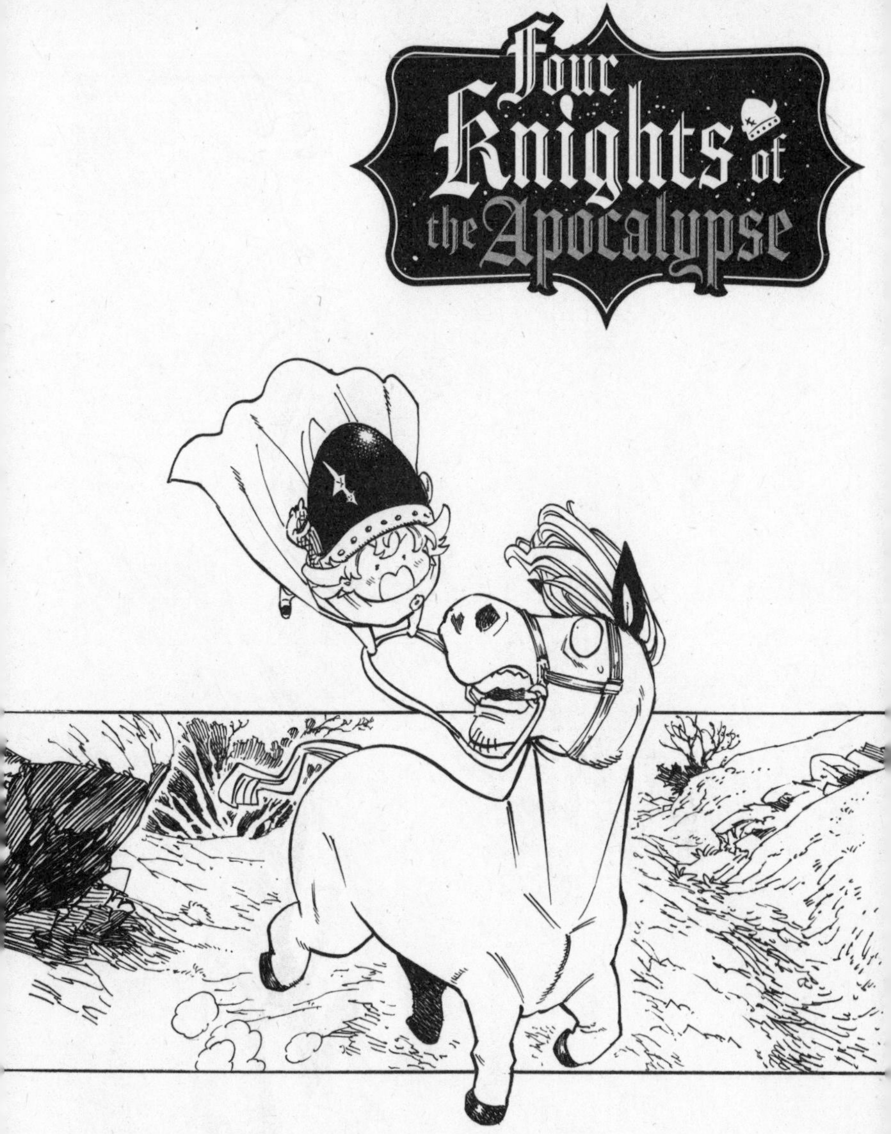

CHAPTER 63: TAMING A WILD HORSE

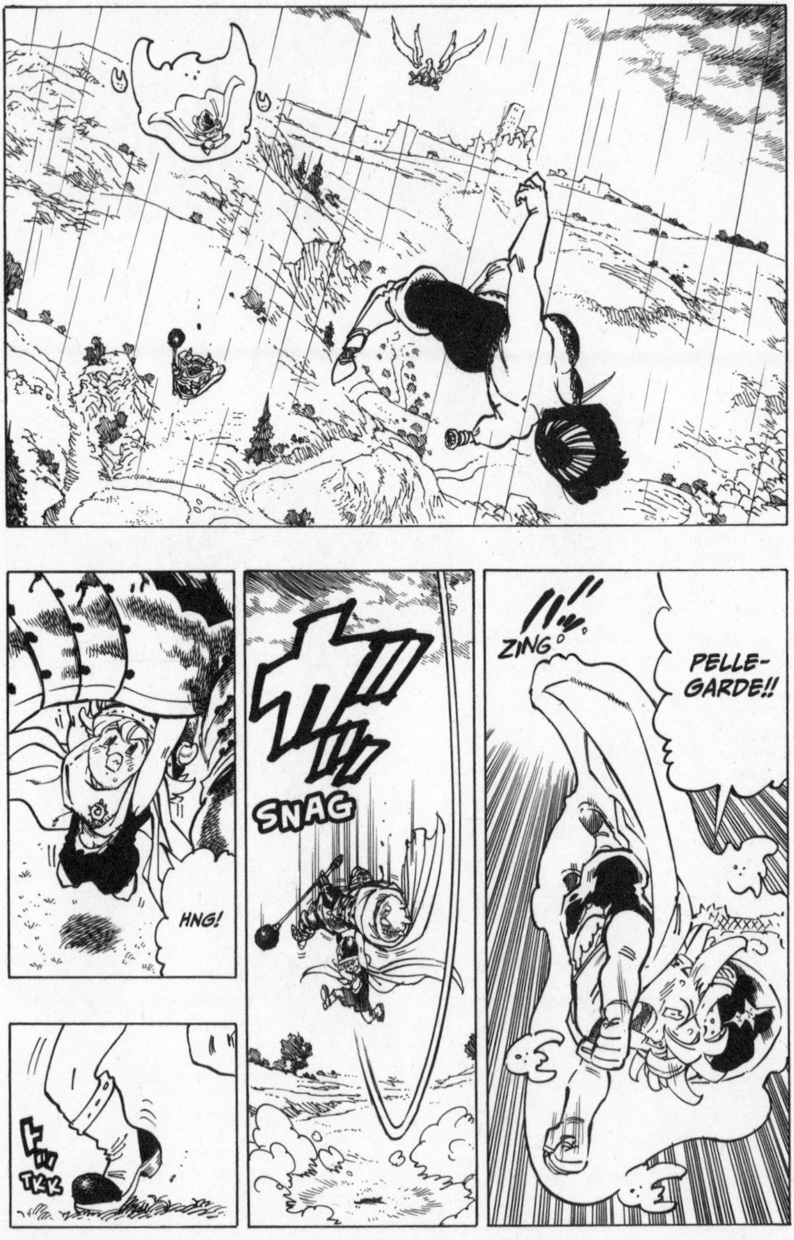
PELLE-
GARDE!!
ZING
SNAG
HNG!
TKK

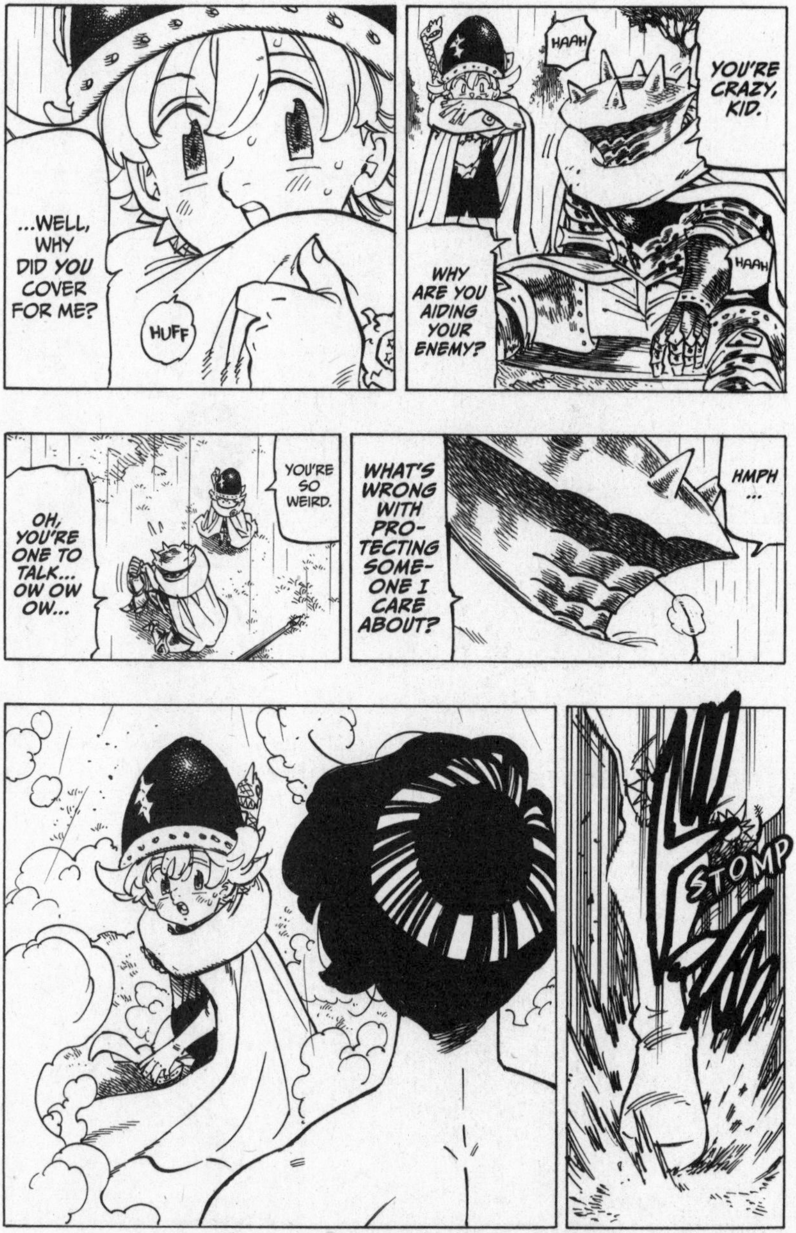
HAAH
YOU'RE CRAZY, KID.
HAAH
WHY ARE YOU AIDING YOUR ENEMY?
...WELL, WHY DID YOU COVER FOR ME?
HUFF
HMPH ...
WHAT'S WRONG WITH PROTECTING SOMEONE I CARE ABOUT?
YOU'RE SO WEIRD.
OH, YOU'RE ONE TO TALK... OW OW OW...
STOMP

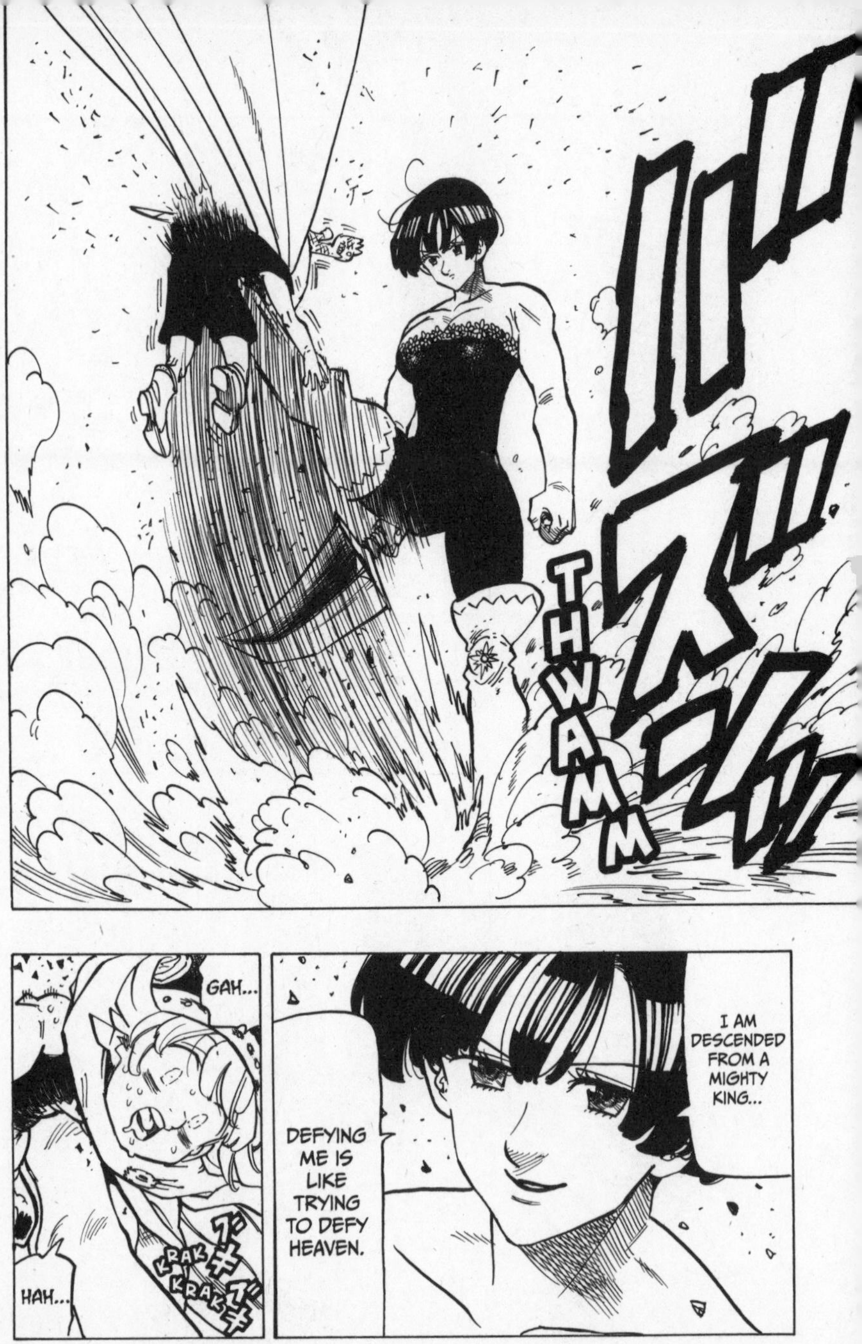
THWAMM
I AM DESCENDED FROM A MIGHTY KING...
DEFYING ME IS LIKE TRYING TO DEFY HEAVEN.
GAH...
KRAK KRAK
HAH...

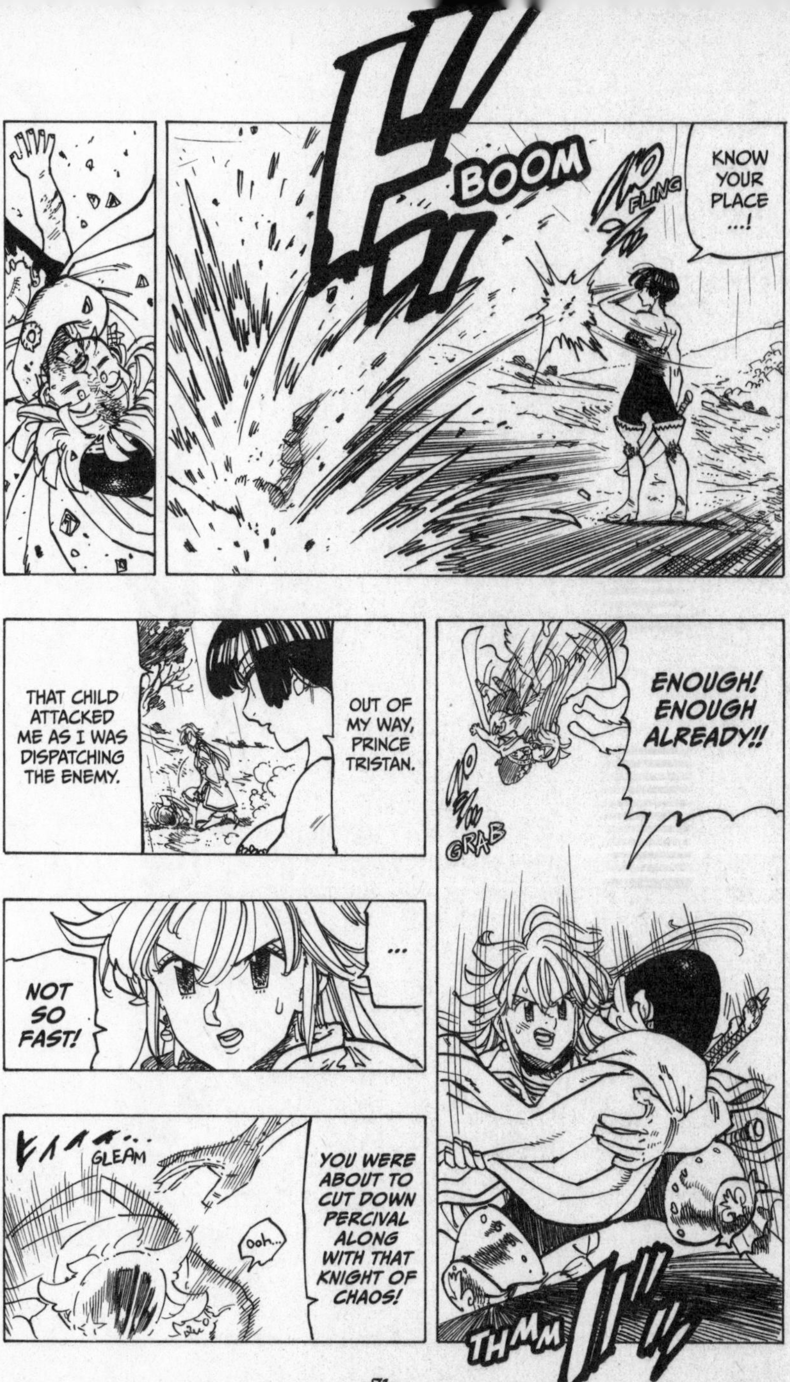
KNOW YOUR PLACE ...!
FLING
BOOM
ENOUGH! ENOUGH ALREADY!!
GRAB
THMM
OUT OF MY WAY, PRINCE TRISTAN.
THAT CHILD ATTACKED ME AS I WAS DISPATCHING THE ENEMY.
...
NOT SO FAST!
YOU WERE ABOUT TO CUT DOWN PERCIVAL ALONG WITH THAT KNIGHT OF CHAOS!
ooh...
GLEAM

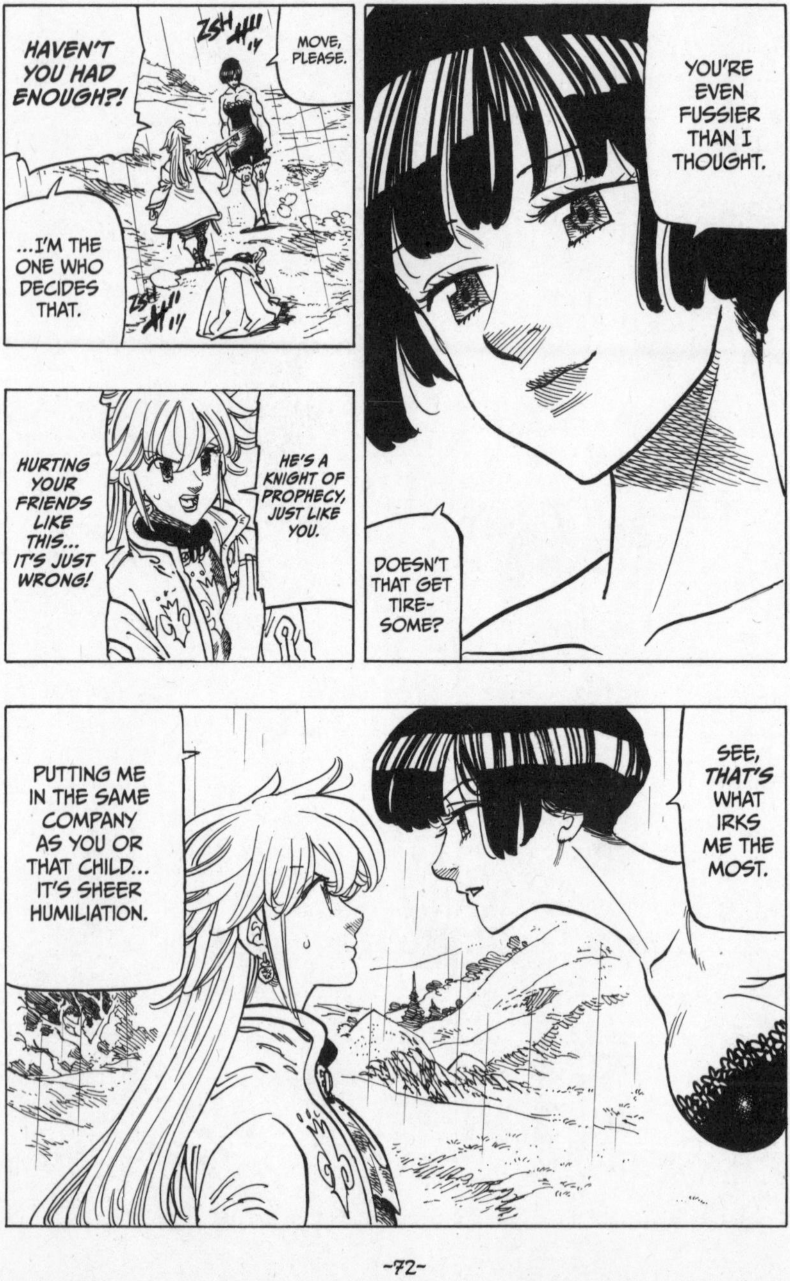
YOU'RE EVEN FUSSIER THAN I THOUGHT.
DOESN'T THAT GET TIRE-SOME?
MOVE, PLEASE.
ZSH
HAVEN'T YOU HAD ENOUGH?!
...I'M THE ONE WHO DECIDES THAT.
ZSH
HE'S A KNIGHT OF PROPHECY, JUST LIKE YOU.
HURTING YOUR FRIENDS LIKE THIS... IT'S JUST WRONG!
SEE, THAT'S WHAT IRKS ME THE MOST.
PUTTING ME IN THE SAME COMPANY AS YOU OR THAT CHILD... IT'S SHEER HUMILIATION.

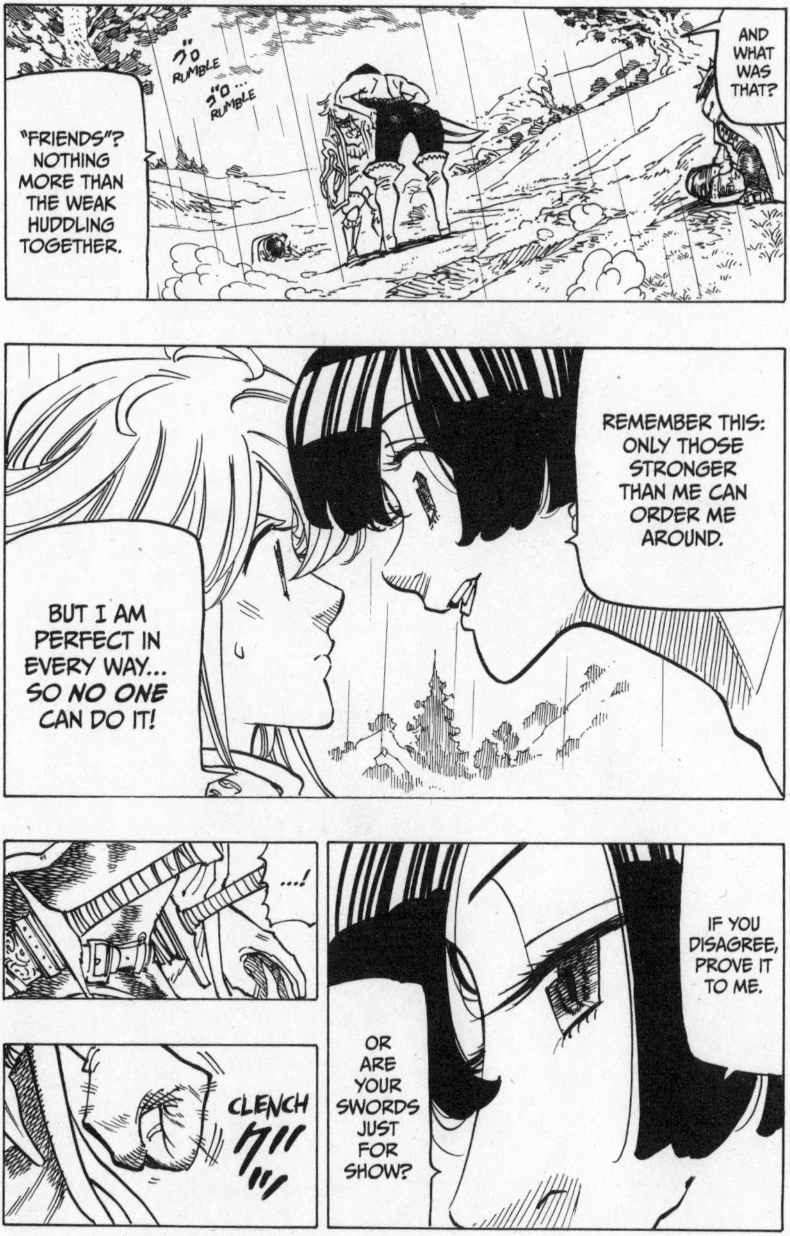
AND WHAT WAS THAT?
ゴロ RUMBLE
ゴロ... RUMBLE
"FRIENDS"? NOTHING MORE THAN THE WEAK HUDDLING TOGETHER.
REMEMBER THIS: ONLY THOSE STRONGER THAN ME CAN ORDER ME AROUND.
BUT I AM PERFECT IN EVERY WAY... SO *NO ONE* CAN DO IT!
IF YOU DISAGREE, PROVE IT TO ME.
OR ARE YOUR SWORDS JUST FOR SHOW?
...!
CLENCH

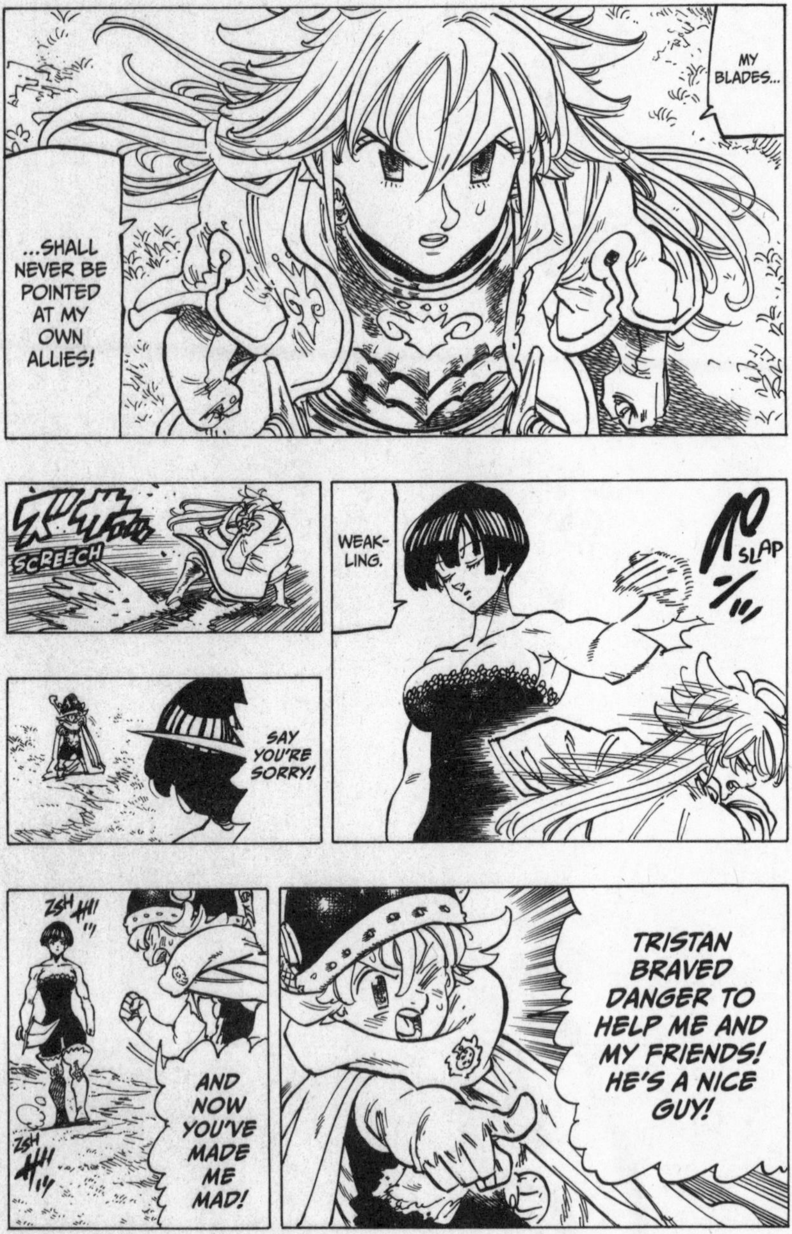
MY BLADES...
...SHALL NEVER BE POINTED AT MY OWN ALLIES!
WEAK-LING.
SLAP
SCREECH
SAY YOU'RE SORRY!
TRISTAN BRAVED DANGER TO HELP ME AND MY FRIENDS! HE'S A NICE GUY!
ZSH
ZSH
AND NOW YOU'VE MADE ME MAD!

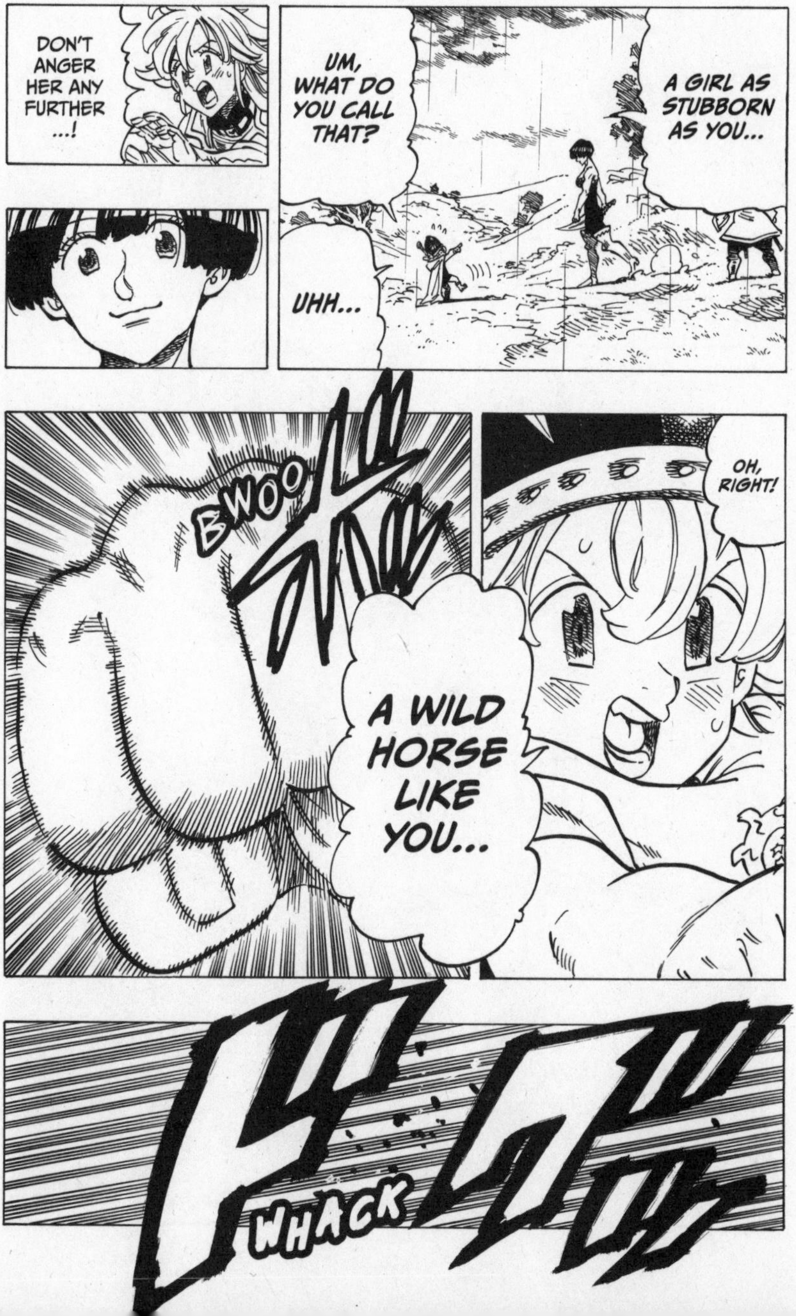
A GIRL AS STUBBORN AS YOU...
UM, WHAT DO YOU CALL THAT?
UHH...
DON'T ANGER HER ANY FURTHER ...!
OH, RIGHT!
A WILD HORSE LIKE YOU...
BWOO
WHACK

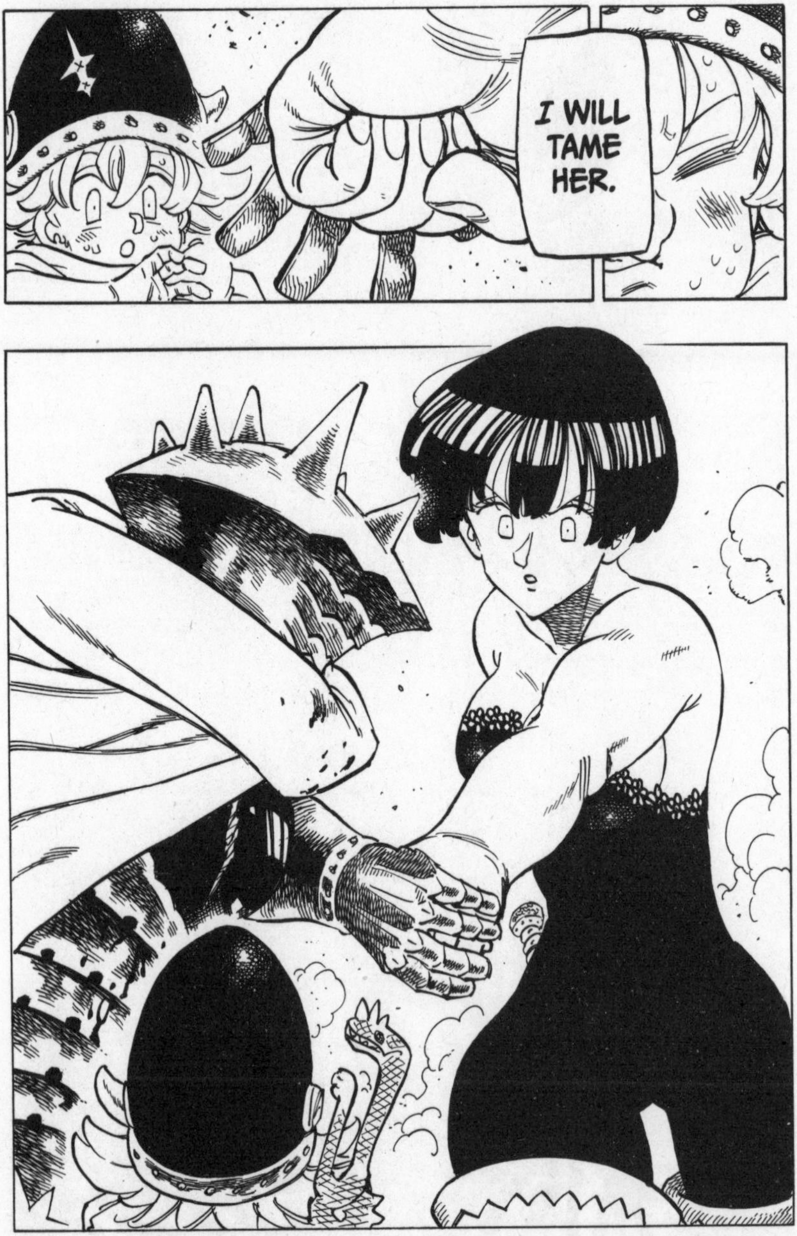
I WILL TAME HER.

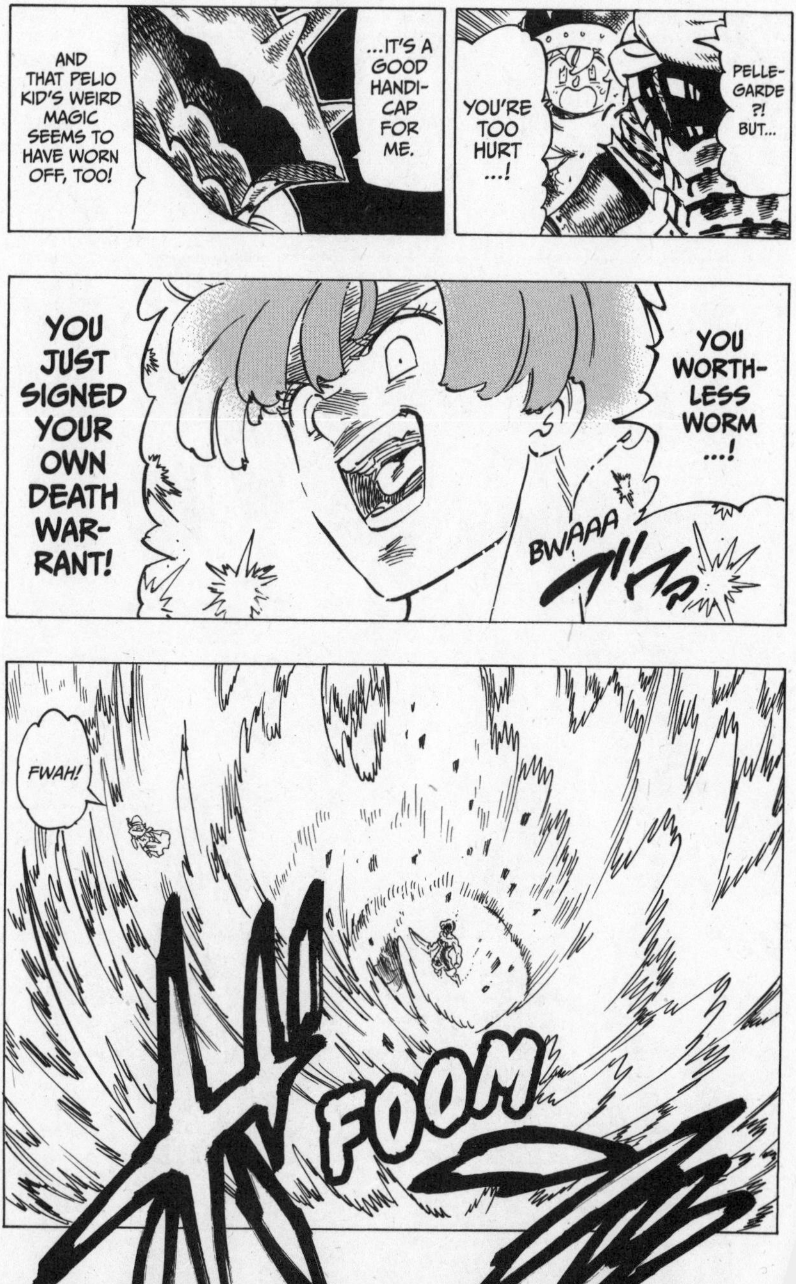
PELLE-GARDE?! BUT...
YOU'RE TOO HURT...!
...IT'S A GOOD HANDI-CAP FOR ME.
AND THAT PELIO KID'S WEIRD MAGIC SEEMS TO HAVE WORN OFF, TOO!
YOU WORTH-LESS WORM...!
BWAAA
YOU JUST SIGNED YOUR OWN DEATH WAR-RANT!
FWAH!
FOOM

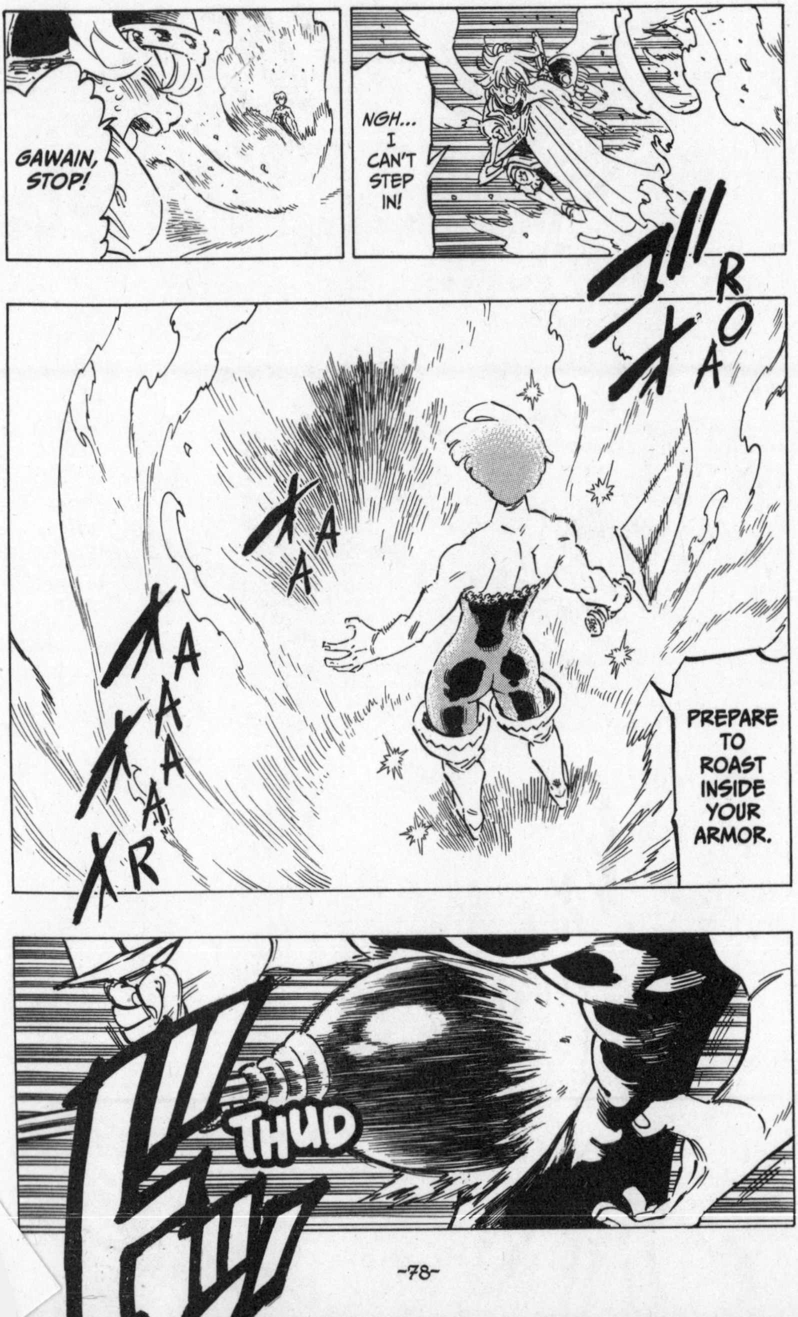
NGH... I CAN'T STEP IN!
GAWAIN, STOP!
ROA
AA
AAAAR
PREPARE TO ROAST INSIDE YOUR ARMOR.
THUD

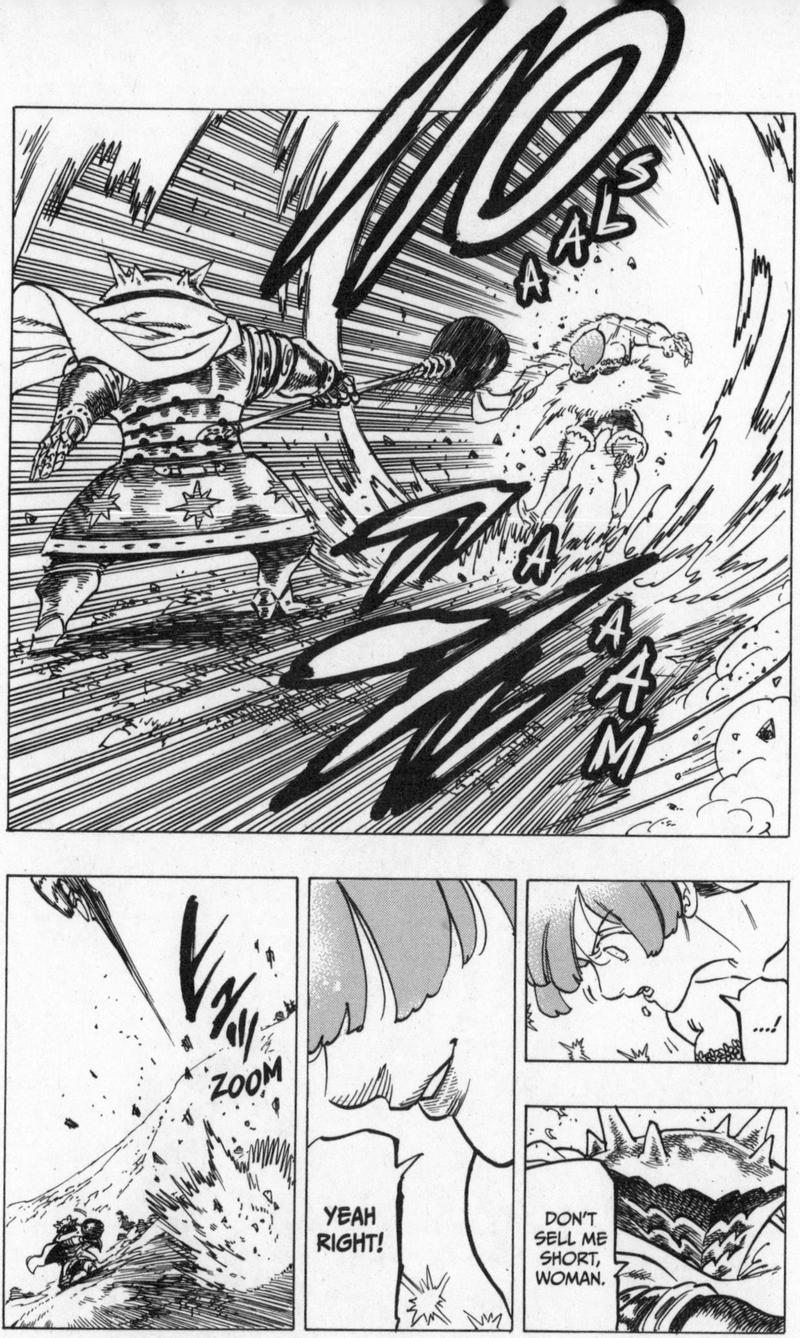
SLAAAAAAM
...!
DON'T SELL ME SHORT, WOMAN.
YEAH RIGHT!
ZOOM

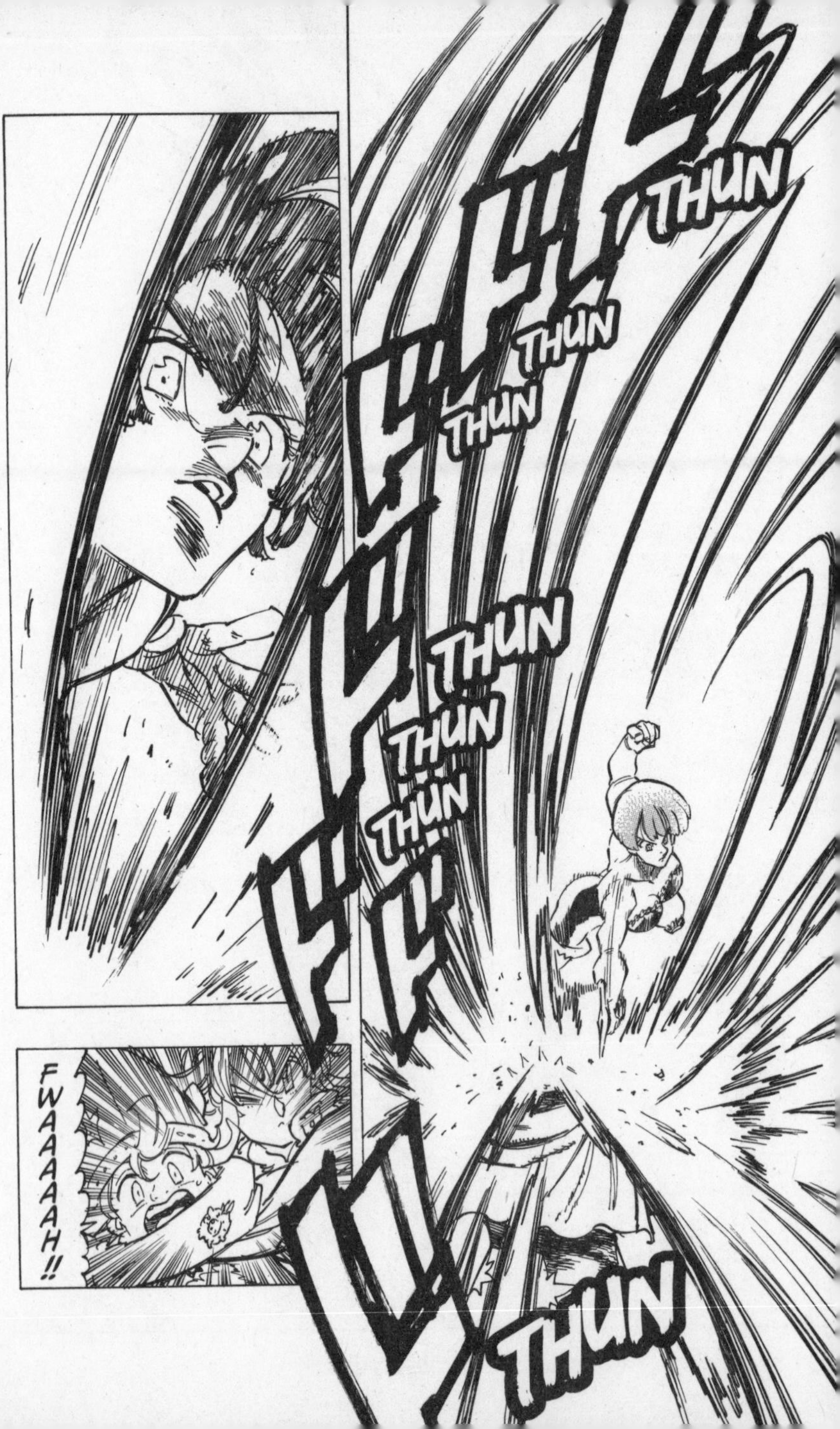
THUN
THUN
THUN
THUN
THUN
THUN
THUN
FWAAAAAAH!!

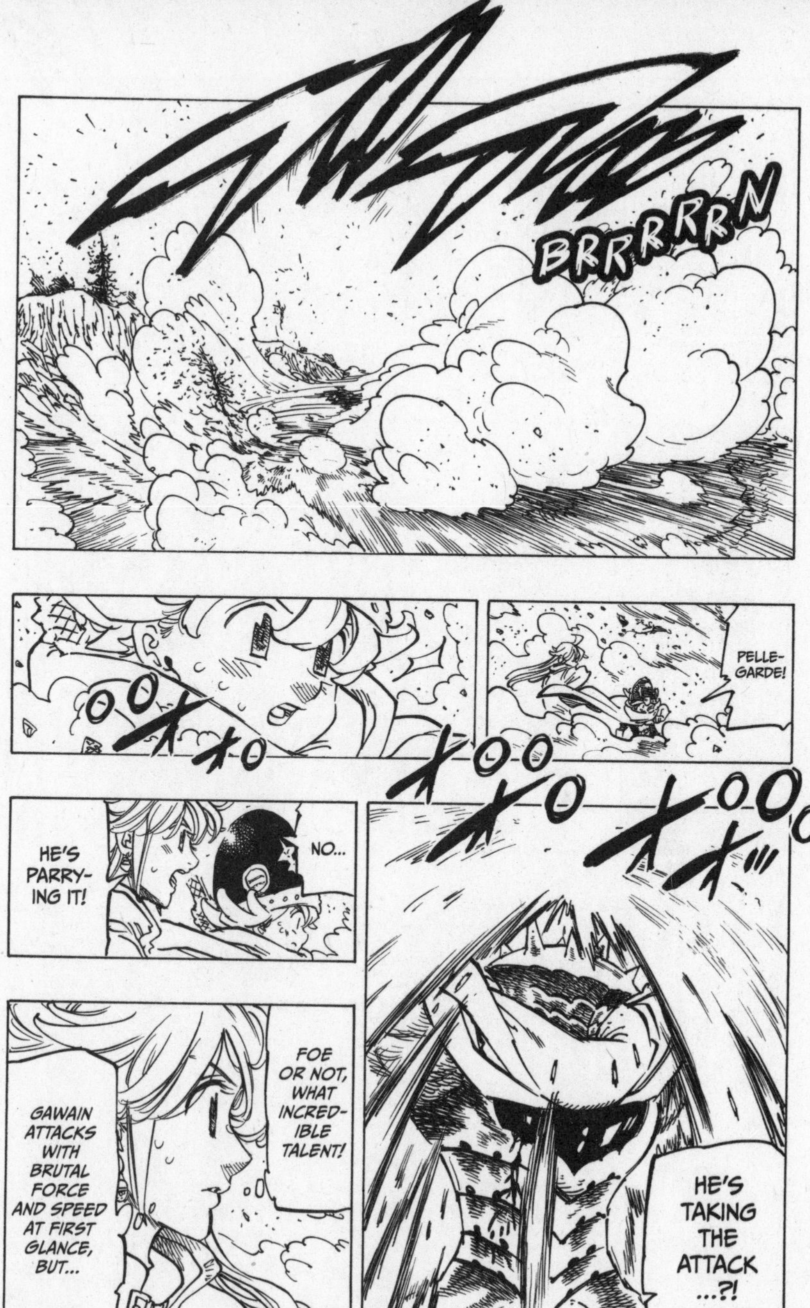
BRRRRRRN
PELLE-GARDE!
HE'S TAKING THE ATTACK ...?!
NO...
HE'S PARRY-ING IT!
FOE OR NOT, WHAT INCRED-IBLE TALENT!
GAWAIN ATTACKS WITH BRUTAL FORCE AND SPEED AT FIRST GLANCE, BUT...

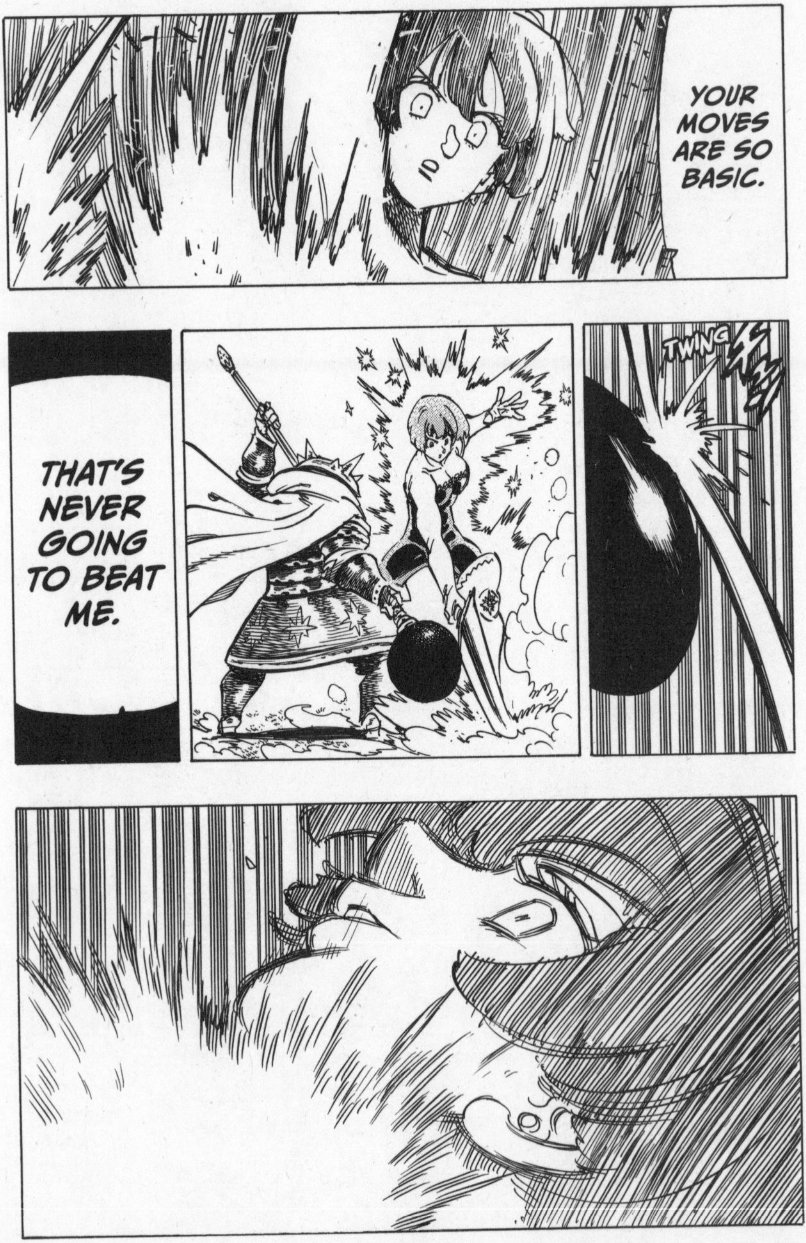
YOUR MOVES ARE SO BASIC.
TWING
THAT'S NEVER GOING TO BEAT ME.

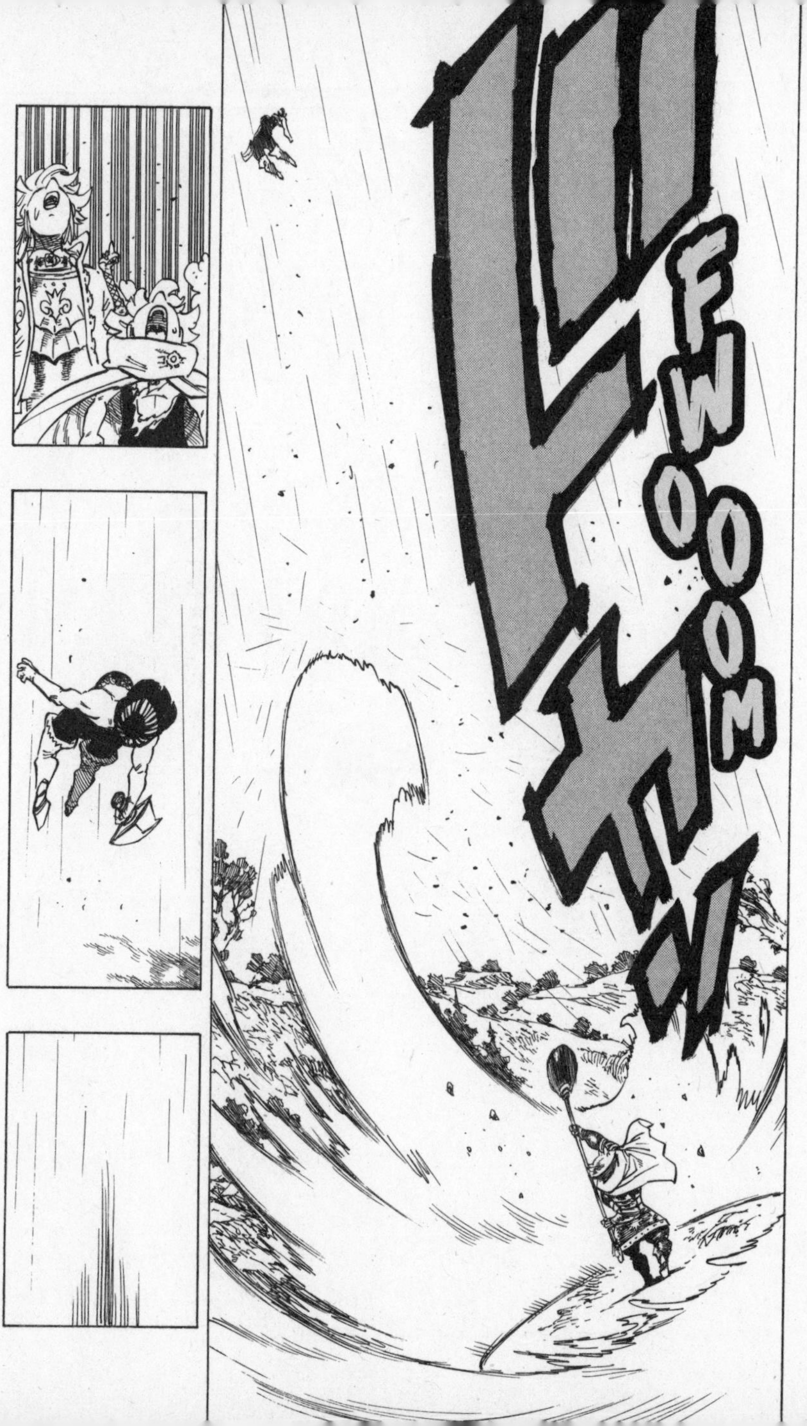
FWOOOM

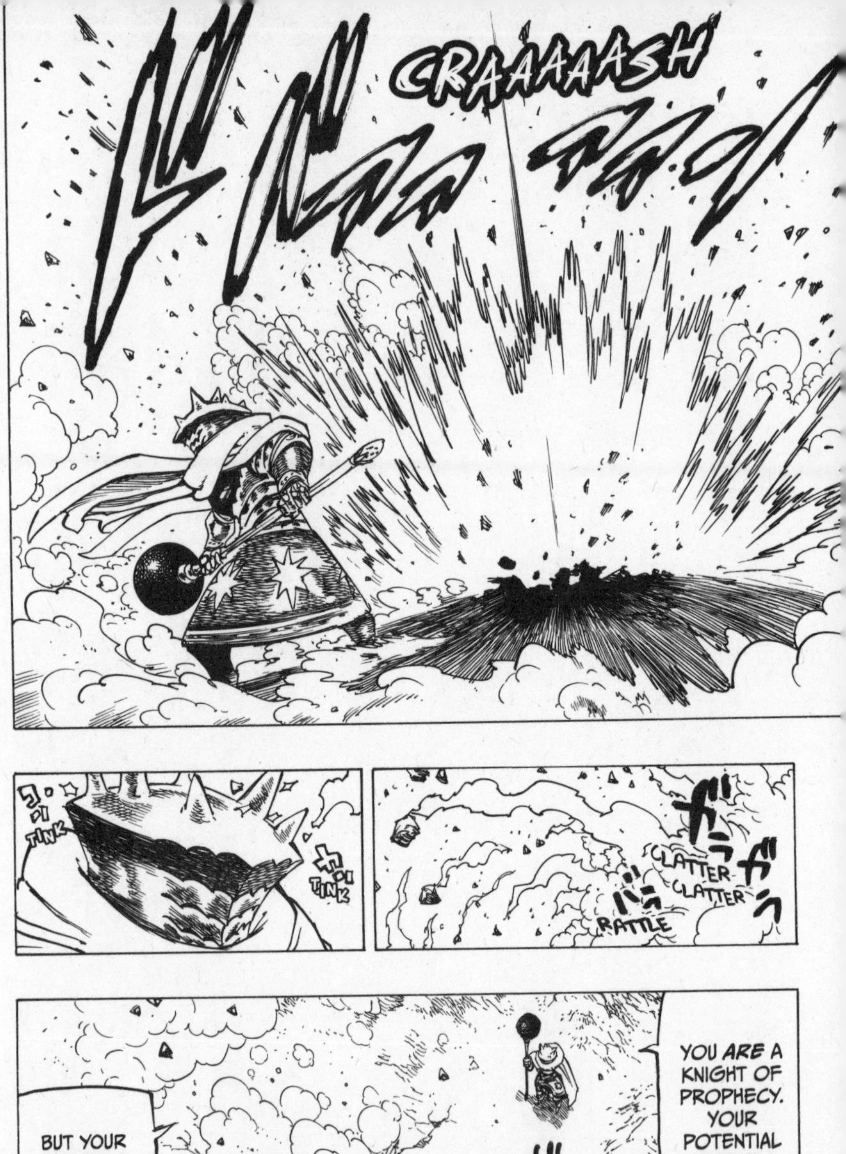
CRAAAAASH
CLATTER CLATTER
RATTLE
TINK
TINK
YOU *ARE* A KNIGHT OF PROPHECY. YOUR POTENTIAL IS TRULY BOUND-LESS.
CLATTER
CLATTER
BUT YOUR ABILITIES HAVEN'T CAUGHT UP YET. YOU'RE STILL AN AMATEUR.

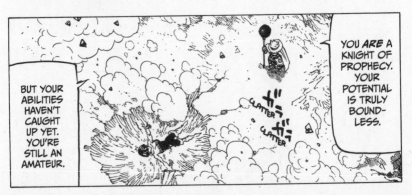

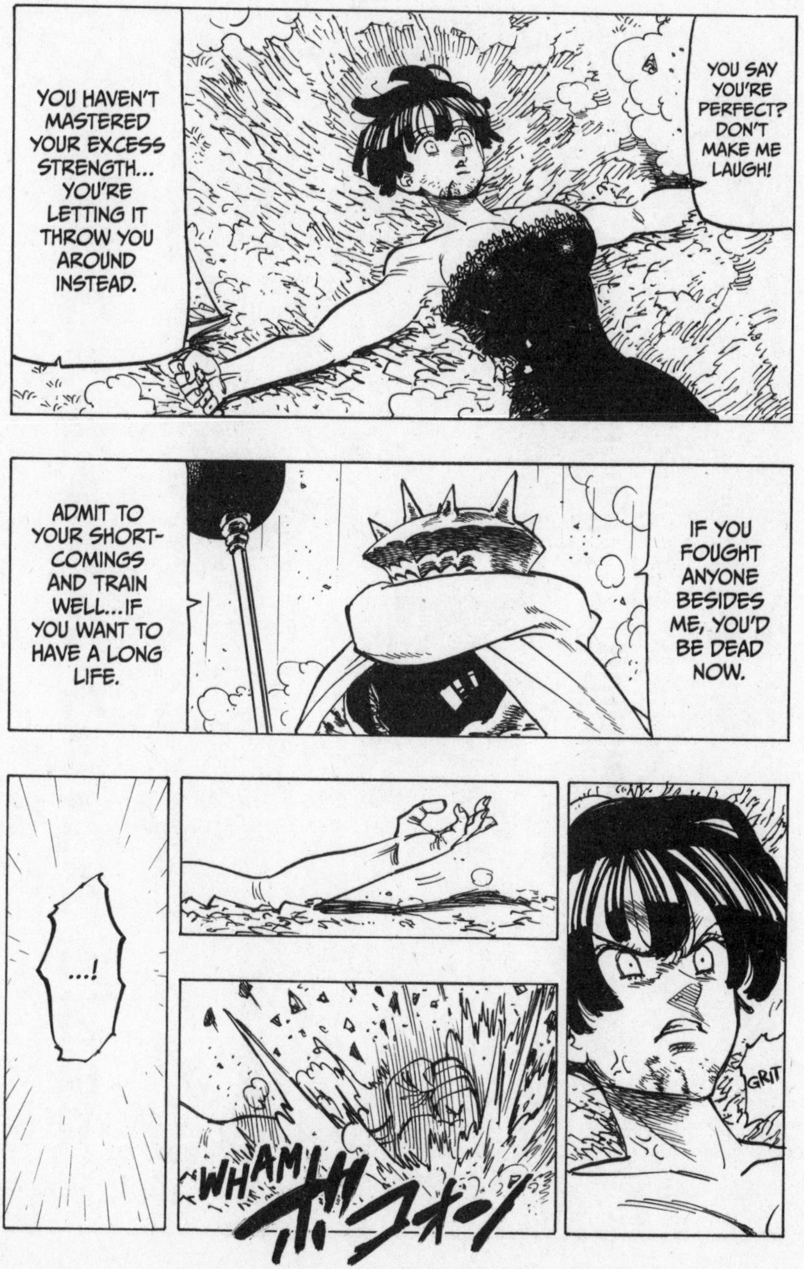
YOU SAY YOU'RE PERFECT? DON'T MAKE ME LAUGH!
YOU HAVEN'T MASTERED YOUR EXCESS STRENGTH... YOU'RE LETTING IT THROW YOU AROUND INSTEAD.
IF YOU FOUGHT ANYONE BESIDES ME, YOU'D BE DEAD NOW.
ADMIT TO YOUR SHORT-COMINGS AND TRAIN WELL...IF YOU WANT TO HAVE A LONG LIFE.
GRIT
WHAM!!
...!

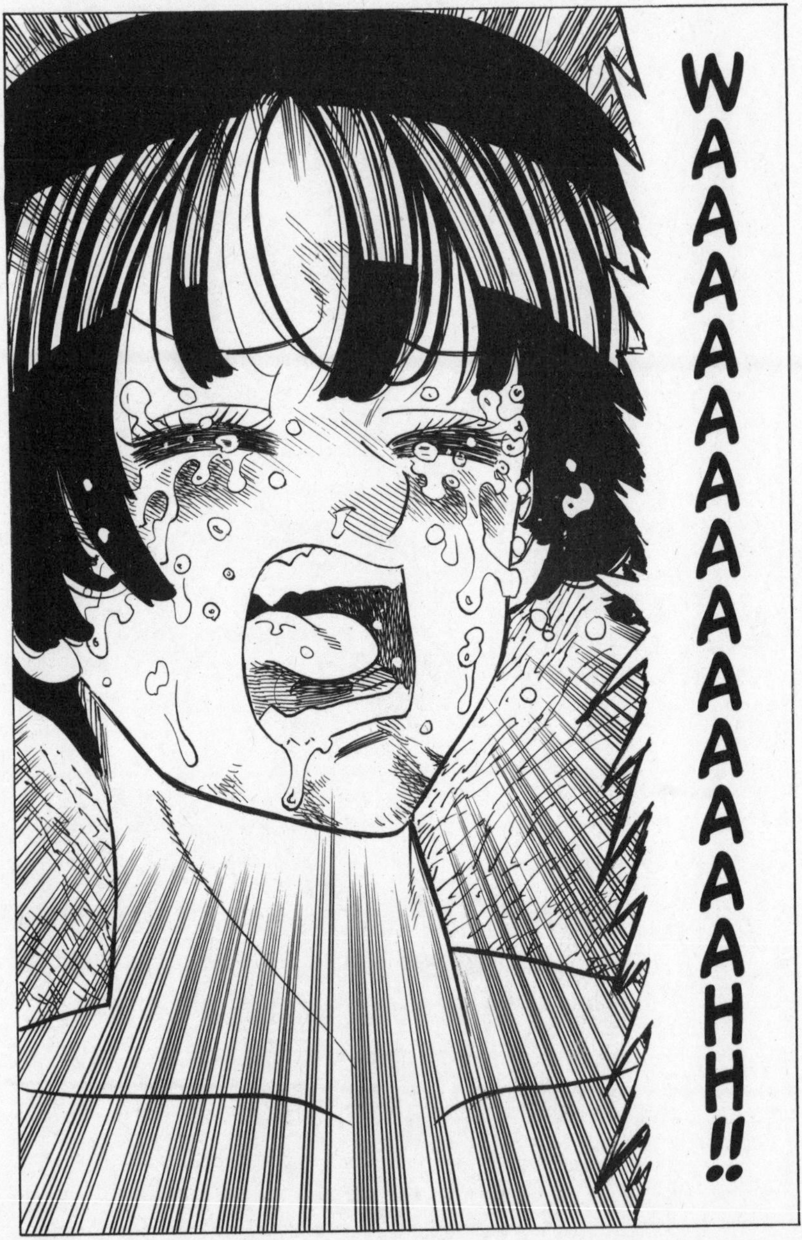
WAAAAAAAAAAAAAAAAHH!!

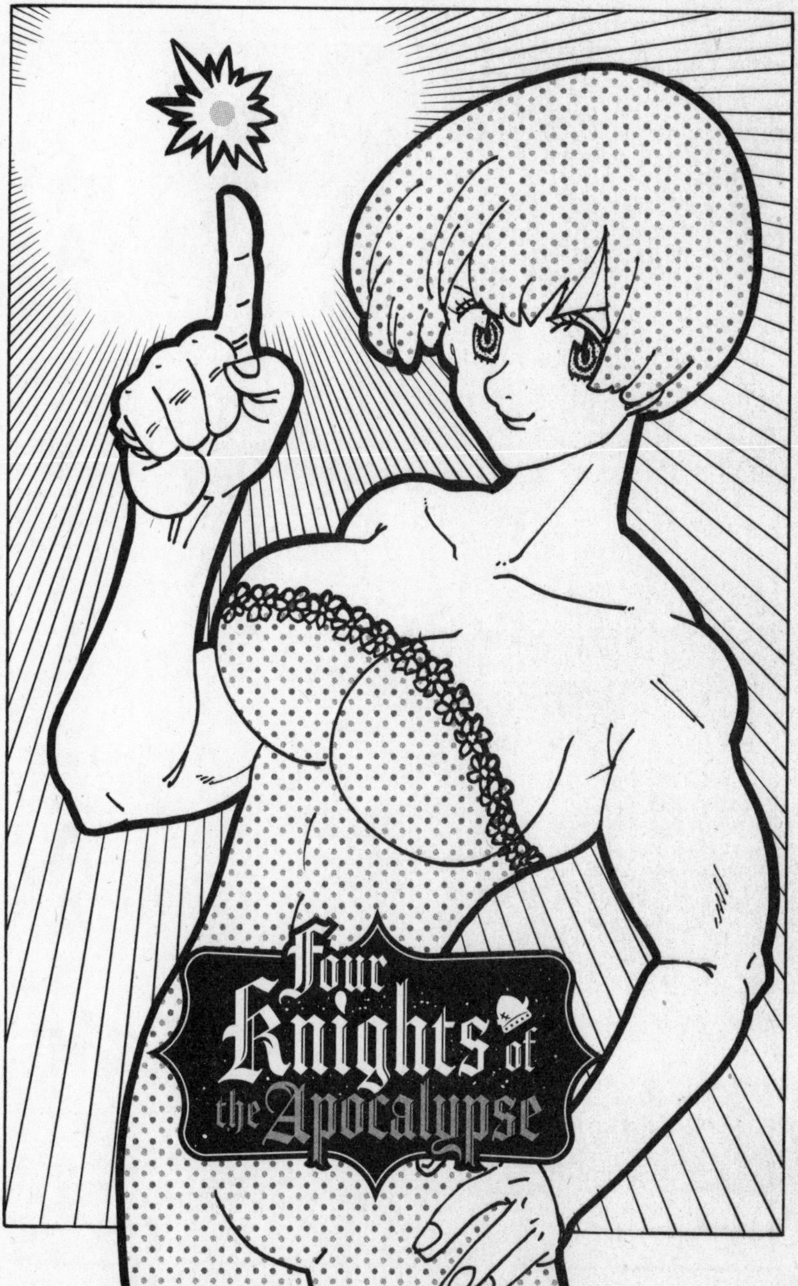
Four Knights of the Apocalypse

CHAPTER 64: THOSE SEEKING REVENGE

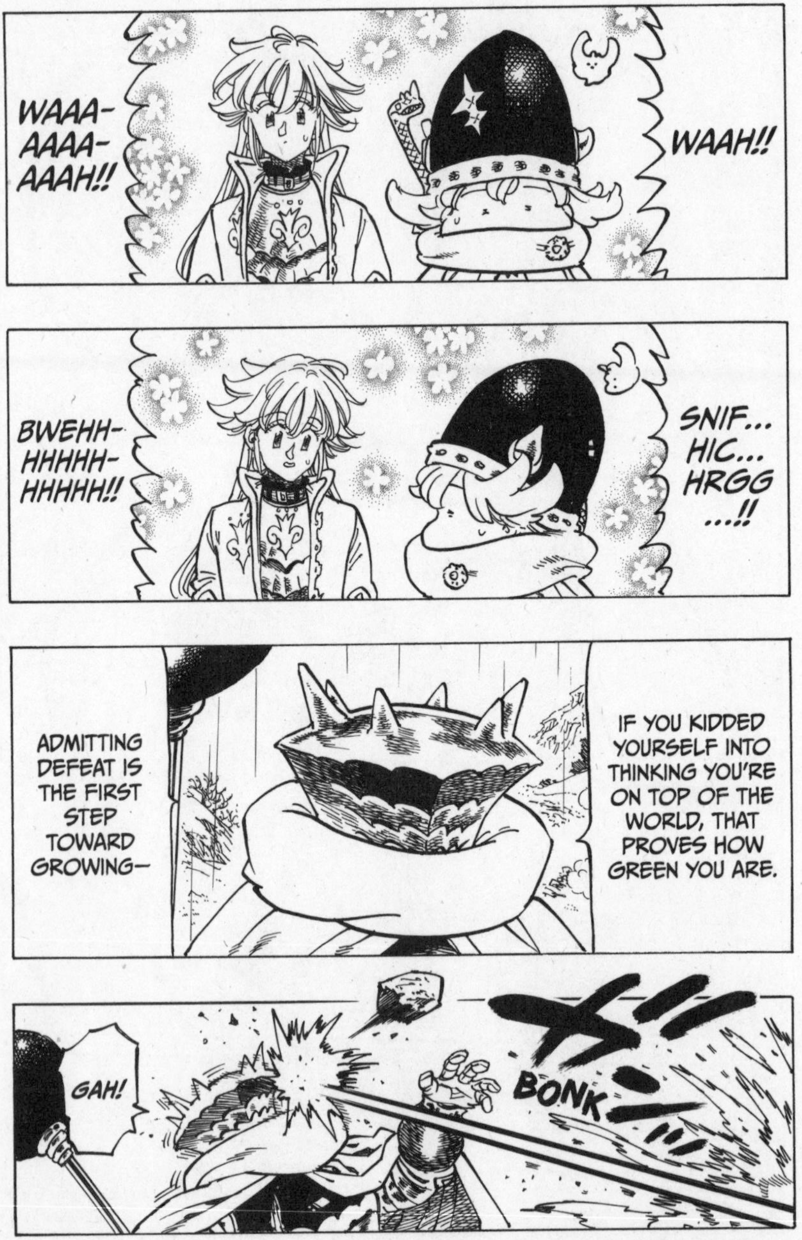
WAAH!!
WAAA-AAAA-AAAH!!
SNIF... HIC... HRGG ...!!
BWEHH-HHHHH-HHHHH!!
IF YOU KIDDED YOURSELF INTO THINKING YOU'RE ON TOP OF THE WORLD, THAT PROVES HOW GREEN YOU ARE.
ADMITTING DEFEAT IS THE FIRST STEP TOWARD GROWING—
BONK
GAH!

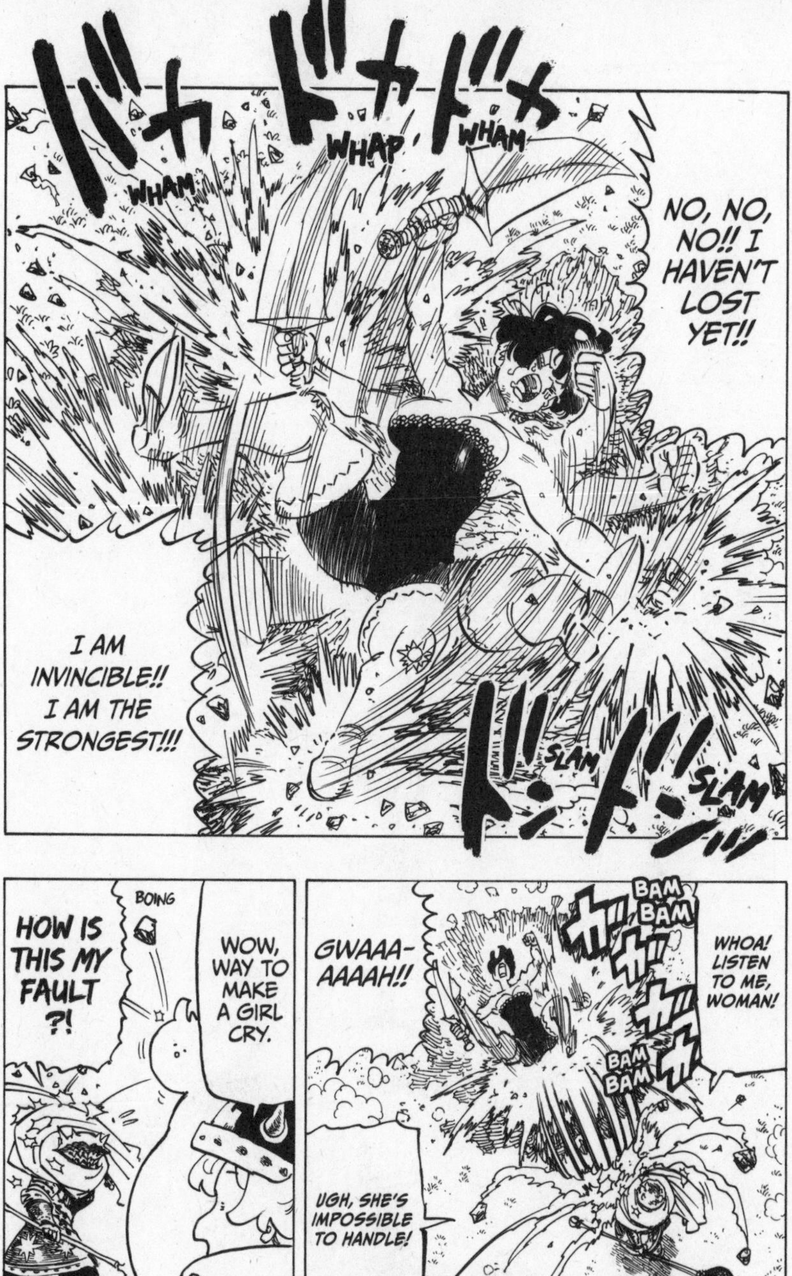
WHAM
WHAP
WHAM
NO, NO, NO!! I HAVEN'T LOST YET!!
I AM INVINCIBLE!! I AM THE STRONGEST!!!
SLAM
SLAM
BAM BAM
WHOA! LISTEN TO ME, WOMAN!
GWAAA-AAAAH!!
BAM BAM
UGH, SHE'S IMPOSSIBLE TO HANDLE!
WOW, WAY TO MAKE A GIRL CRY.
BOING
HOW IS THIS MY FAULT?!

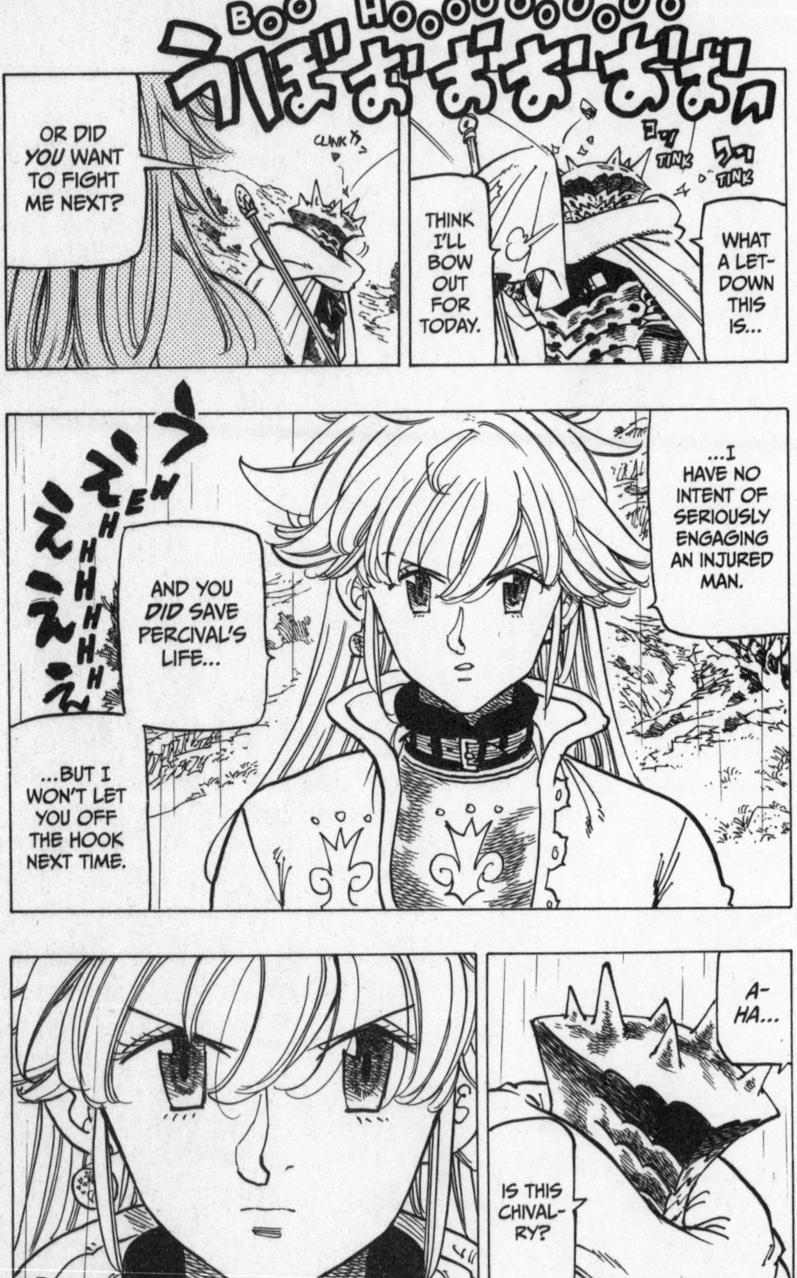
BOO HOOOOOOOOOO
WHAT A LET-DOWN THIS IS...
TINK
TINK
THINK I'LL BOW OUT FOR TODAY.
CLINK
OR DID YOU WANT TO FIGHT ME NEXT?
...I HAVE NO INTENT OF SERIOUSLY ENGAGING AN INJURED MAN.
AND YOU DID SAVE PERCIVAL'S LIFE...
EWHHHHHHH
...BUT I WON'T LET YOU OFF THE HOOK NEXT TIME.
A-HA...
IS THIS CHIVAL-RY?

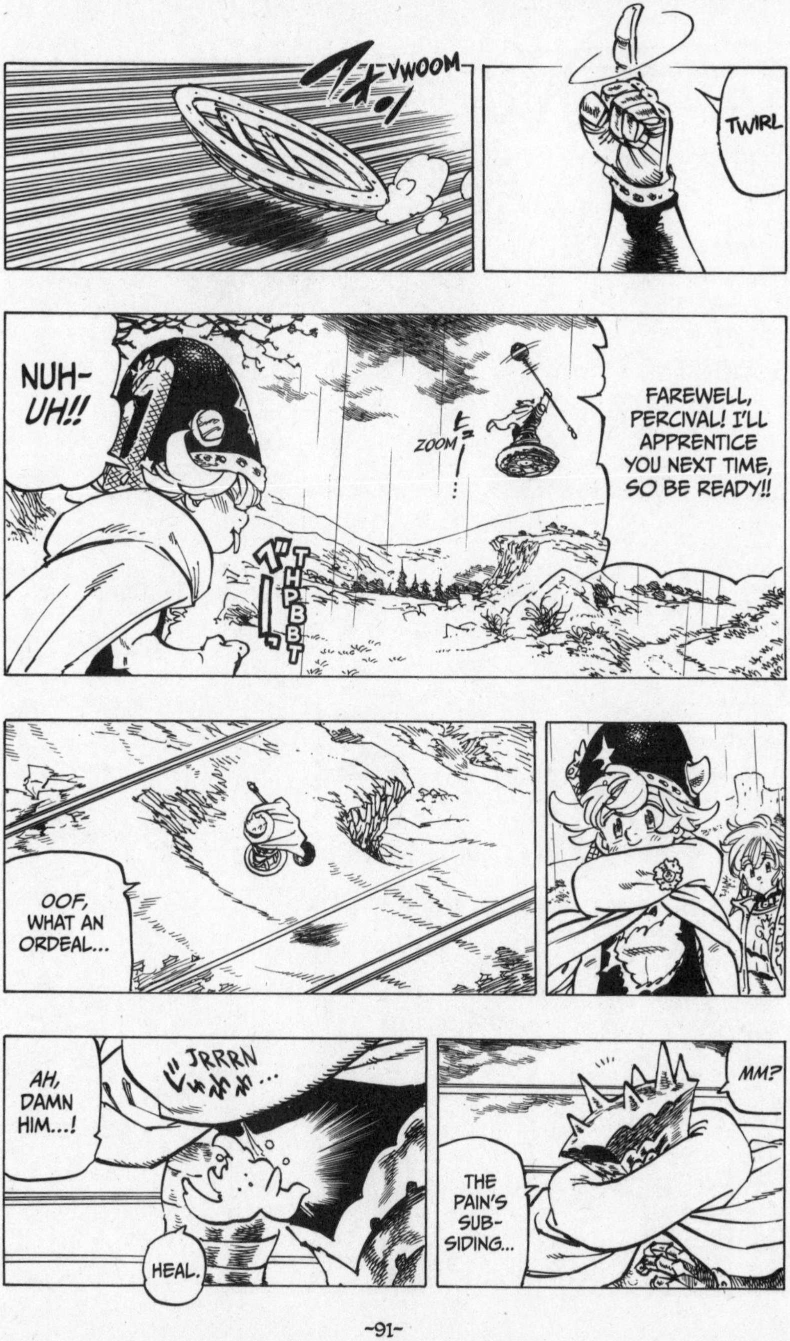
TWIRL
VWOOM
FAREWELL, PERCIVAL! I'LL APPRENTICE YOU NEXT TIME, SO BE READY!!
ZOOM
NUH-UH!!
THPBBT
OOF, WHAT AN ORDEAL...
MM?
THE PAIN'S SUB-SIDING...
AH, DAMN HIM...!
JRRRN
HEAL.

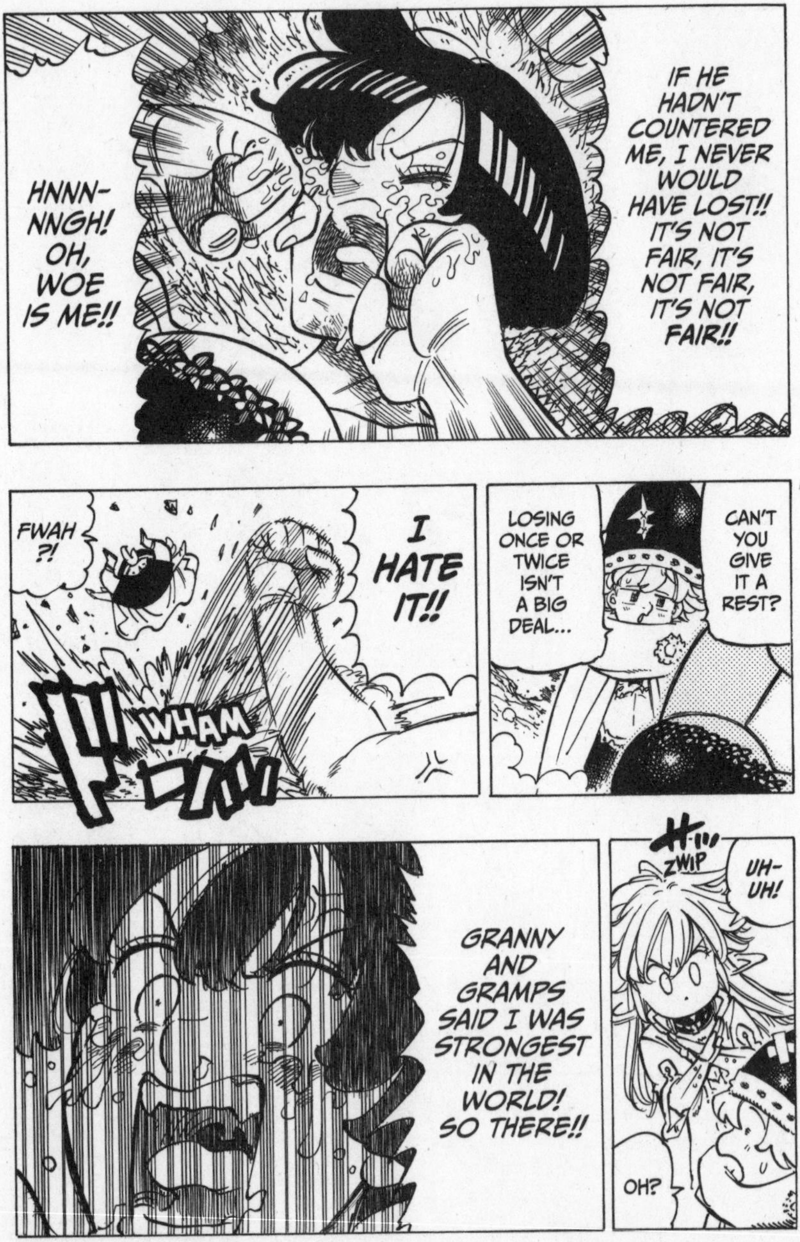
IF HE HADN'T COUNTERED ME, I NEVER WOULD HAVE LOST!! IT'S NOT FAIR, IT'S NOT FAIR, IT'S NOT FAIR!!
HNNN-NNGH! OH, WOE IS ME!!
CAN'T YOU GIVE IT A REST?
LOSING ONCE OR TWICE ISN'T A BIG DEAL...
I HATE IT!!
FWAH ?!
WHAM
ZWIP
UH-UH!
OH?
GRANNY AND GRAMPS SAID I WAS STRONGEST IN THE WORLD! SO THERE!!

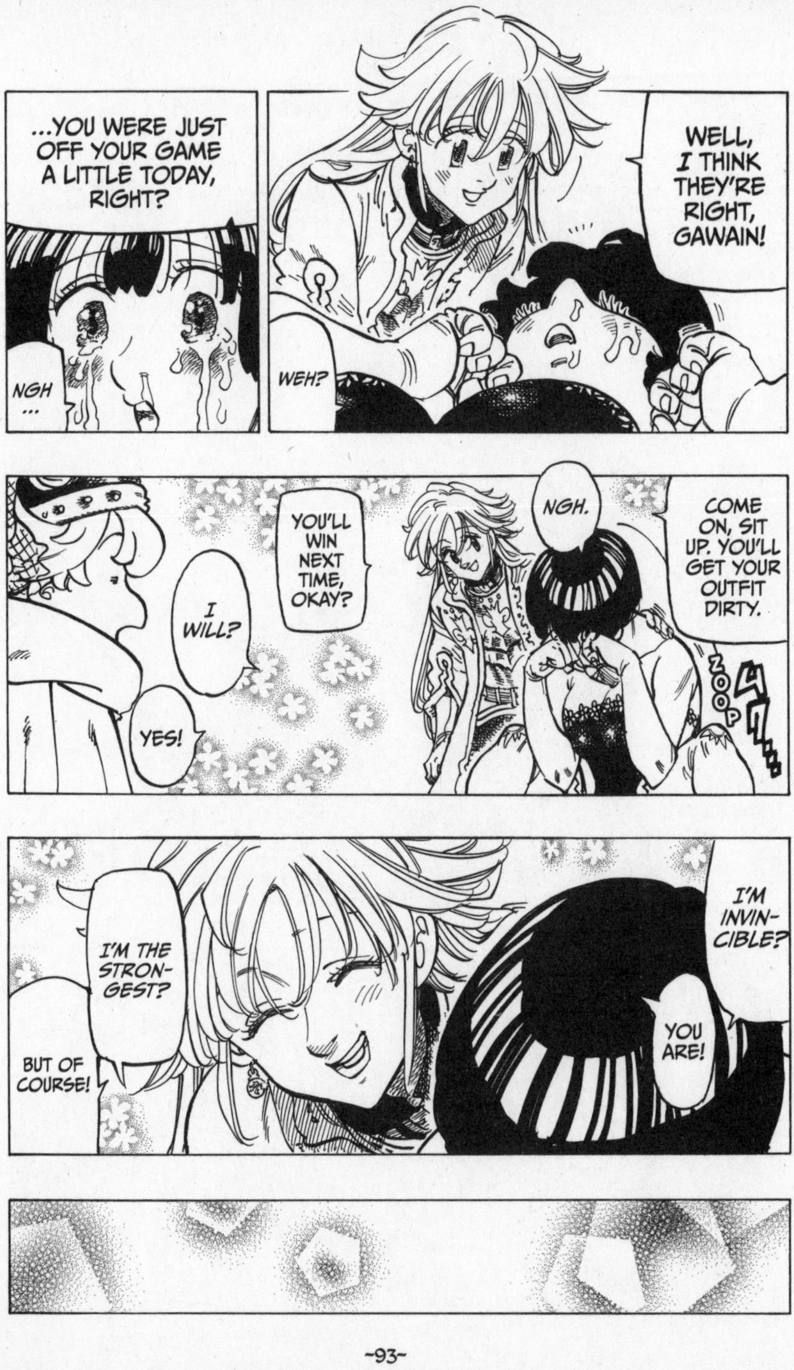
WELL, I THINK THEY'RE RIGHT, GAWAIN!
WEH?
...YOU WERE JUST OFF YOUR GAME A LITTLE TODAY, RIGHT?
NGH ...
COME ON, SIT UP. YOU'LL GET YOUR OUTFIT DIRTY.
ZOOP
NGH.
YOU'LL WIN NEXT TIME, OKAY?
I WILL?
YES!
I'M INVINCIBLE?
YOU ARE!
I'M THE STRONGEST?
BUT OF COURSE!

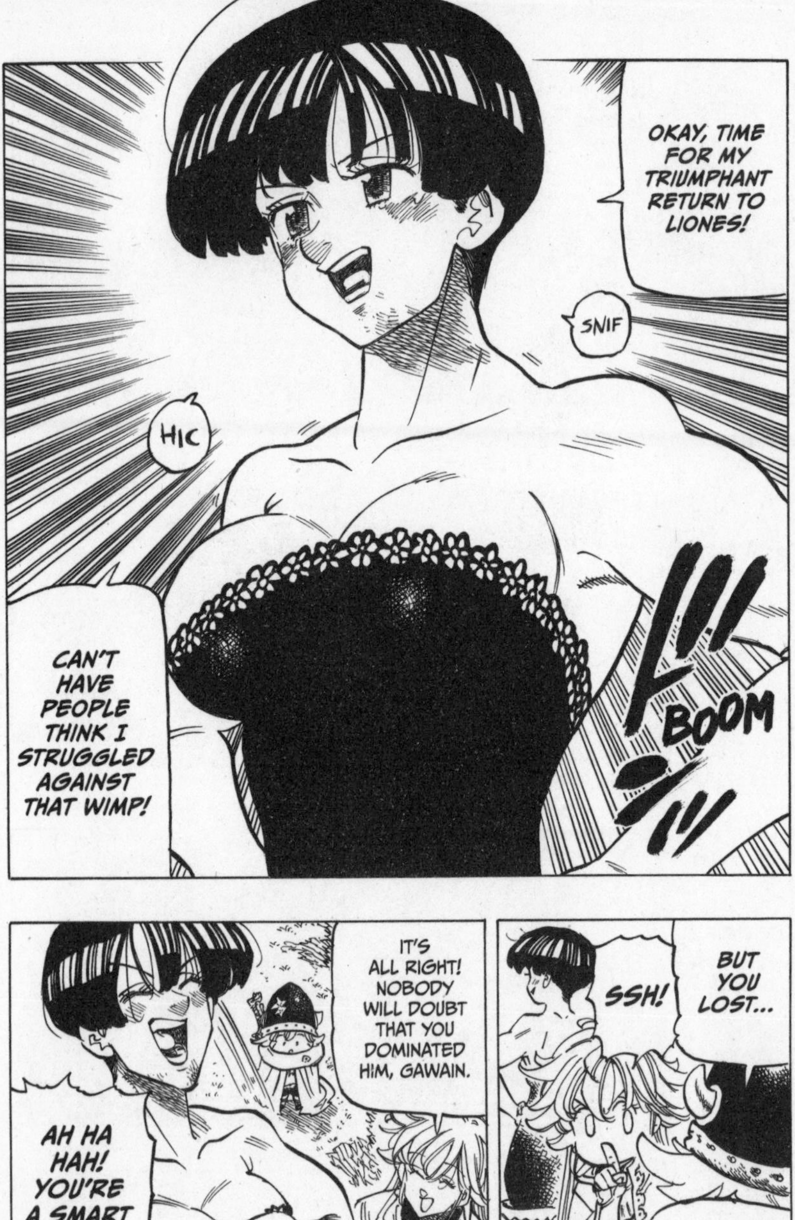
OKAY, TIME FOR MY TRIUMPHANT RETURN TO LIONES!
SNIF
HIC
BOOM
CAN'T HAVE PEOPLE THINK I STRUGGLED AGAINST THAT WIMP!
BUT YOU LOST...
SSH!
IT'S ALL RIGHT! NOBODY WILL DOUBT THAT YOU DOMINATED HIM, GAWAIN.
AH HA HAH! YOU'RE A SMART LAD!

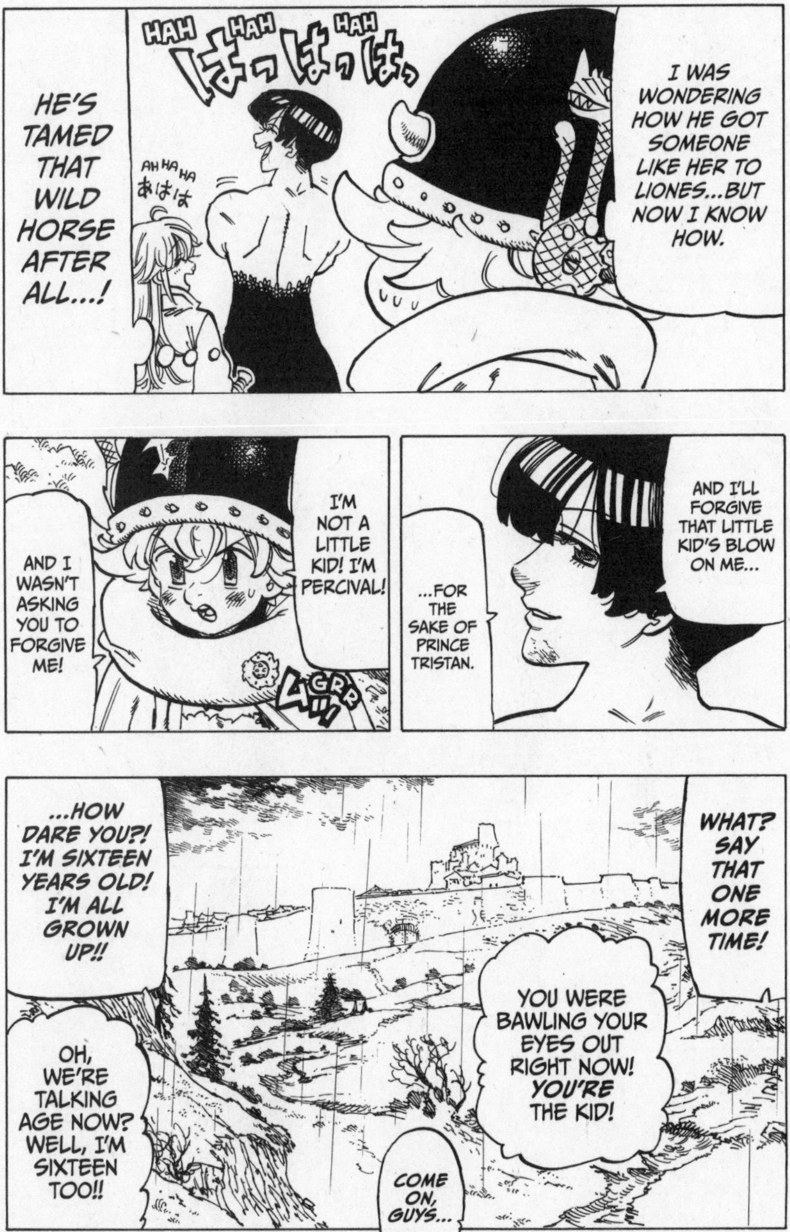
I WAS WONDERING HOW HE GOT SOMEONE LIKE HER TO LIONES...BUT NOW I KNOW HOW.
HAH HAH HAH
はっはっはっ
AH HA HA
あはは
HE'S TAMED THAT WILD HORSE AFTER ALL...!
AND I'LL FORGIVE THAT LITTLE KID'S BLOW ON ME...
...FOR THE SAKE OF PRINCE TRISTAN.
I'M NOT A LITTLE KID! I'M PERCIVAL!
AND I WASN'T ASKING YOU TO FORGIVE ME!
GRR
ムッ
WHAT? SAY THAT ONE MORE TIME!
...HOW DARE YOU?! I'M SIXTEEN YEARS OLD! I'M ALL GROWN UP!!
YOU WERE BAWLING YOUR EYES OUT RIGHT NOW! YOU'RE THE KID!
OH, WE'RE TALKING AGE NOW? WELL, I'M SIXTEEN TOO!!
COME ON, GUYS...

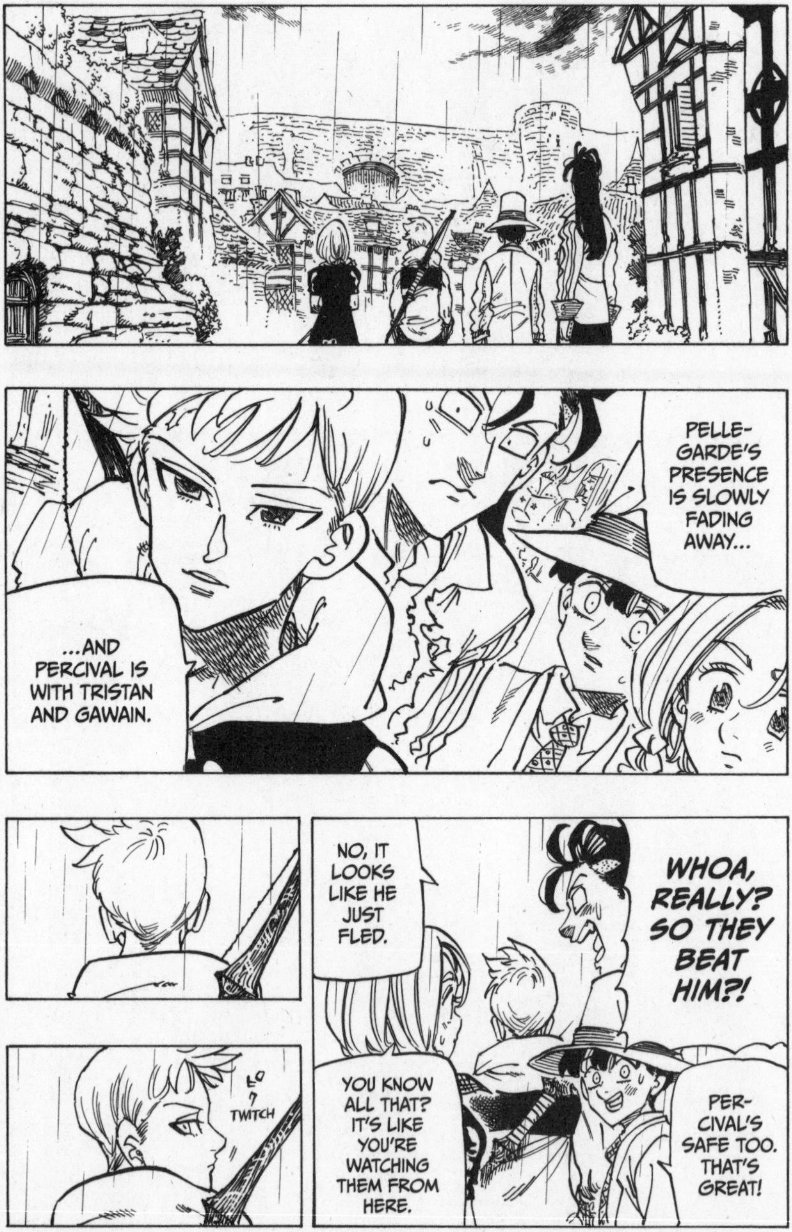
PELLE-GARDE'S PRESENCE IS SLOWLY FADING AWAY...
...AND PERCIVAL IS WITH TRISTAN AND GAWAIN.
WHOA, REALLY? SO THEY BEAT HIM?!
NO, IT LOOKS LIKE HE JUST FLED.
PER-CIVAL'S SAFE TOO. THAT'S GREAT!
YOU KNOW ALL THAT? IT'S LIKE YOU'RE WATCHING THEM FROM HERE.
TWITCH

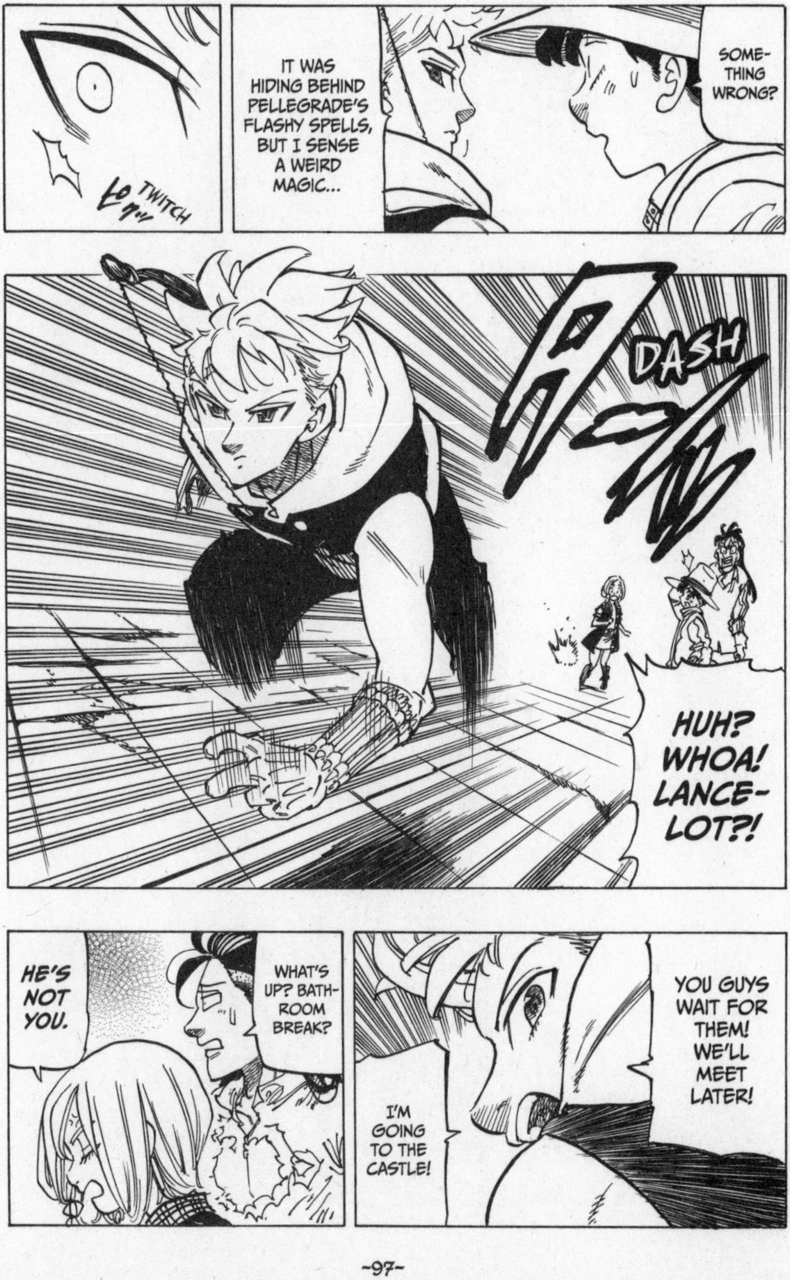
SOME-THING WRONG?
IT WAS HIDING BEHIND PELLEGRADE'S FLASHY SPELLS, BUT I SENSE A WEIRD MAGIC...
TWITCH
DASH
HUH? WHOA! LANCE-LOT?!
YOU GUYS WAIT FOR THEM! WE'LL MEET LATER!
I'M GOING TO THE CASTLE!
WHAT'S UP? BATH-ROOM BREAK?
HE'S NOT YOU.

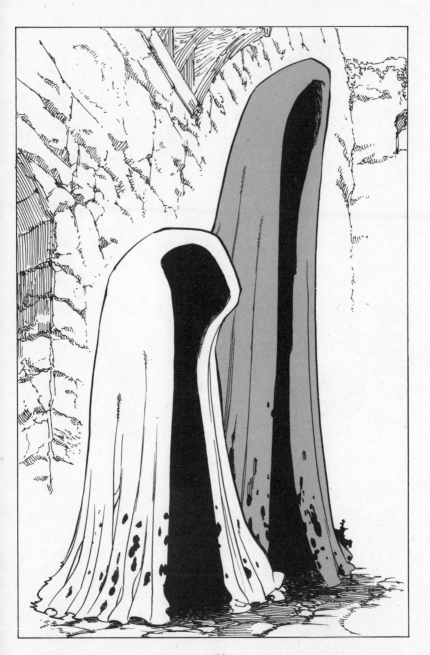

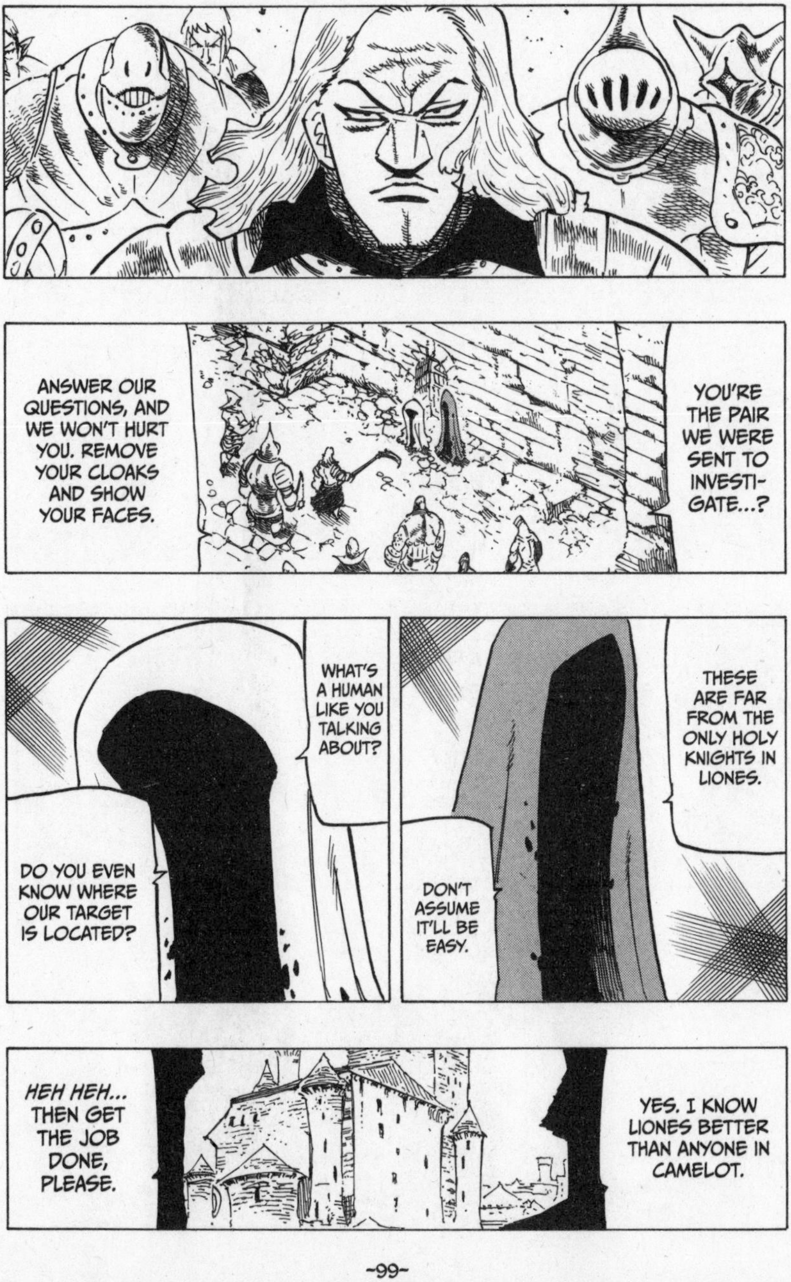
YOU'RE THE PAIR WE WERE SENT TO INVESTI-GATE...?
ANSWER OUR QUESTIONS, AND WE WON'T HURT YOU. REMOVE YOUR CLOAKS AND SHOW YOUR FACES.
THESE ARE FAR FROM THE ONLY HOLY KNIGHTS IN LIONES.
DON'T ASSUME IT'LL BE EASY.
WHAT'S A HUMAN LIKE YOU TALKING ABOUT?
DO YOU EVEN KNOW WHERE OUR TARGET IS LOCATED?
YES. I KNOW LIONES BETTER THAN ANYONE IN CAMELOT.
HEH HEH... THEN GET THE JOB DONE, PLEASE.

BWOOF

YOU WILL BE DEALING WITH US.

AFTER IT!!

IT'S GONE!

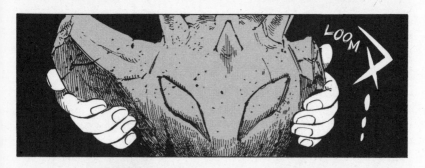

LOOM

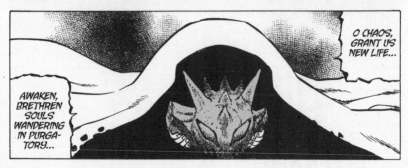

O CHAOS, GRANT US NEW LIFE...

AWAKEN, BRETHREN SOULS WANDERING IN PURGATORY...

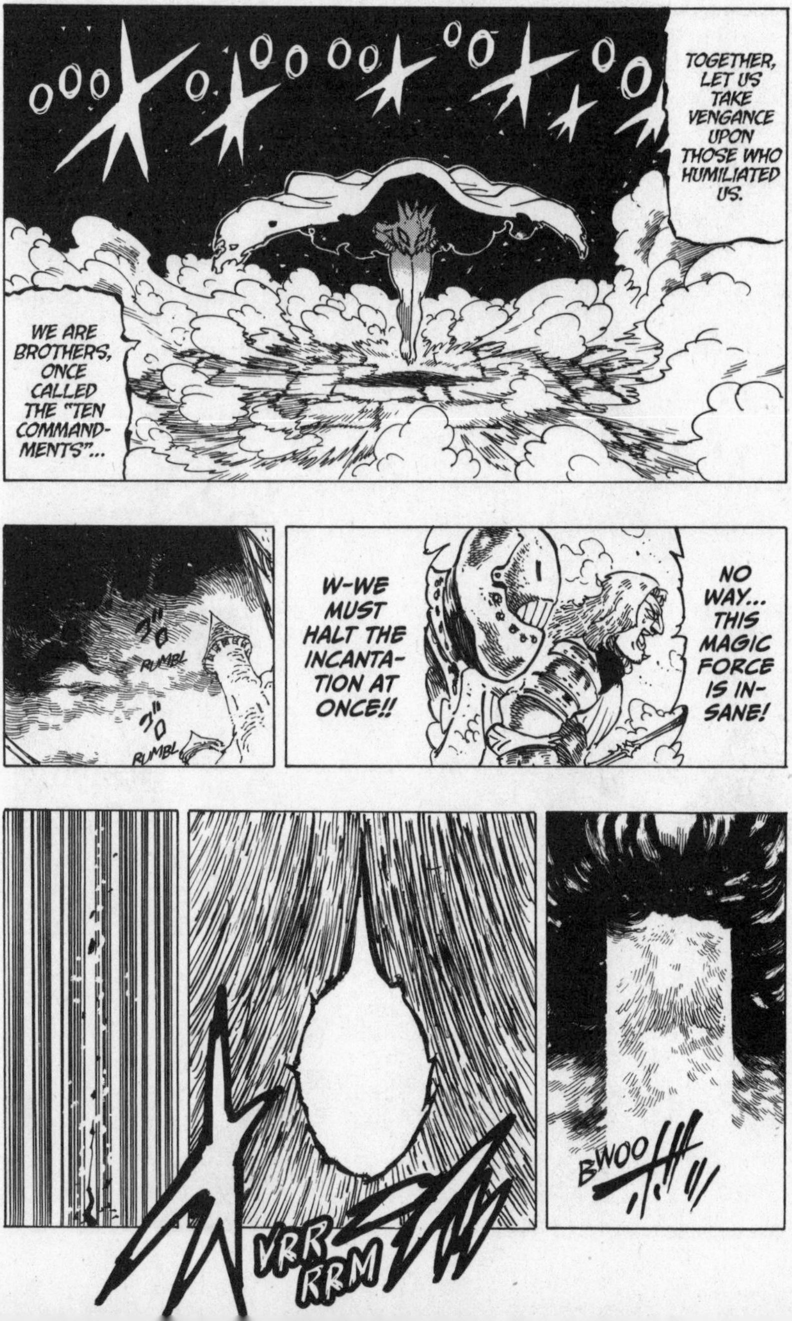
TOGETHER, LET US TAKE VENGANCE UPON THOSE WHO HUMILIATED US.
WE ARE BROTHERS, ONCE CALLED THE "TEN COMMANDMENTS"...
NO WAY... THIS MAGIC FORCE IS INSANE!
W-WE MUST HALT THE INCANTATION AT ONCE!!
RUMBL
RUMBL
BWOO
VRR RRM

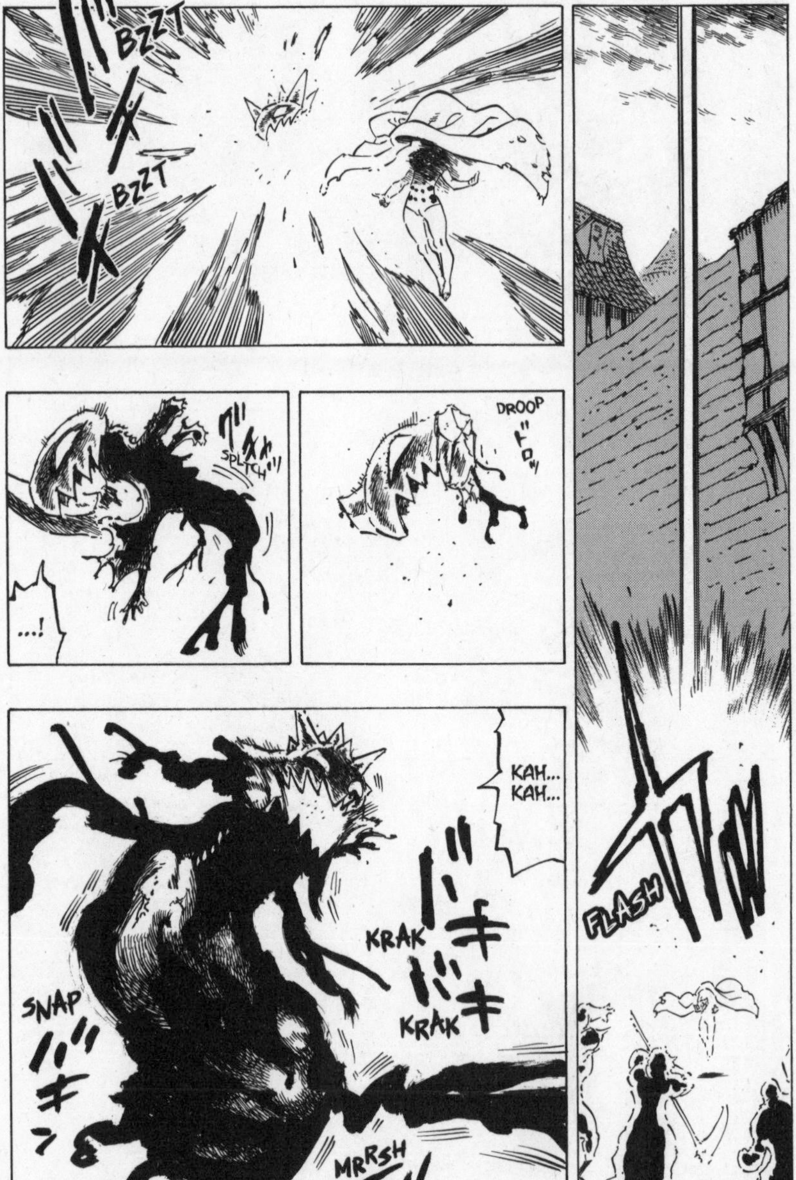
FLASH
BZZT
BZZT
DROOP
SPLTCH
...!
KAH... KAH...
KRAK
KRAK
SNAP
MRRSH

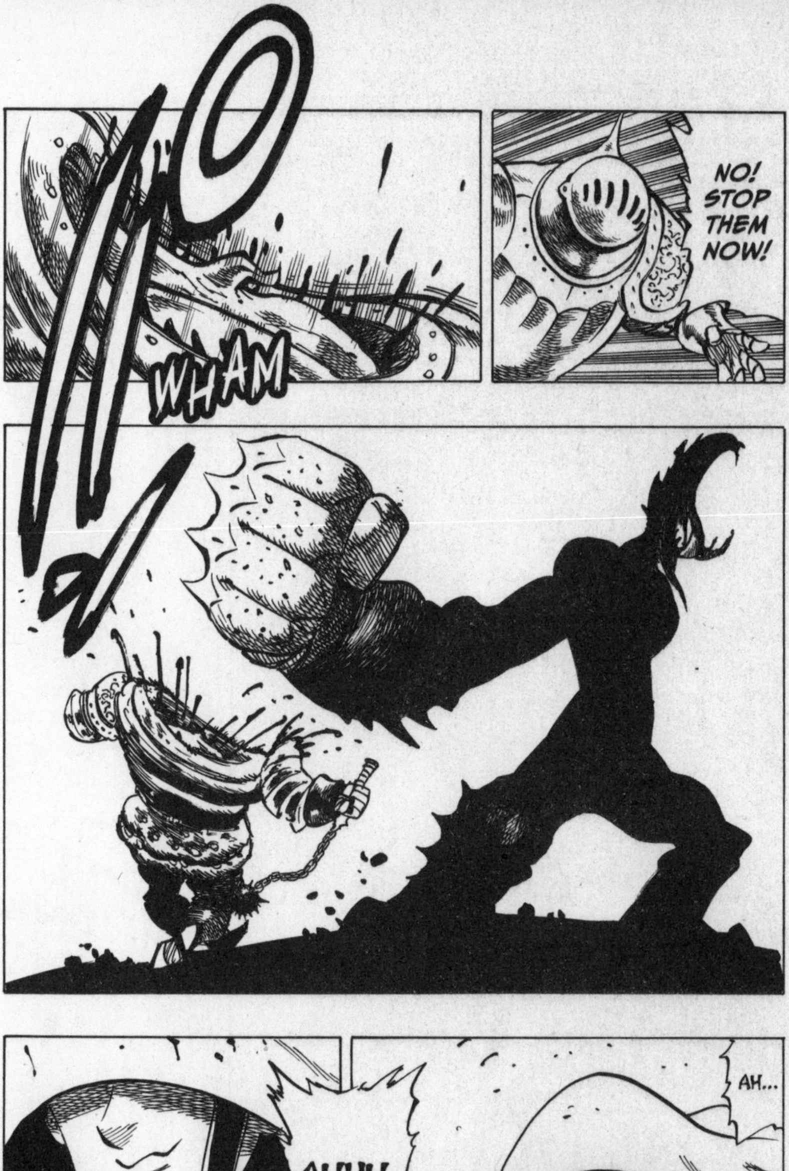

NO! STOP THEM NOW!
WHAM
AH...
AHHH-HHH!!

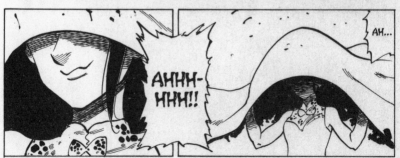

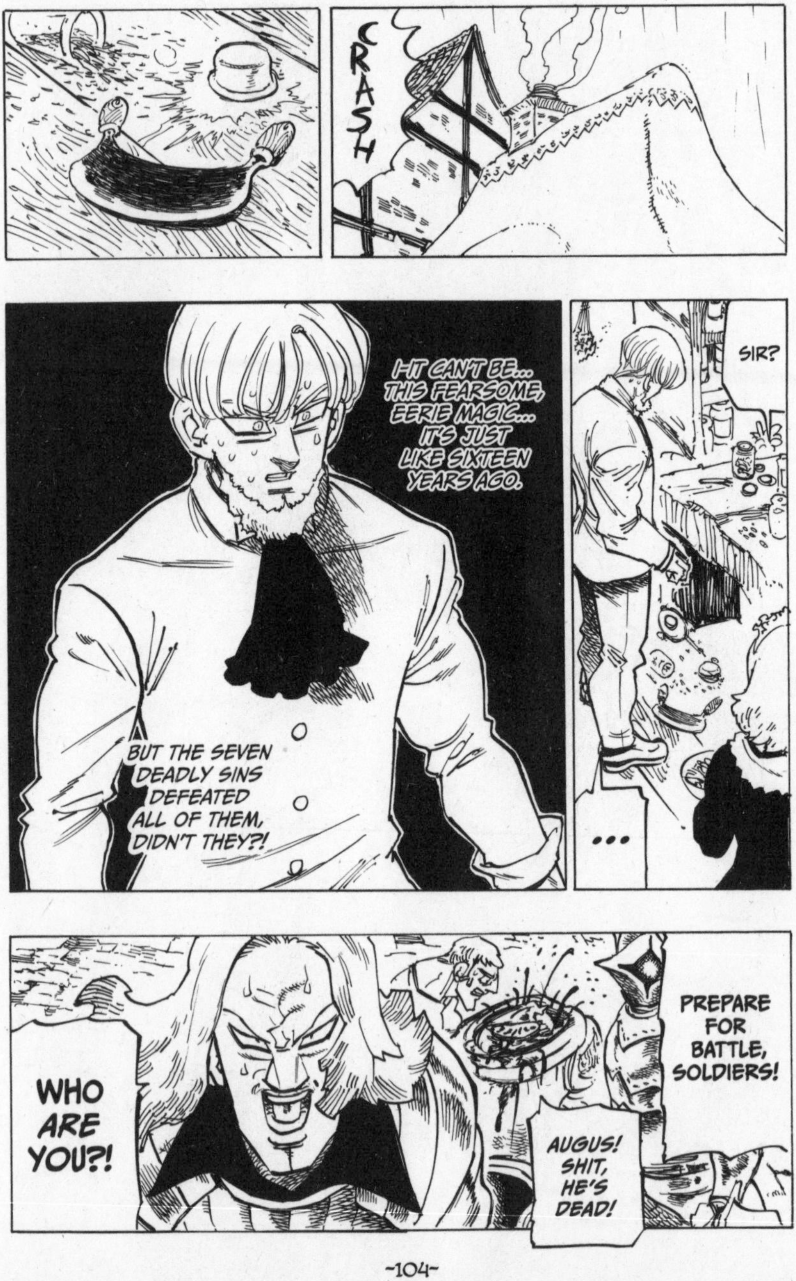
CRASH
SIR?
...
I-IT CAN'T BE... THIS FEARSOME, EERIE MAGIC... IT'S JUST LIKE SIXTEEN YEARS AGO.
BUT THE SEVEN DEADLY SINS DEFEATED ALL OF THEM, DIDN'T THEY?!
PREPARE FOR BATTLE, SOLDIERS!
AUGUS! SHIT, HE'S DEAD!
WHO ARE YOU?!

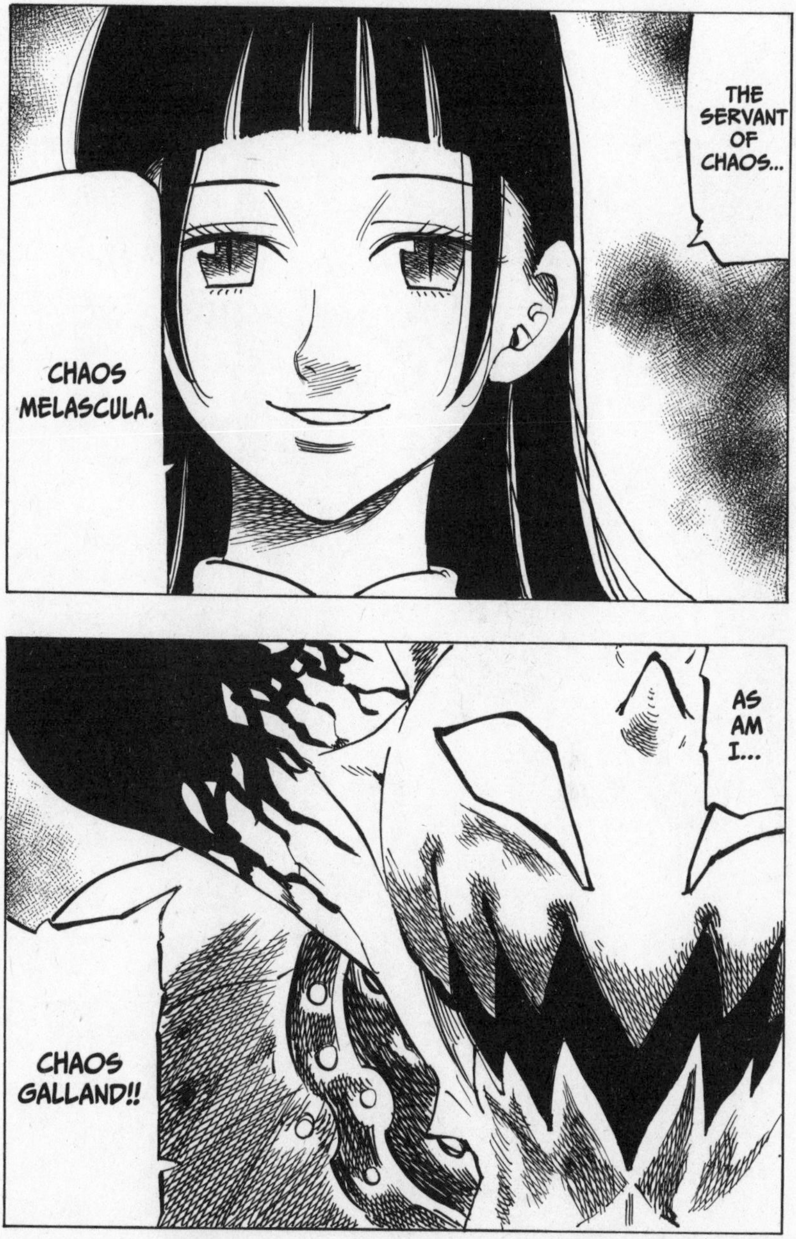
THE SERVANT OF CHAOS...
CHAOS MELASCULA.
AS AM I...
CHAOS GALLAND!!

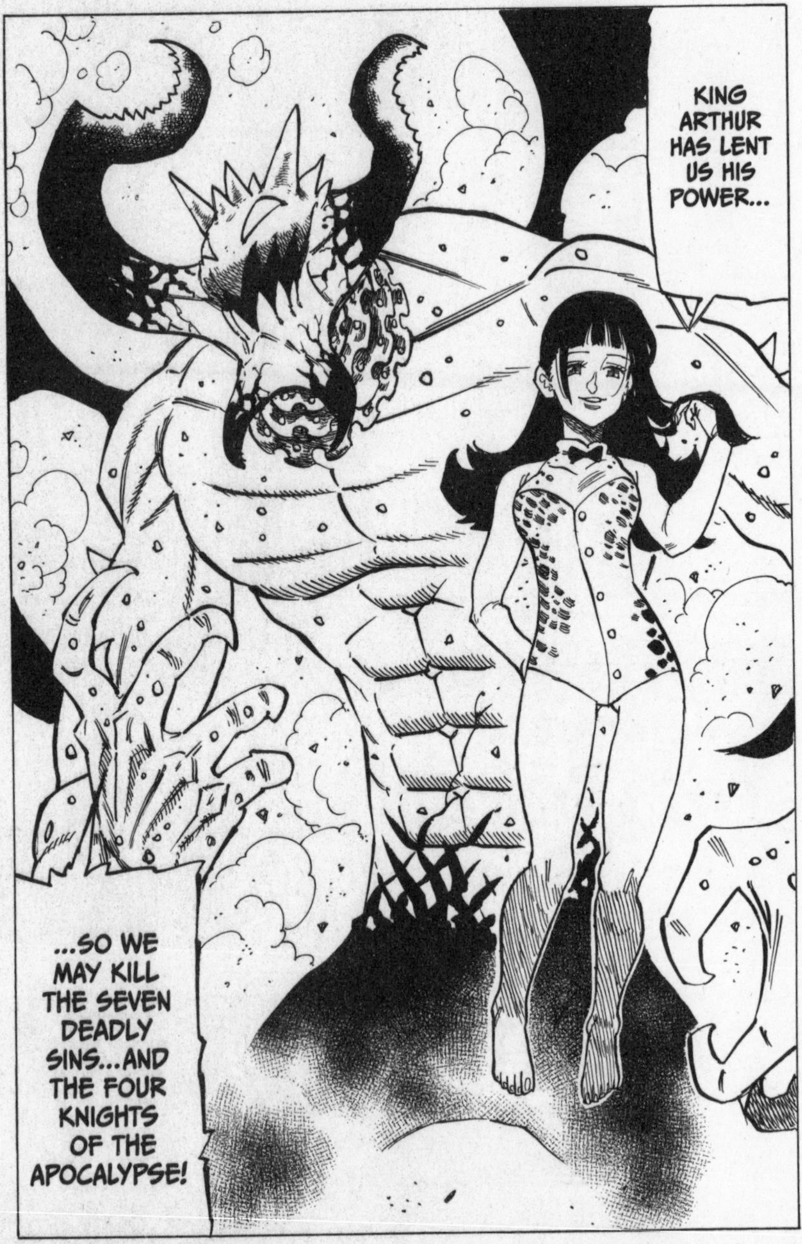
KING ARTHUR HAS LENT US HIS POWER...
...SO WE MAY KILL THE SEVEN DEADLY SINS...AND THE FOUR KNIGHTS OF THE APOCALYPSE!

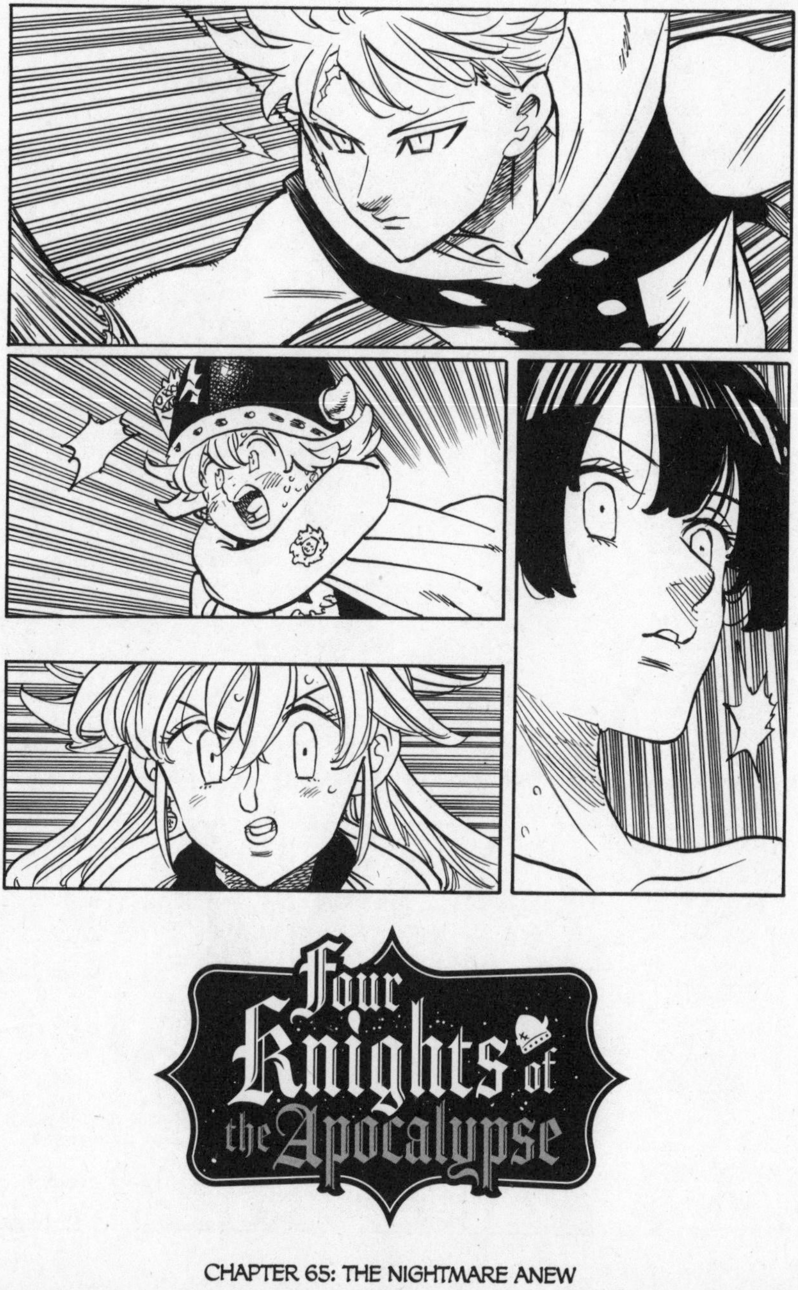

Four Knights of the Apocalypse

CHAPTER 65: THE NIGHTMARE ANEW

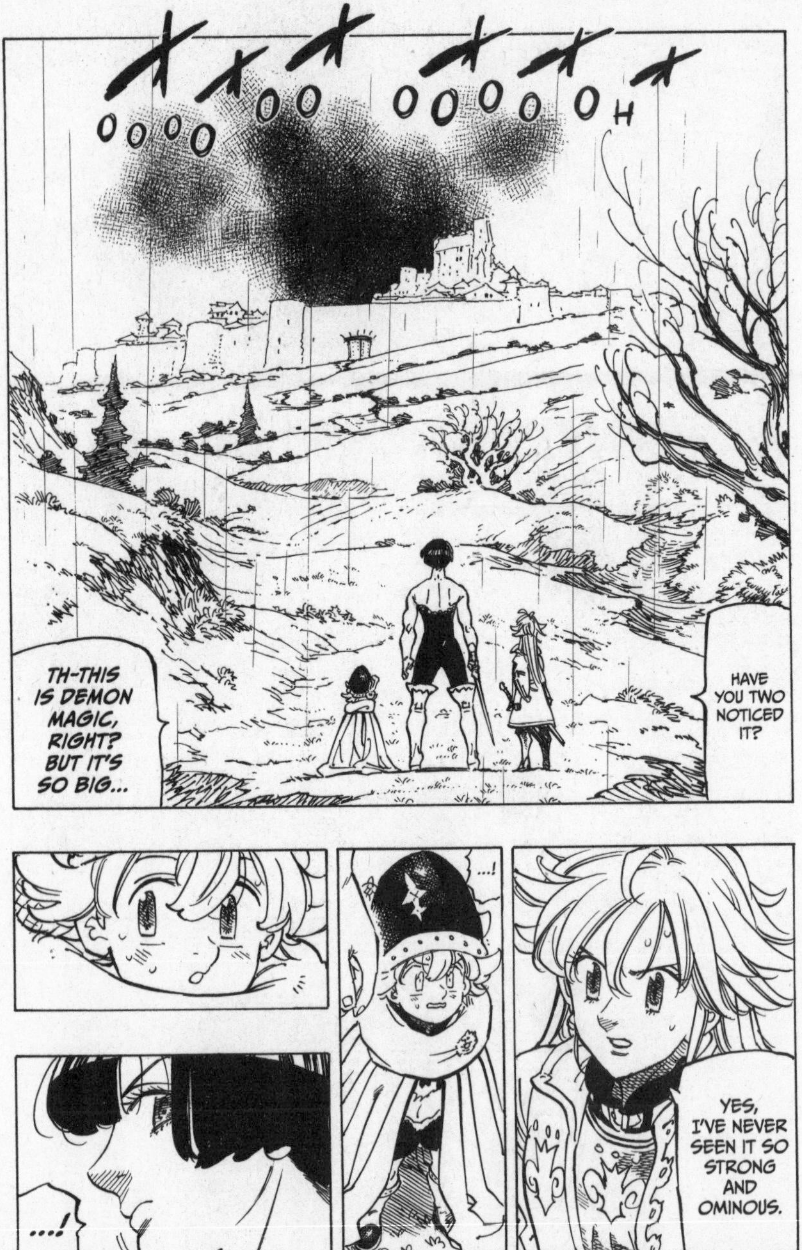
OOOOOOOOOOOH
HAVE YOU TWO NOTICED IT?
TH-THIS IS DEMON MAGIC, RIGHT? BUT IT'S SO BIG...
YES, I'VE NEVER SEEN IT SO STRONG AND OMINOUS.
...!
...!

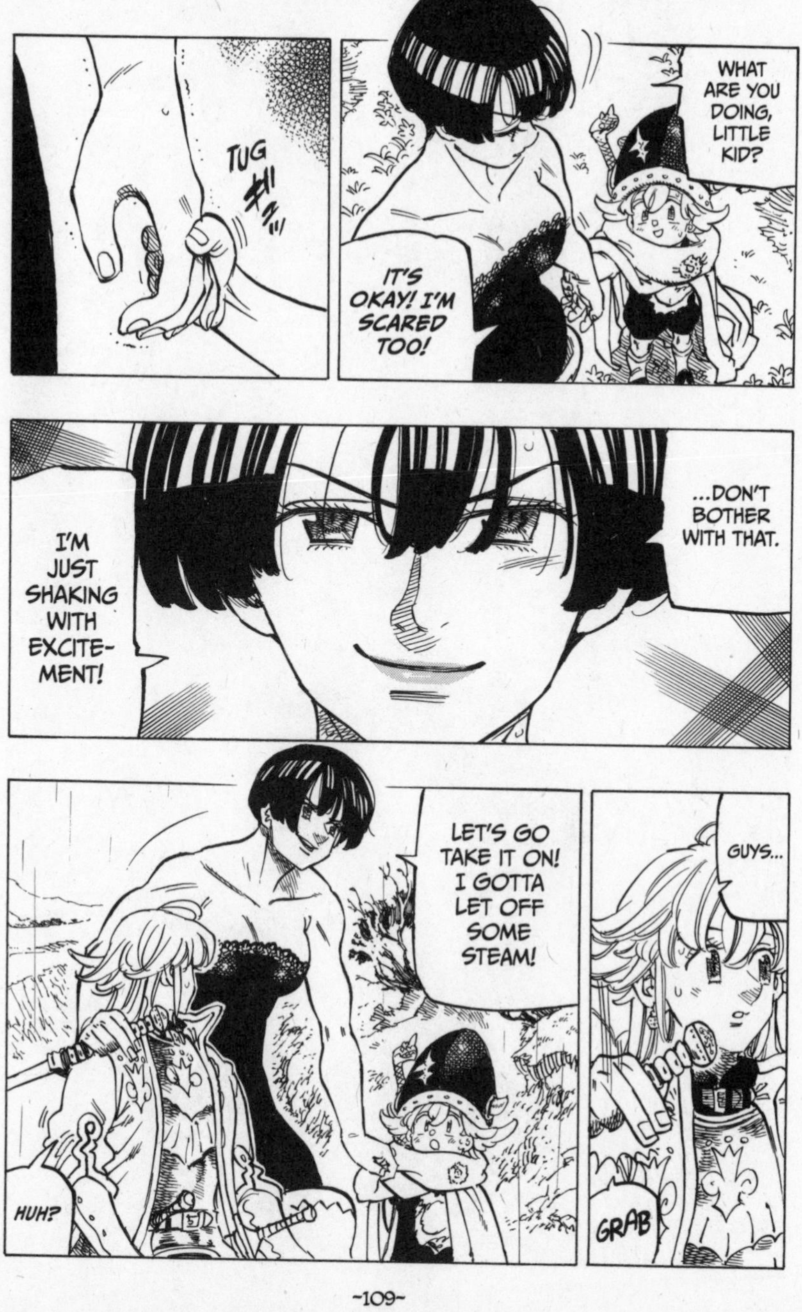
WHAT ARE YOU DOING, LITTLE KID?
IT'S OKAY! I'M SCARED TOO!
TUG
...DON'T BOTHER WITH THAT.
I'M JUST SHAKING WITH EXCITE-MENT!
GUYS...
GRAB
LET'S GO TAKE IT ON! I GOTTA LET OFF SOME STEAM!
HUH?

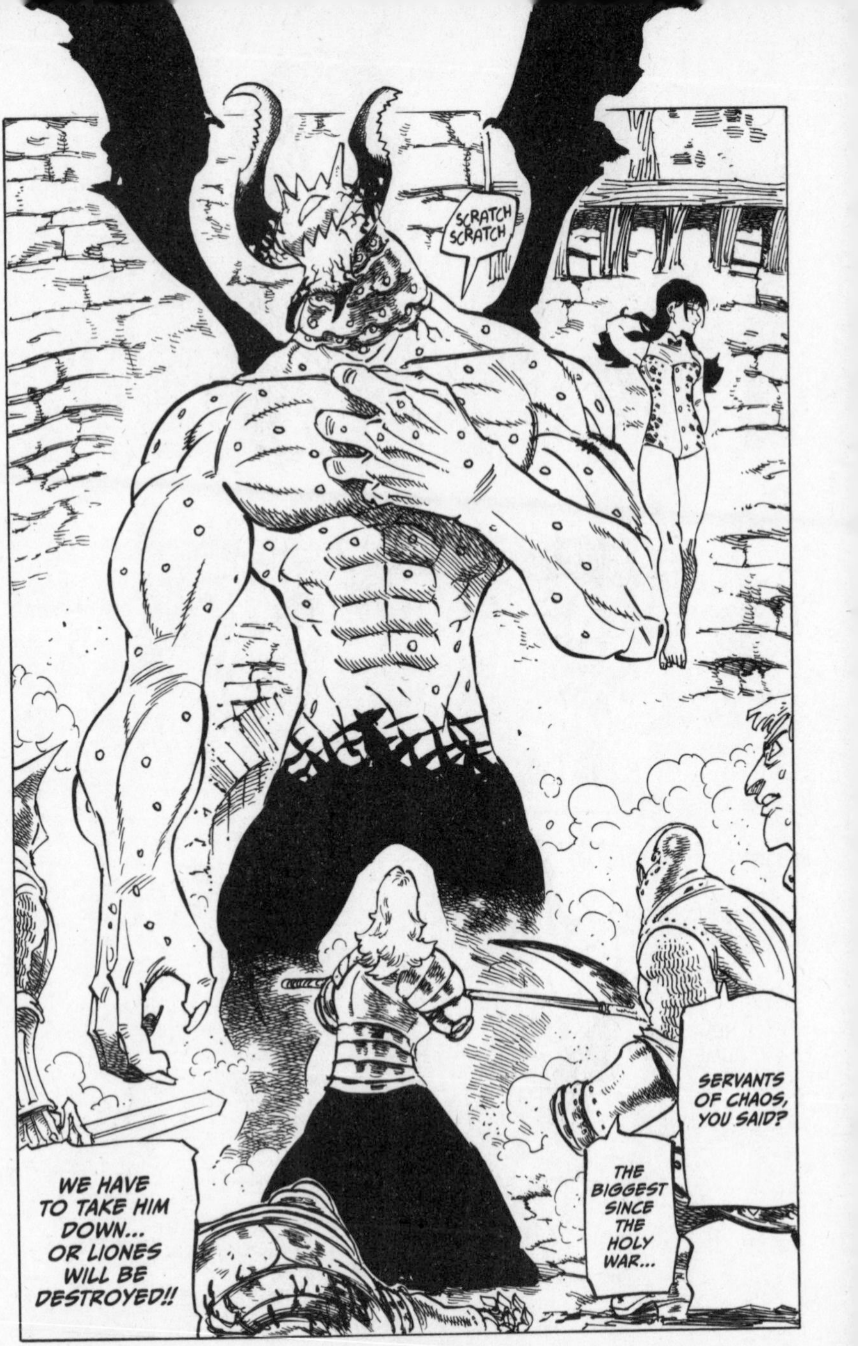
SCRATCH SCRATCH
SERVANTS OF CHAOS, YOU SAID?
THE BIGGEST SINCE THE HOLY WAR...
WE HAVE TO TAKE HIM DOWN... OR LIONES WILL BE DESTROYED!!

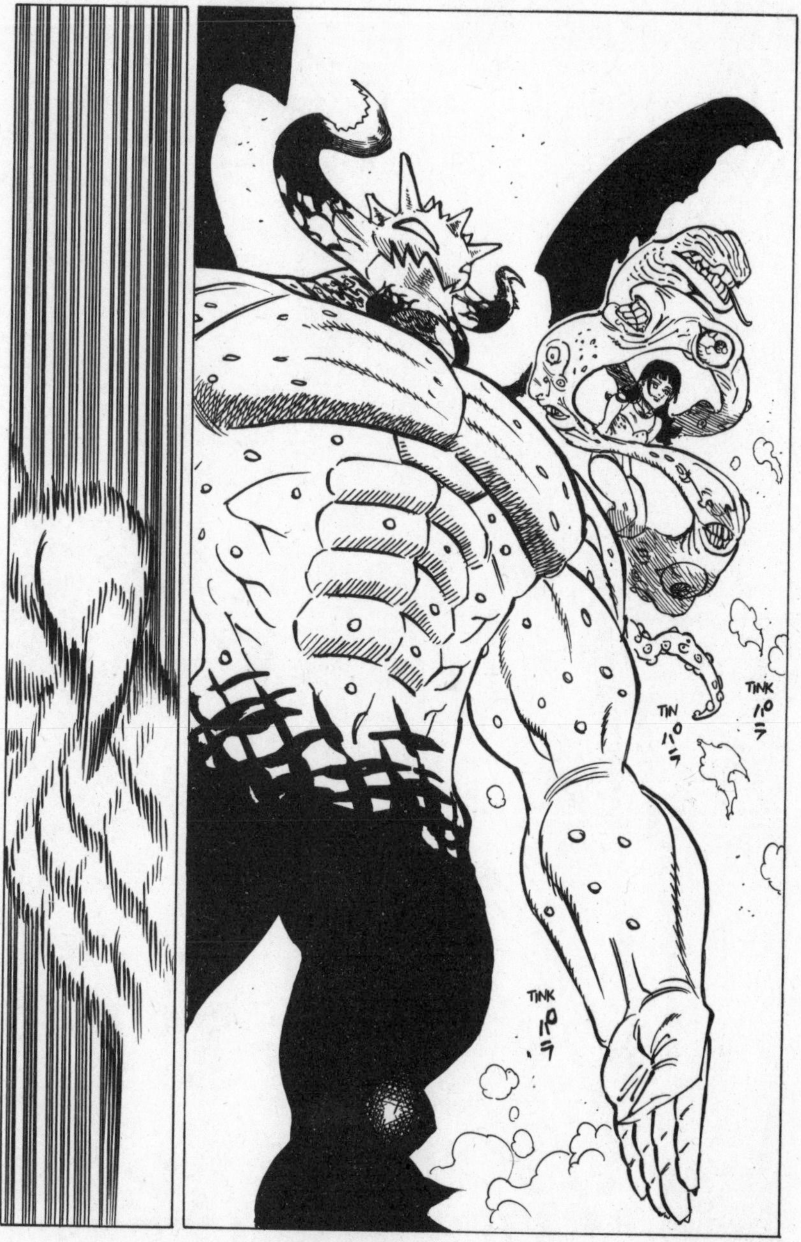
TINK
パラ
TIN
パラ
TINK
パラ

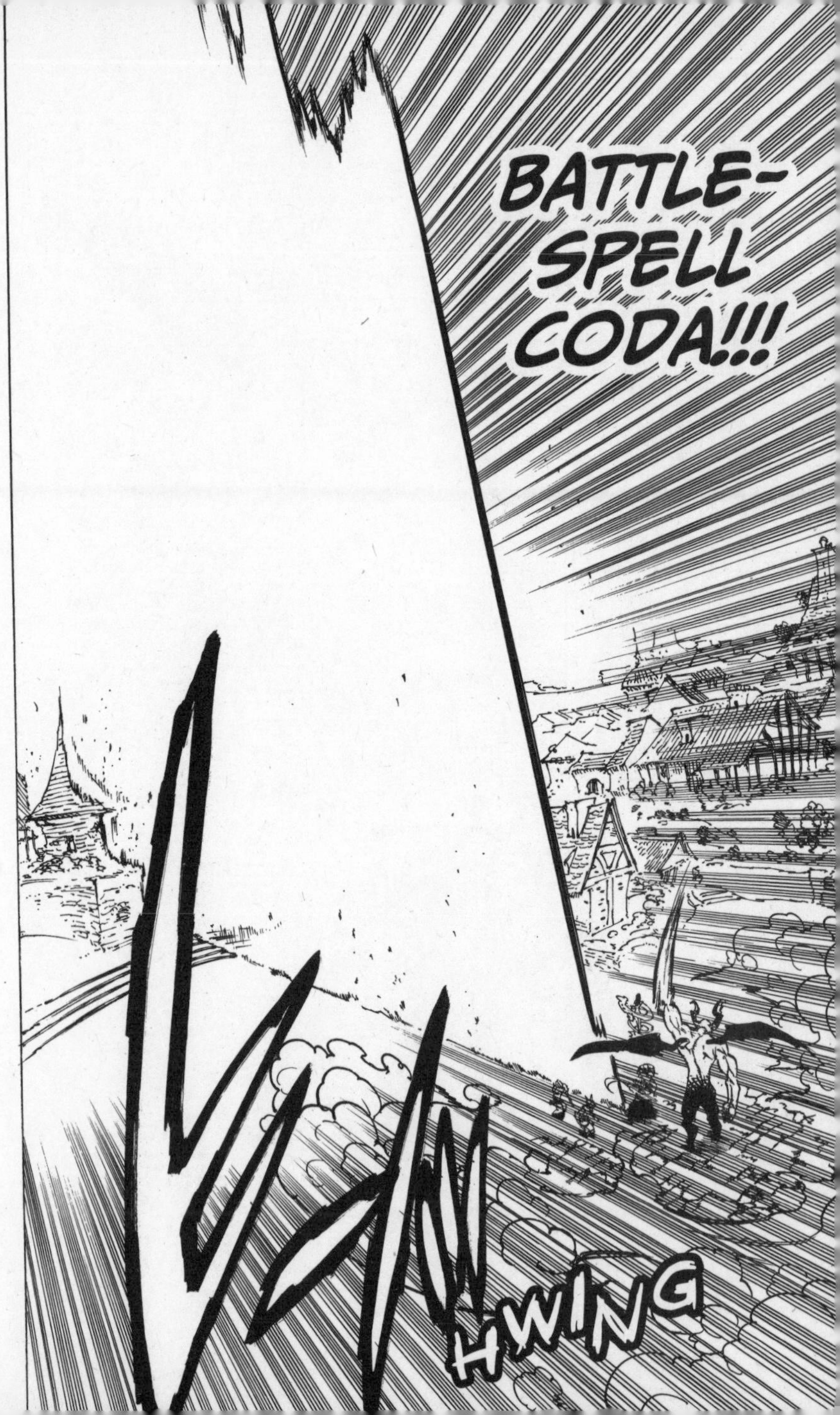
BATTLE-SPELL CODA!!!
HWING

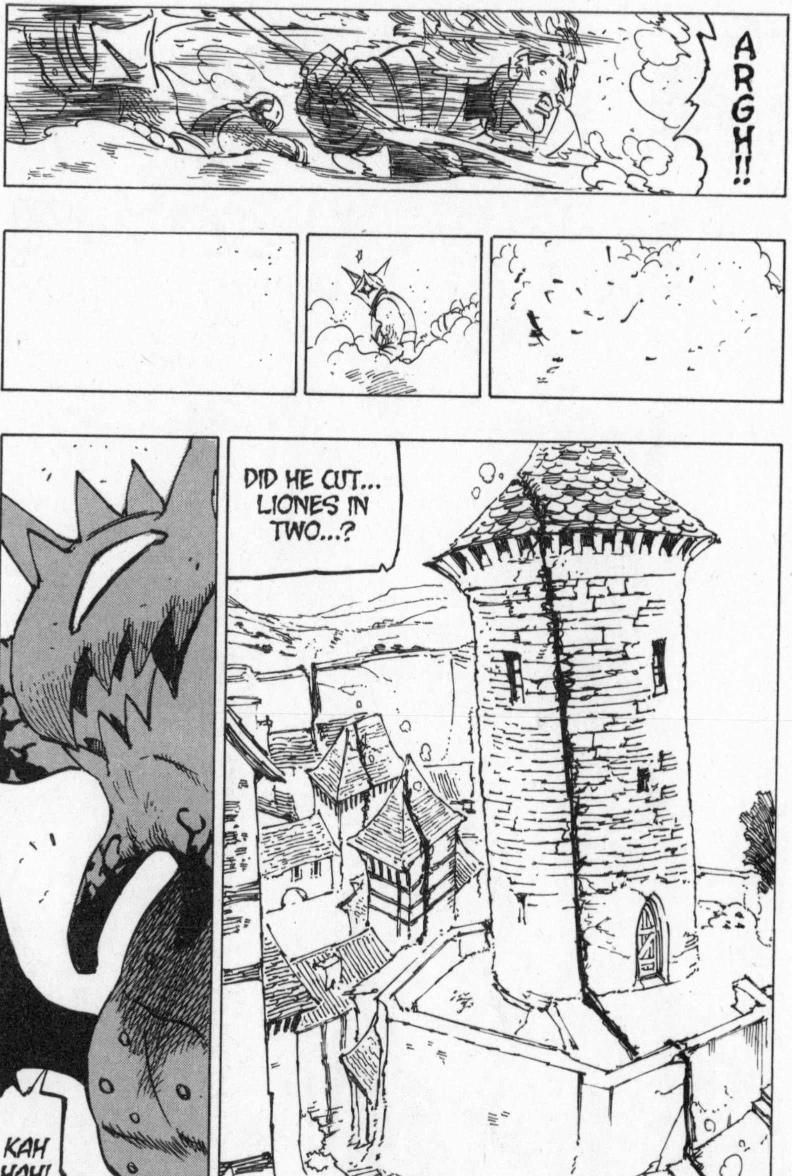
ARGH!!
DID HE CUT... LIONES IN TWO...?
KAH HAH!

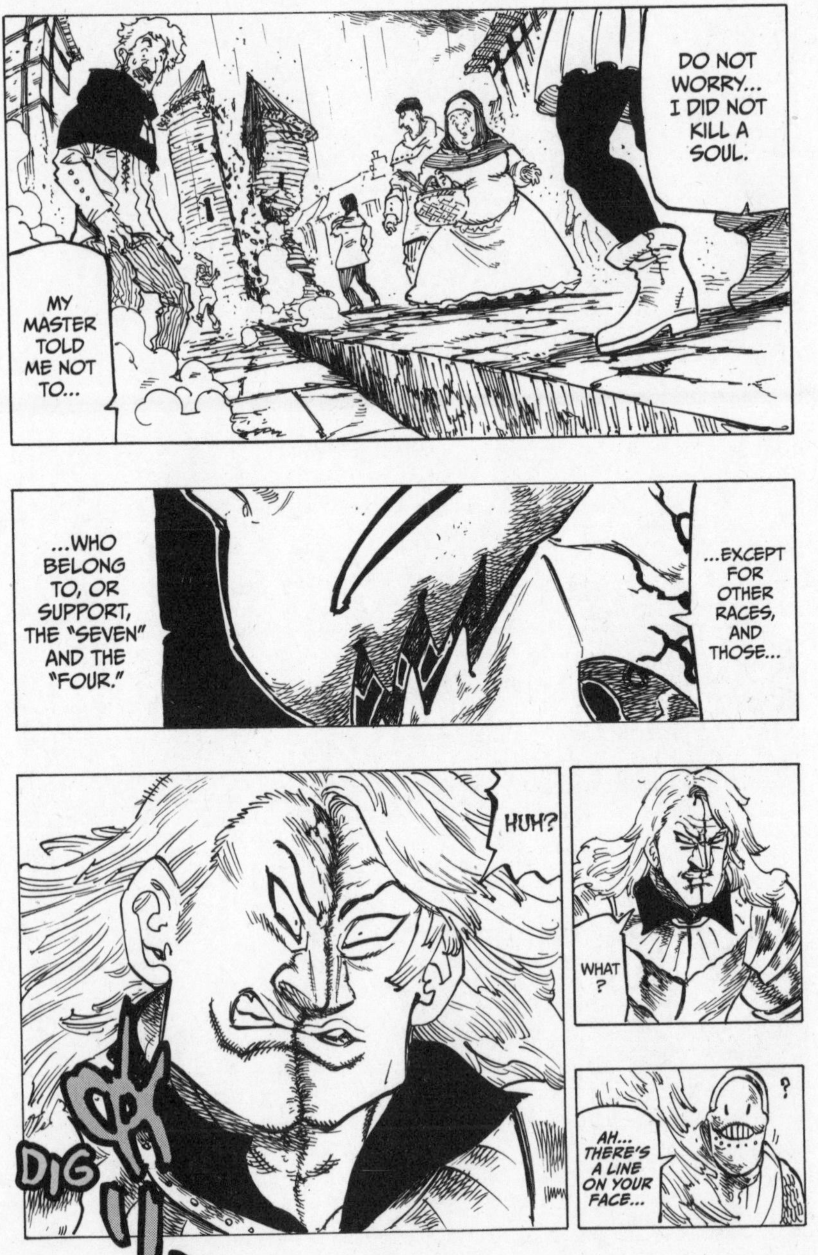
DO NOT WORRY... I DID NOT KILL A SOUL.
MY MASTER TOLD ME NOT TO...
...EXCEPT FOR OTHER RACES, AND THOSE...
...WHO BELONG TO, OR SUPPORT, THE "SEVEN" AND THE "FOUR."
WHAT?
?
AH... THERE'S A LINE ON YOUR FACE...
HUH?
DIG

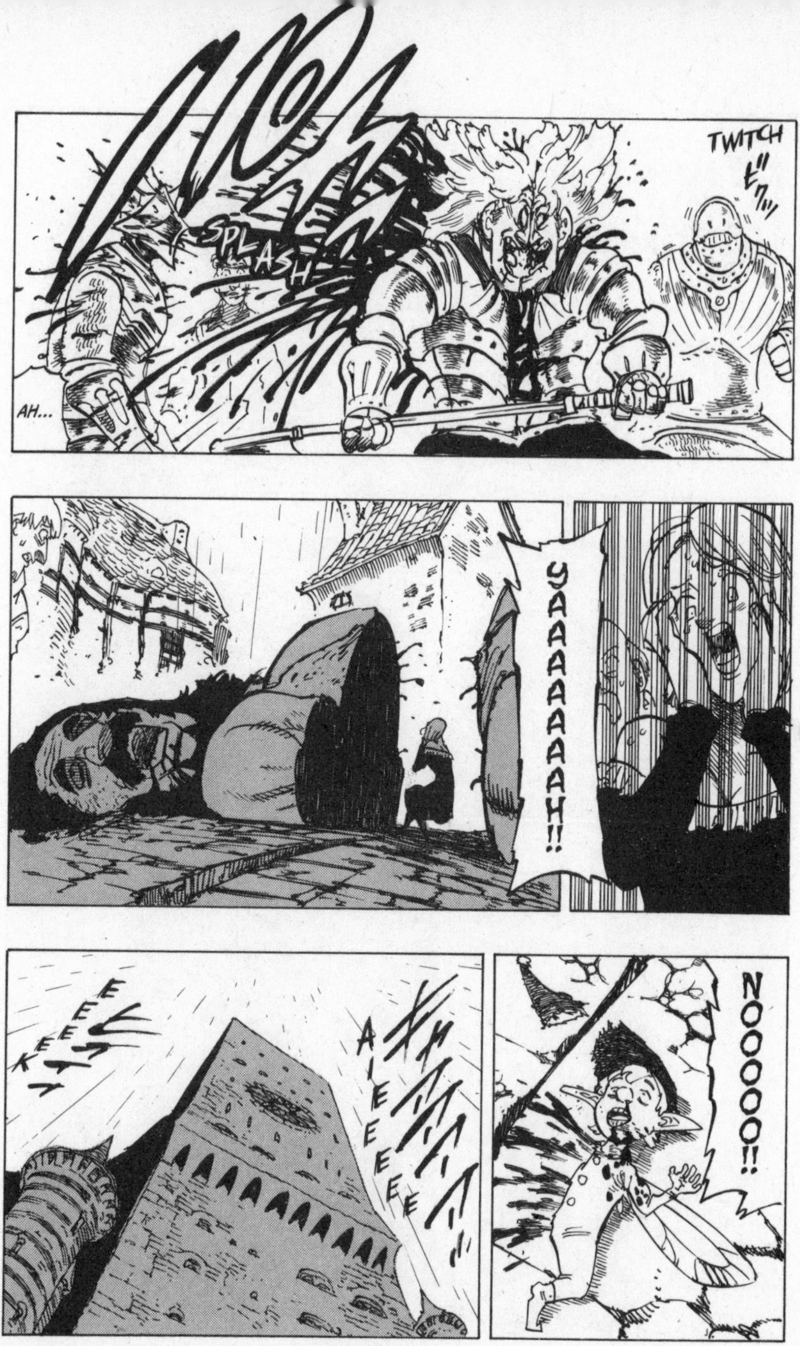
TWITCH
SPLASH
AH...
YAAAAAAAAAAH!!
NOOOOOO!!
AIEEEEEE!!
EEEEK
AAAAAAAAAAA

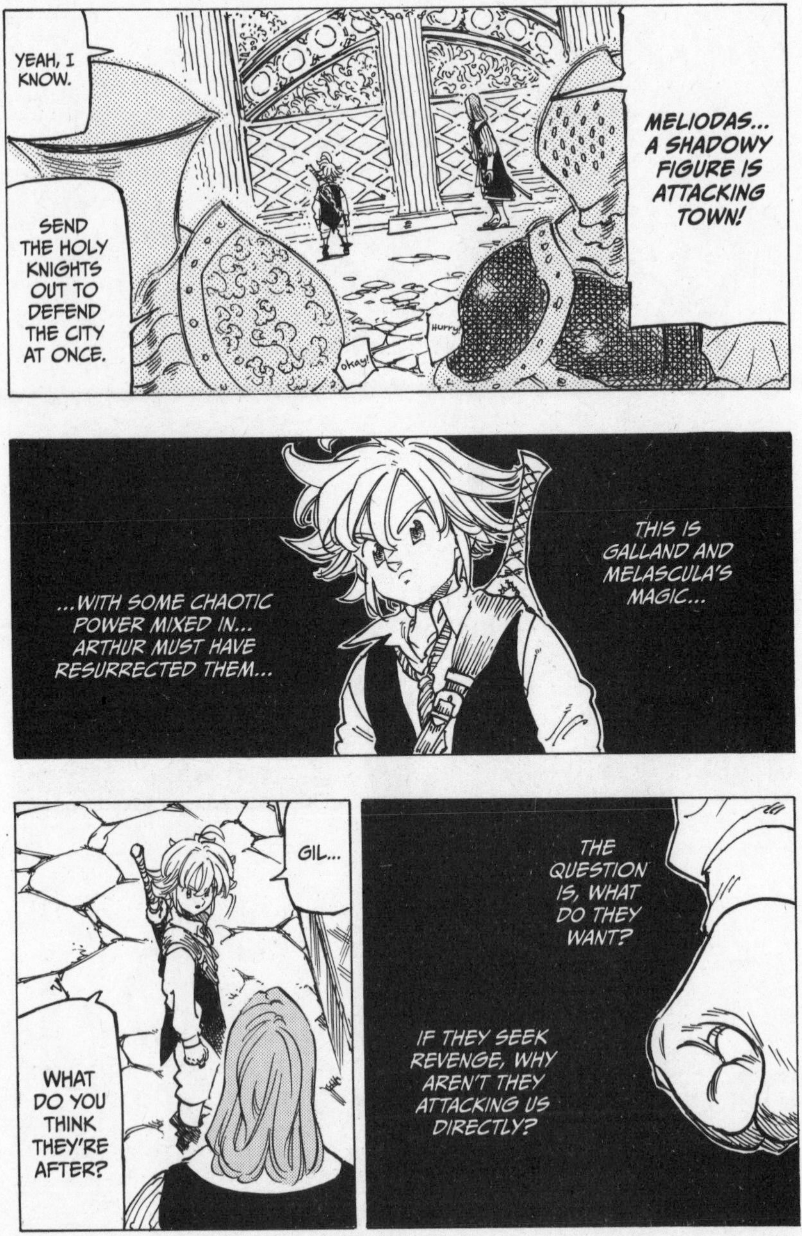
MELIODAS... A SHADOWY FIGURE IS ATTACKING TOWN!
YEAH, I KNOW.
Hurry!
SEND THE HOLY KNIGHTS OUT TO DEFEND THE CITY AT ONCE.
okay!
THIS IS GALLAND AND MELASCULA'S MAGIC...
...WITH SOME CHAOTIC POWER MIXED IN... ARTHUR MUST HAVE RESURRECTED THEM...
THE QUESTION IS, WHAT DO THEY WANT?
IF THEY SEEK REVENGE, WHY AREN'T THEY ATTACKING US DIRECTLY?
GIL...
WHAT DO YOU THINK THEY'RE AFTER?

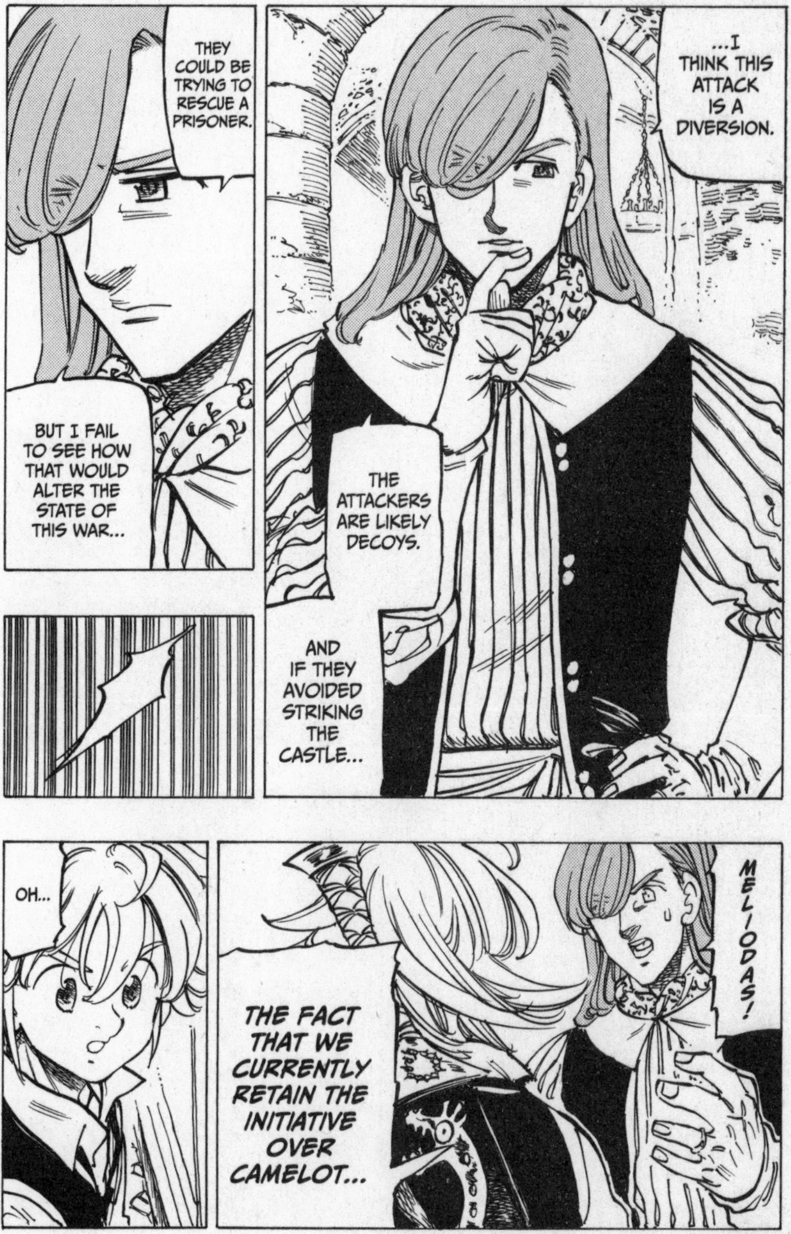
...I THINK THIS ATTACK IS A DIVERSION.
THE ATTACKERS ARE LIKELY DECOYS.
AND IF THEY AVOIDED STRIKING THE CASTLE...
THEY COULD BE TRYING TO RESCUE A PRISONER.
BUT I FAIL TO SEE HOW THAT WOULD ALTER THE STATE OF THIS WAR...
MELIODAS!
THE FACT THAT WE CURRENTLY RETAIN THE INITIATIVE OVER CAMELOT...
OH...

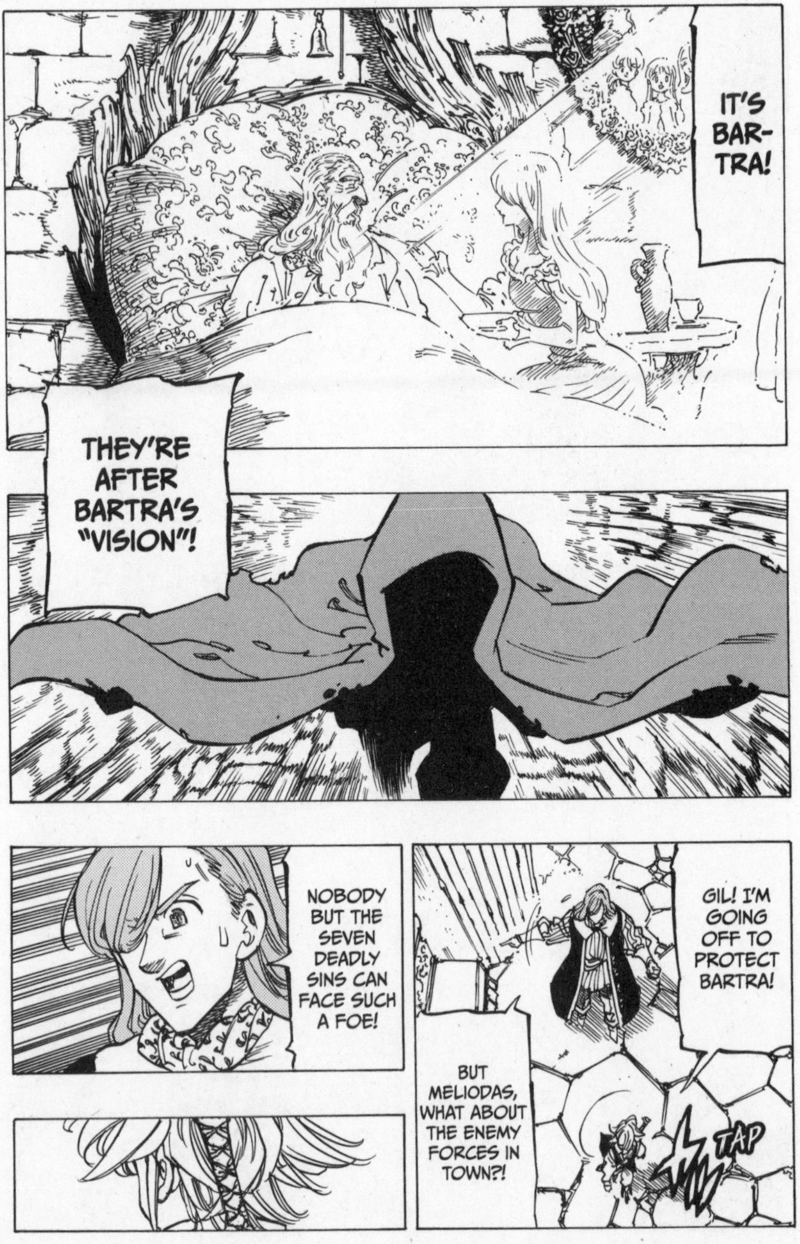
IT'S BAR-TRA!
THEY'RE AFTER BARTRA'S "VISION"!
GIL! I'M GOING OFF TO PROTECT BARTRA!
BUT MELIODAS, WHAT ABOUT THE ENEMY FORCES IN TOWN?!
TAP
NOBODY BUT THE SEVEN DEADLY SINS CAN FACE SUCH A FOE!

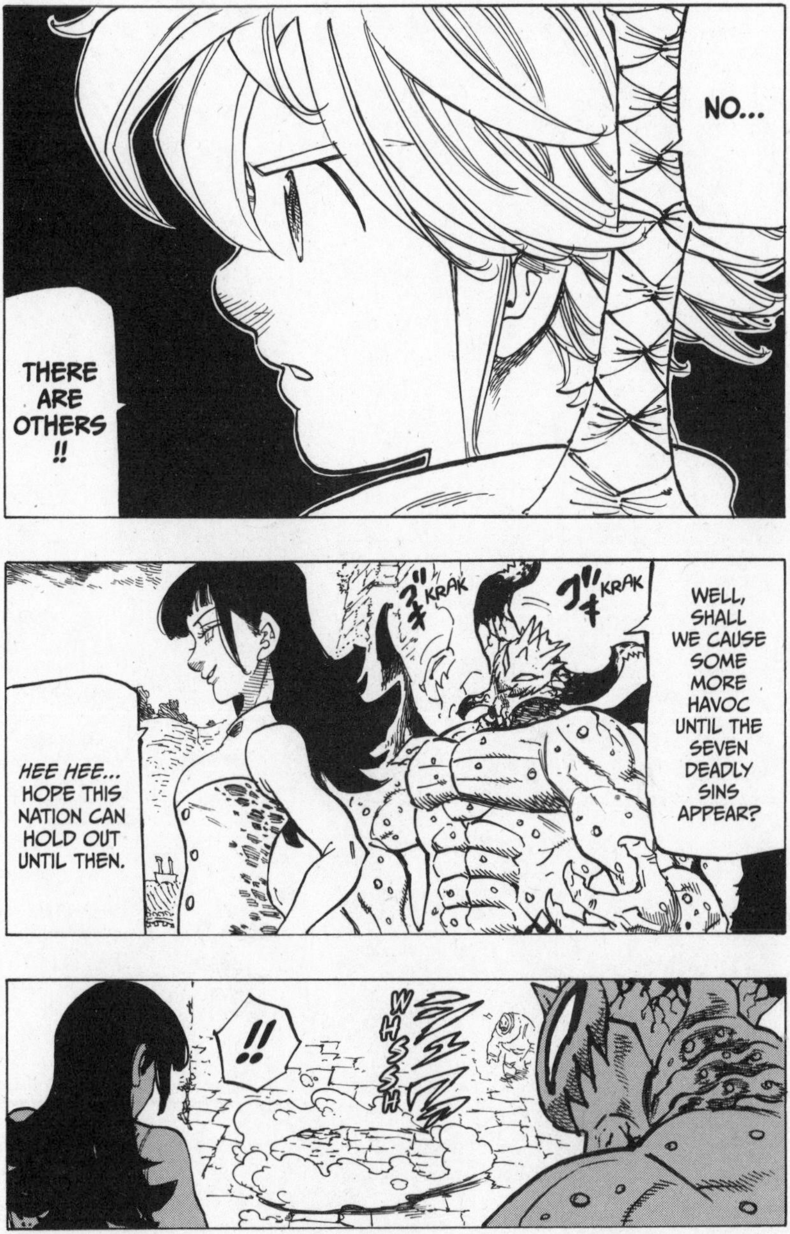
NO...
THERE ARE OTHERS !!
WELL, SHALL WE CAUSE SOME MORE HAVOC UNTIL THE SEVEN DEADLY SINS APPEAR?
KRAK
KRAK
HEE HEE... HOPE THIS NATION CAN HOLD OUT UNTIL THEN.
WHSSH
!!

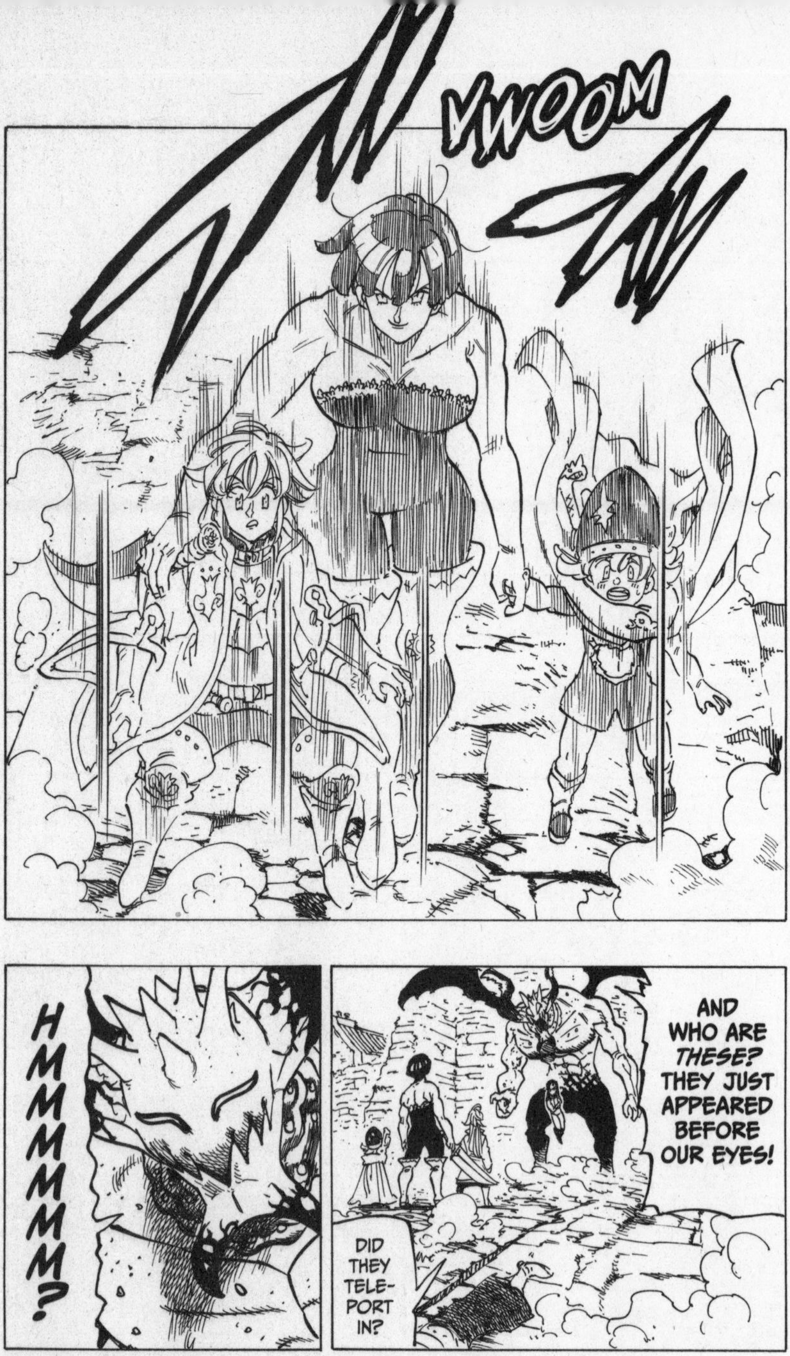
YWOOM
AND WHO ARE *THESE?* THEY JUST APPEARED BEFORE OUR EYES!
DID THEY TELE-PORT IN?
HMMMMMMM?

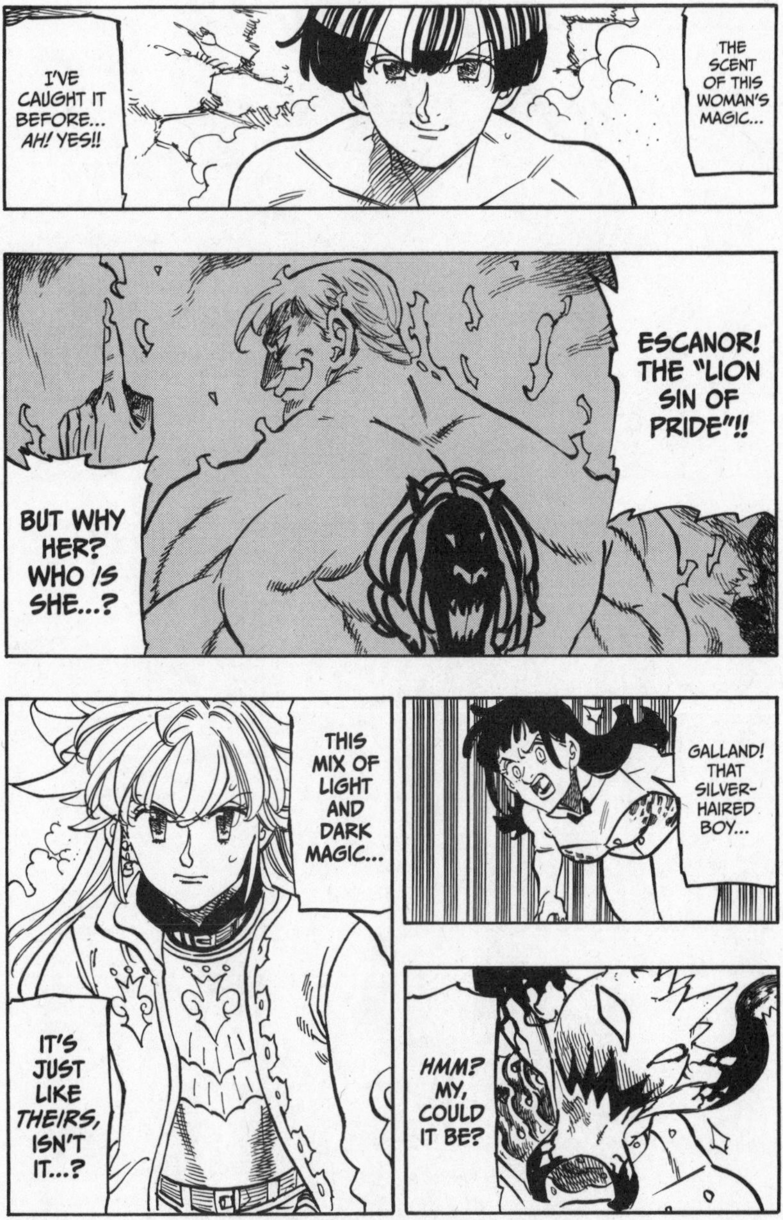
THE SCENT OF THIS WOMAN'S MAGIC...
I'VE CAUGHT IT BEFORE... *AH!* YES!!
ESCANOR! THE "LION SIN OF PRIDE"!!
BUT WHY HER? WHO *IS* SHE...?
GALLAND! THAT SILVER-HAIRED BOY...
HMM? MY, COULD IT BE?
THIS MIX OF LIGHT AND DARK MAGIC...
IT'S JUST LIKE *THEIRS,* ISN'T IT...?

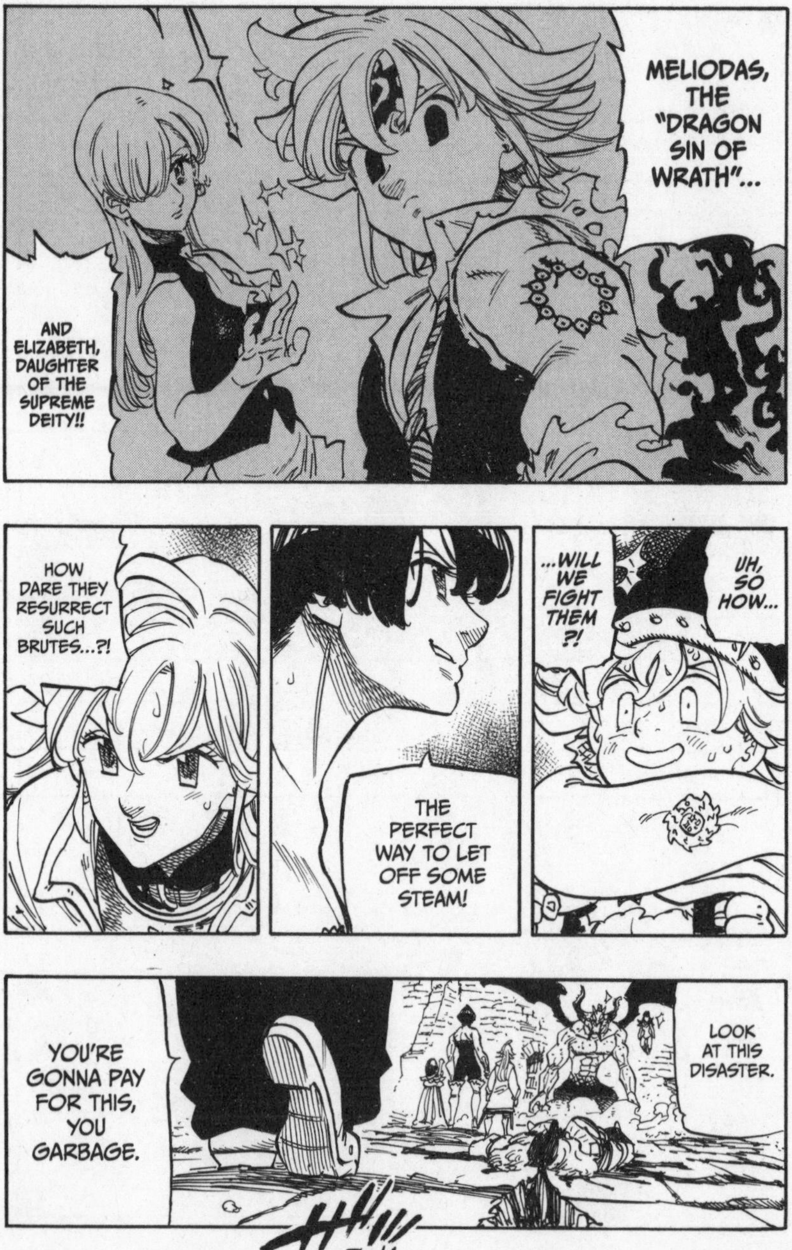
MELIODAS, THE "DRAGON SIN OF WRATH"...
AND ELIZABETH, DAUGHTER OF THE SUPREME DEITY!!
UH, SO HOW...
...WILL WE FIGHT THEM ?!
THE PERFECT WAY TO LET OFF SOME STEAM!
HOW DARE THEY RESURRECT SUCH BRUTES...?!
LOOK AT THIS DISASTER.
YOU'RE GONNA PAY FOR THIS, YOU GARBAGE.
ZSH

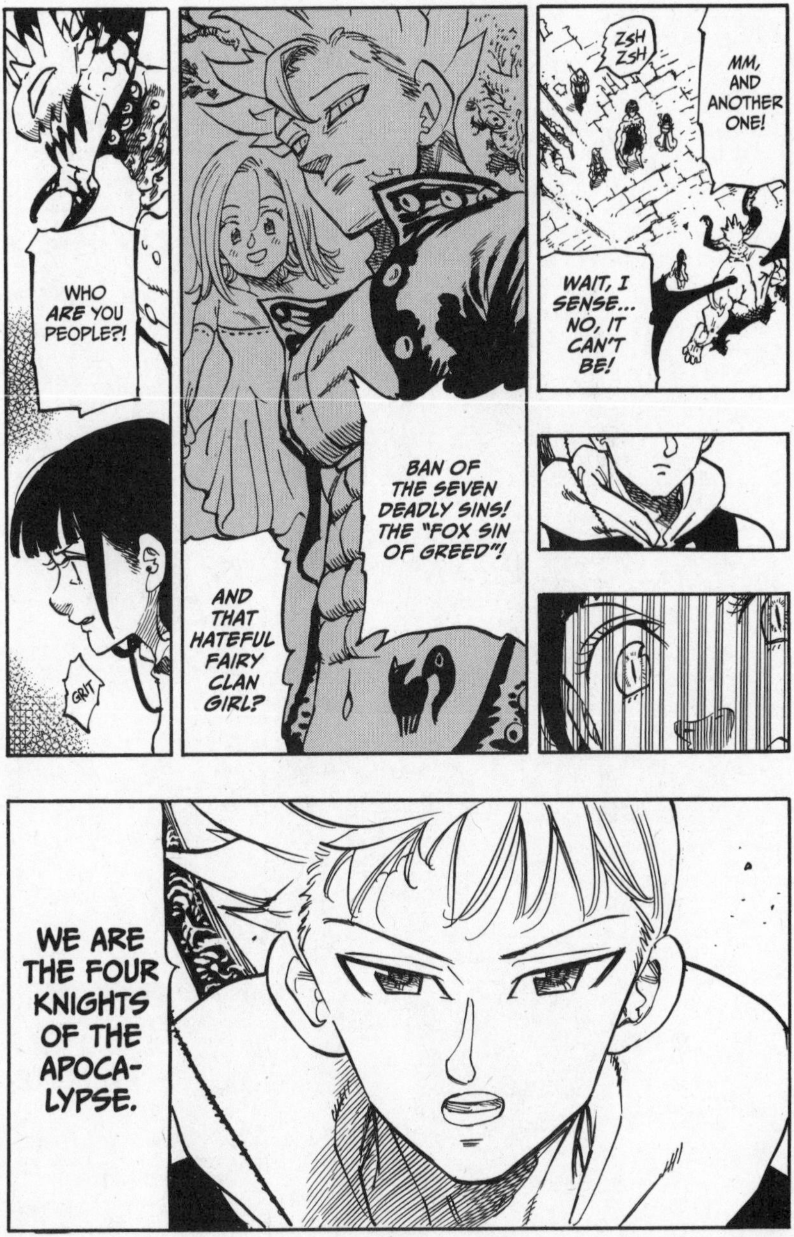
ZSH ZSH
MM, AND ANOTHER ONE!
WAIT, I SENSE... NO, IT CAN'T BE!
BAN OF THE SEVEN DEADLY SINS! THE "FOX SIN OF GREED"!
AND THAT HATEFUL FAIRY CLAN GIRL?
WHO ARE YOU PEOPLE?!
GRIT
WE ARE THE FOUR KNIGHTS OF THE APOCA-LYPSE.

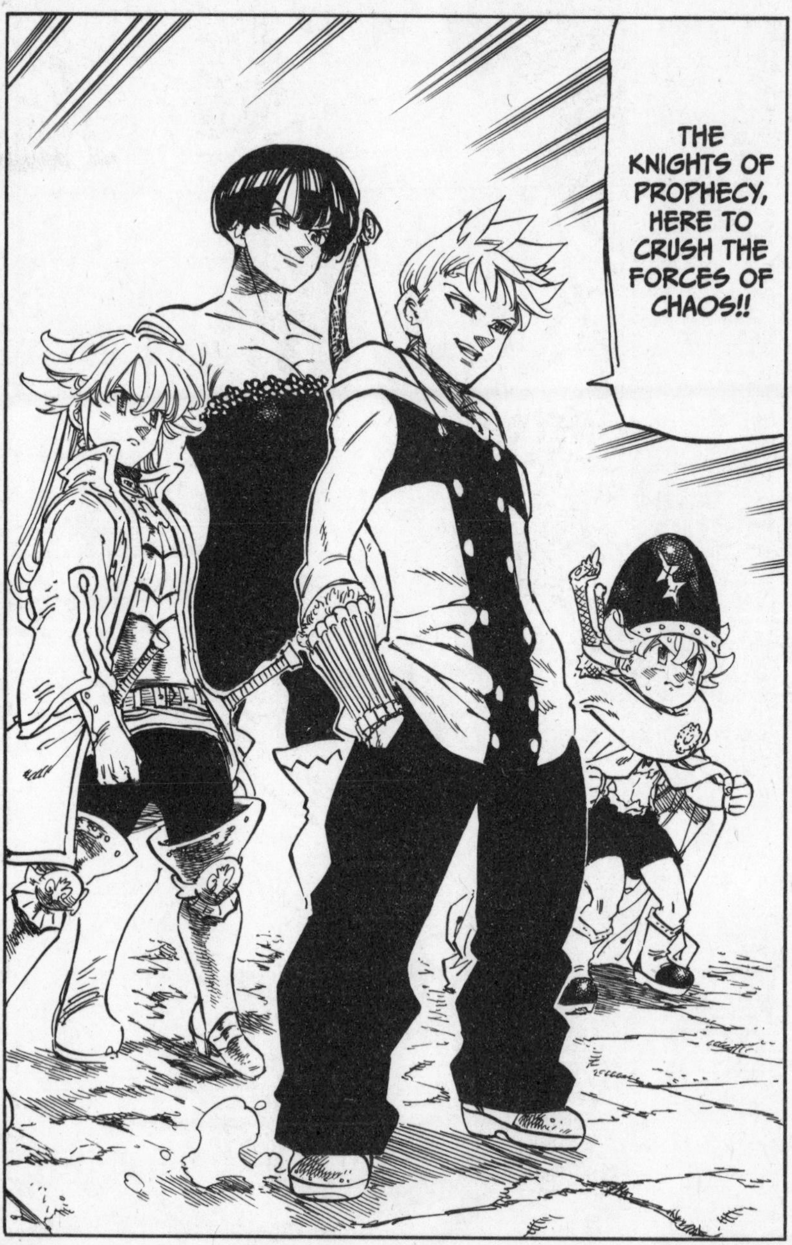
THE KNIGHTS OF PROPHECY, HERE TO CRUSH THE FORCES OF CHAOS!!

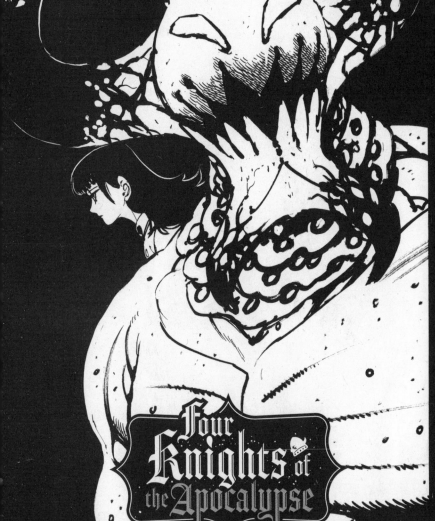

Four Knights of the Apocalypse

CHAPTER 66: THE ASSESSMENT

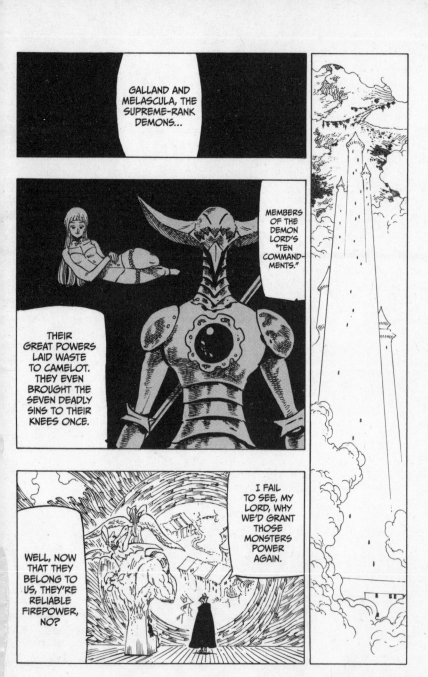

GALLAND AND MELASCULA, THE SUPREME-RANK DEMONS...

MEMBERS OF THE DEMON LORD'S "TEN COMMANDMENTS."

THEIR GREAT POWERS LAID WASTE TO CAMELOT. THEY EVEN BROUGHT THE SEVEN DEADLY SINS TO THEIR KNEES ONCE.

I FAIL TO SEE, MY LORD, WHY WE'D GRANT THOSE MONSTERS POWER AGAIN.

WELL, NOW THAT THEY BELONG TO US, THEY'RE RELIABLE FIREPOWER, NO?

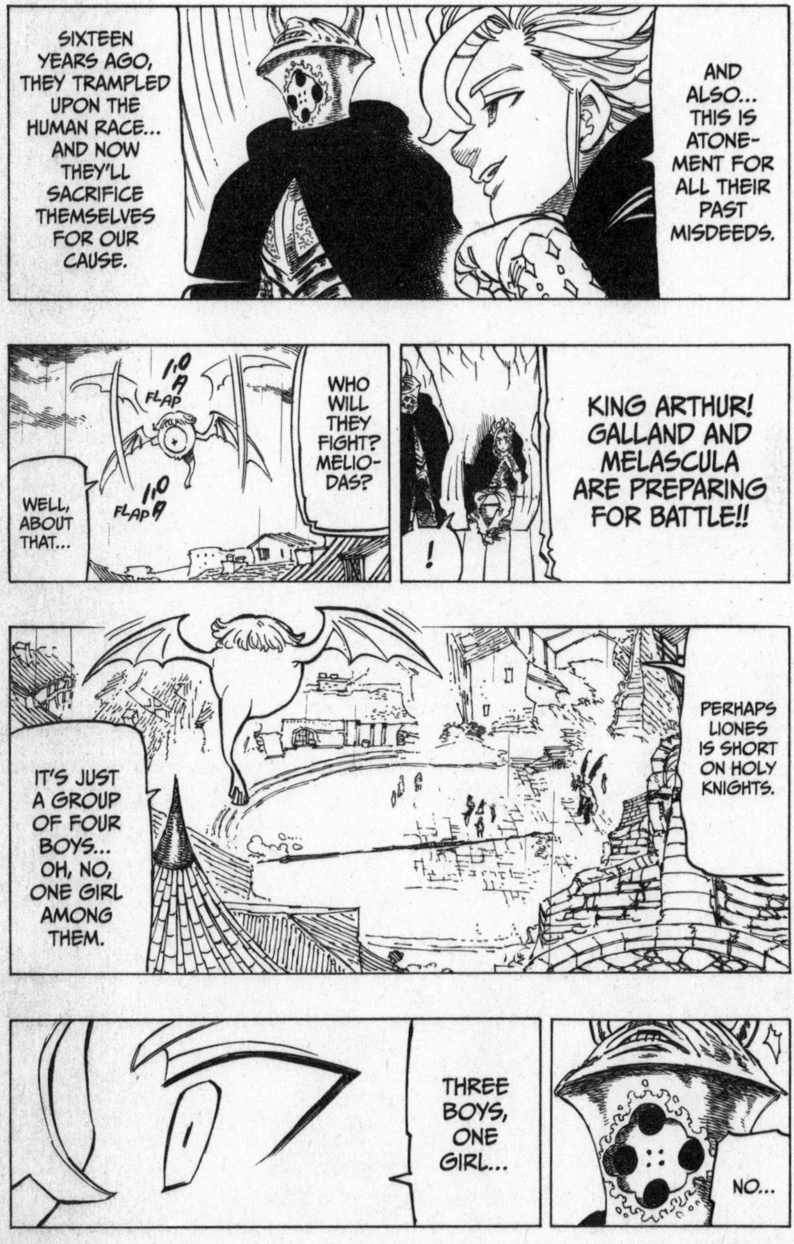
SIXTEEN YEARS AGO, THEY TRAMPLED UPON THE HUMAN RACE... AND NOW THEY'LL SACRIFICE THEMSELVES FOR OUR CAUSE.
AND ALSO... THIS IS ATONE-MENT FOR ALL THEIR PAST MISDEEDS.
KING ARTHUR! GALLAND AND MELASCULA ARE PREPARING FOR BATTLE!!
!
WHO WILL THEY FIGHT? MELIO-DAS?
FLAP
FLAP
WELL, ABOUT THAT...
PERHAPS LIONES IS SHORT ON HOLY KNIGHTS.
IT'S JUST A GROUP OF FOUR BOYS... OH, NO, ONE GIRL AMONG THEM.
NO...
THREE BOYS, ONE GIRL...

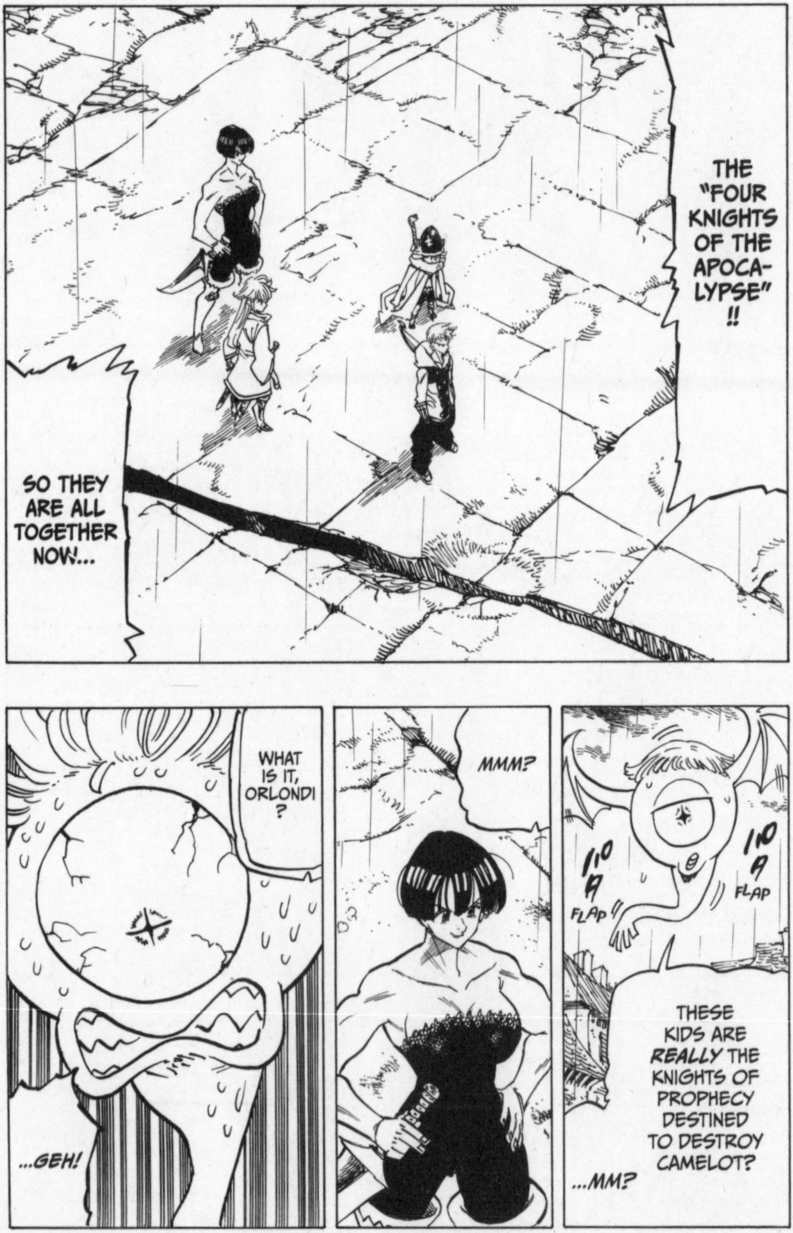

THE "FOUR KNIGHTS OF THE APOCALYPSE" !!
SO THEY ARE ALL TOGETHER NOW...
FLAP
FLAP
THESE KIDS ARE *REALLY* THE KNIGHTS OF PROPHECY DESTINED TO DESTROY CAMELOT?
...MM?
MMM?
WHAT IS IT, ORLONDI ?
...GEH!

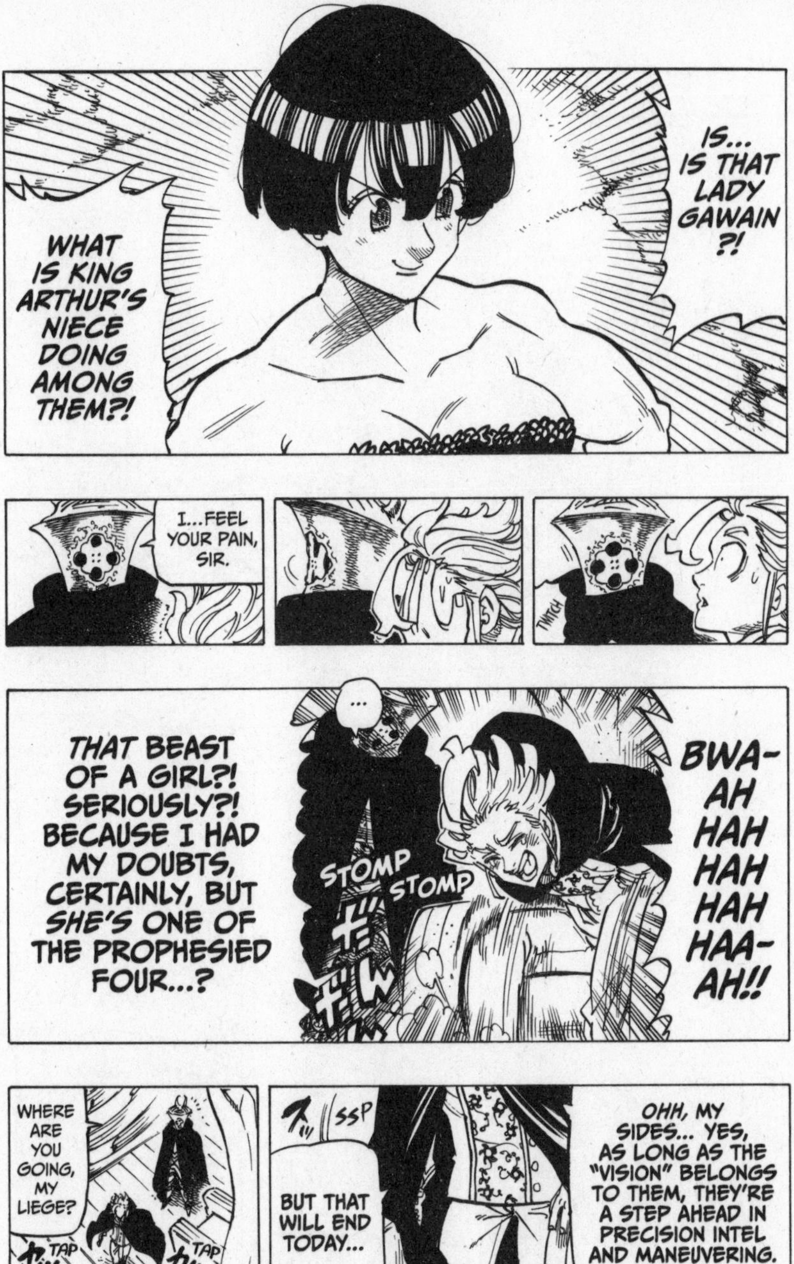

IS... IS THAT LADY GAWAIN ?!
WHAT IS KING ARTHUR'S NIECE DOING AMONG THEM?!
TWITCH
I...FEEL YOUR PAIN, SIR.
BWA-AH HAH HAH HAH HAA-AH!!
...
STOMP STOMP
THAT BEAST OF A GIRL?! SERIOUSLY?! BECAUSE I HAD MY DOUBTS, CERTAINLY, BUT SHE'S ONE OF THE PROPHESIED FOUR...?
OHH, MY SIDES... YES, AS LONG AS THE "VISION" BELONGS TO THEM, THEY'RE A STEP AHEAD IN PRECISION INTEL AND MANEUVERING.
SSP
BUT THAT WILL END TODAY...
WHERE ARE YOU GOING, MY LIEGE?
TAP
TAP

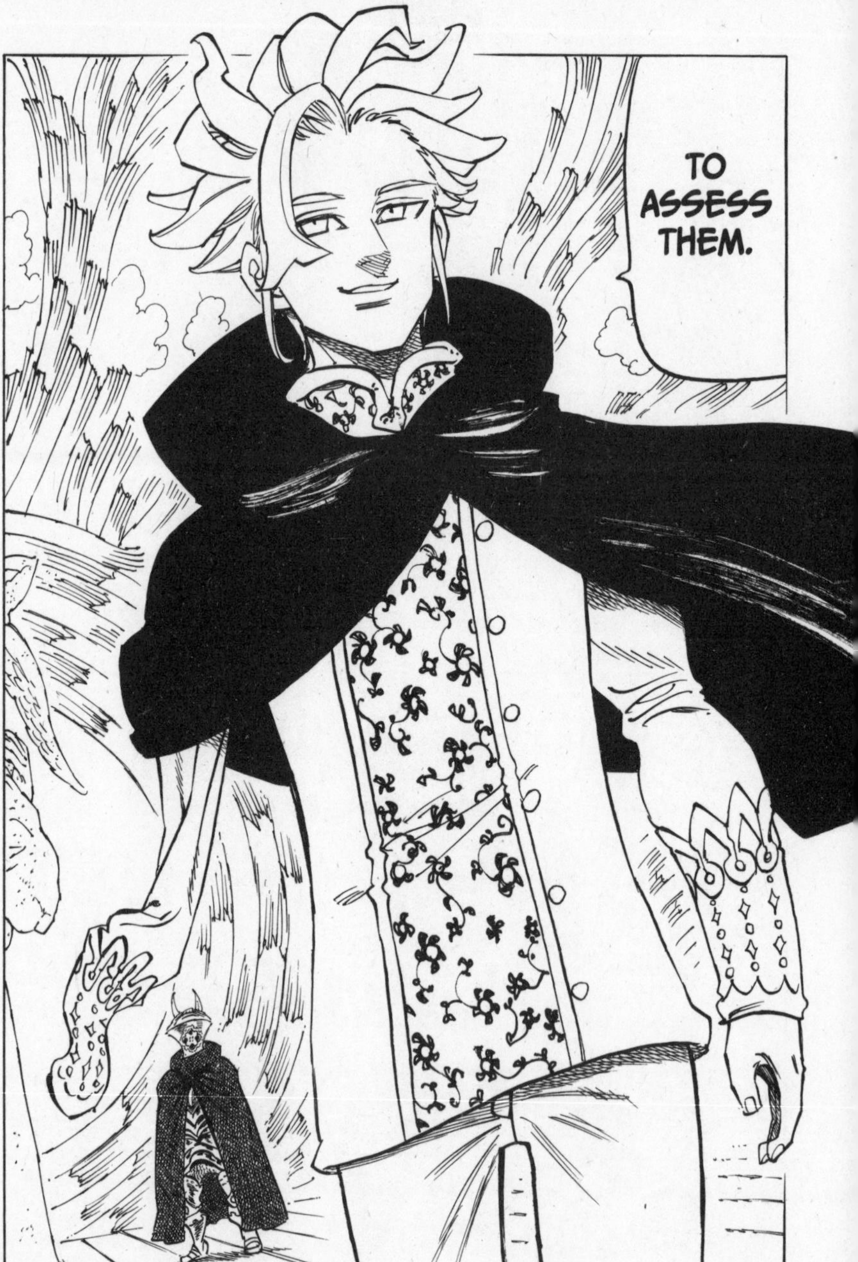
TO ASSESS THEM.

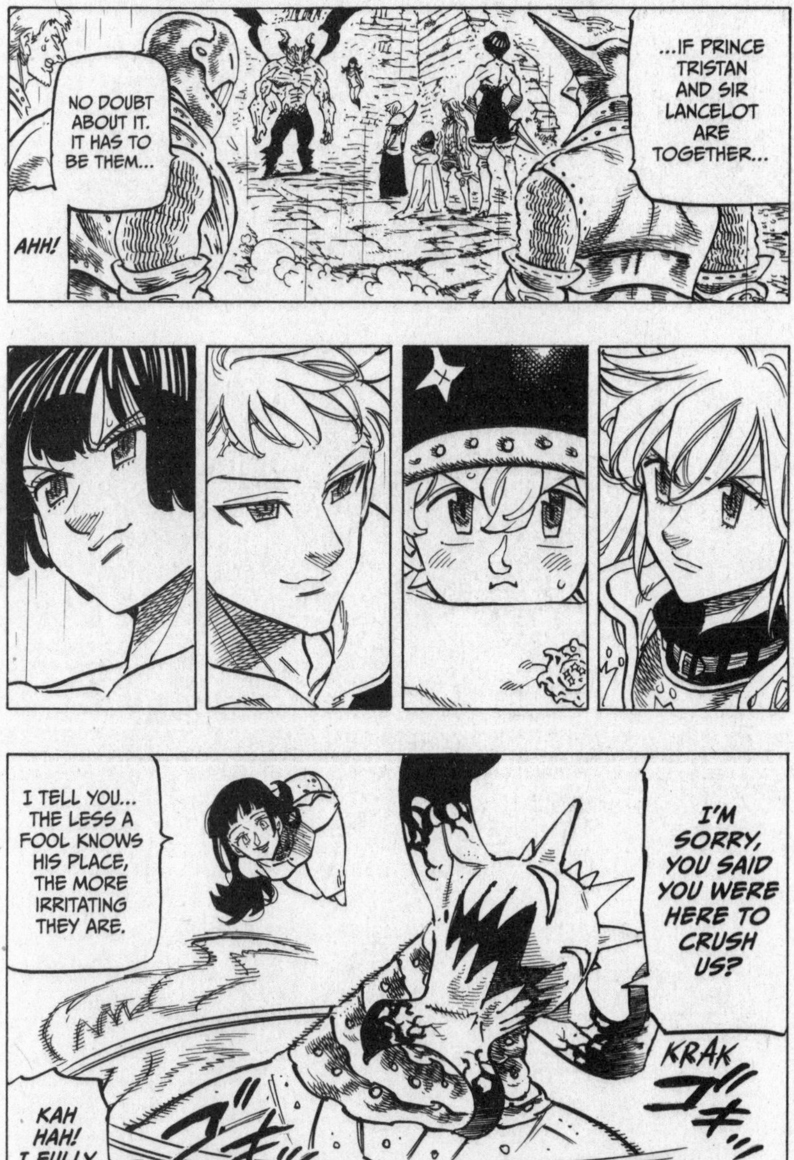
...IF PRINCE TRISTAN AND SIR LANCELOT ARE TOGETHER...
NO DOUBT ABOUT IT. IT HAS TO BE THEM...
AHH!
I'M SORRY, YOU SAID YOU WERE HERE TO CRUSH US?
KRAK
I TELL YOU... THE LESS A FOOL KNOWS HIS PLACE, THE MORE IRRITATING THEY ARE.
KAH HAH! I FULLY AGREE.
KRAK

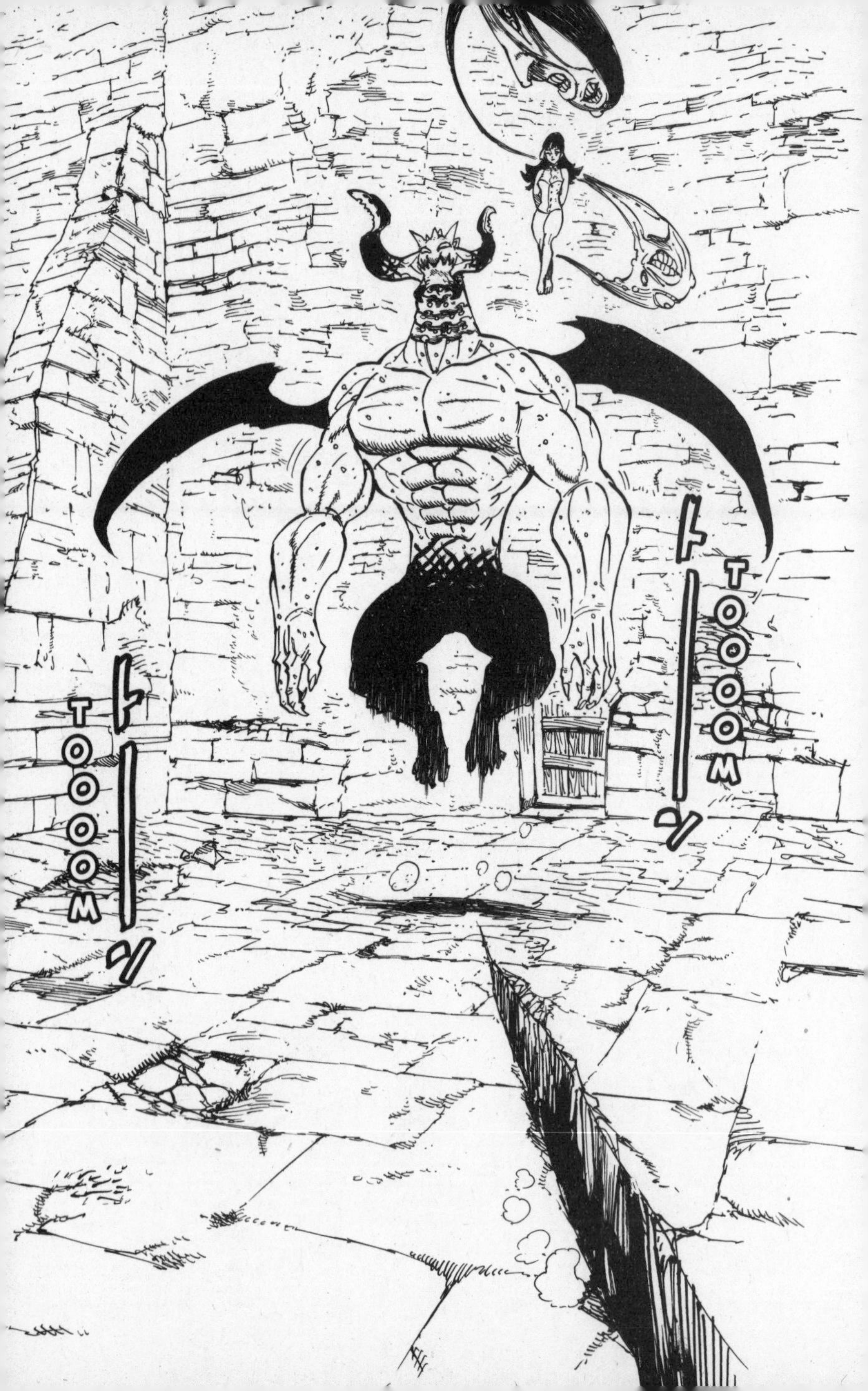
トーン
TOOOOM
トーン
TOOOOM

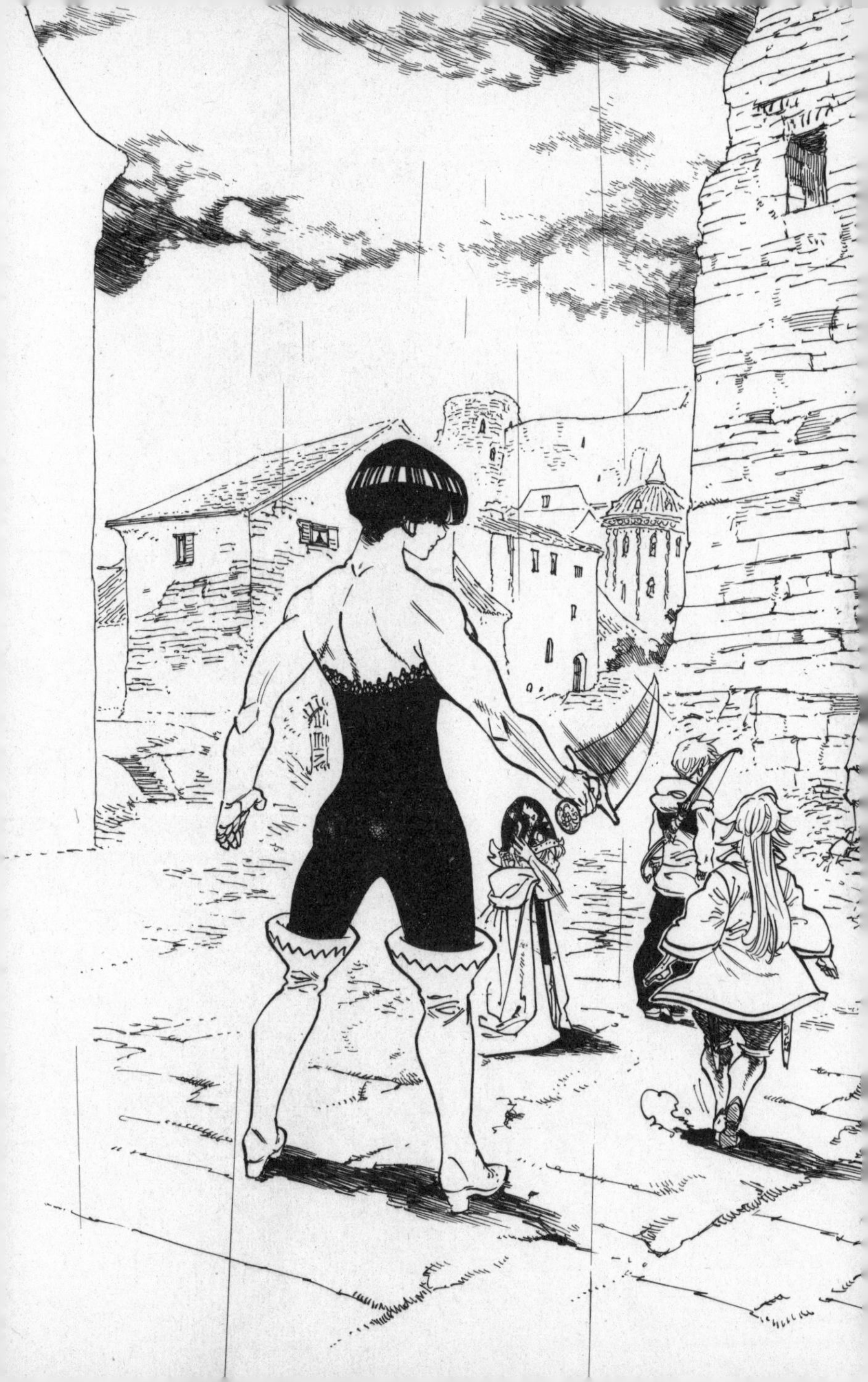

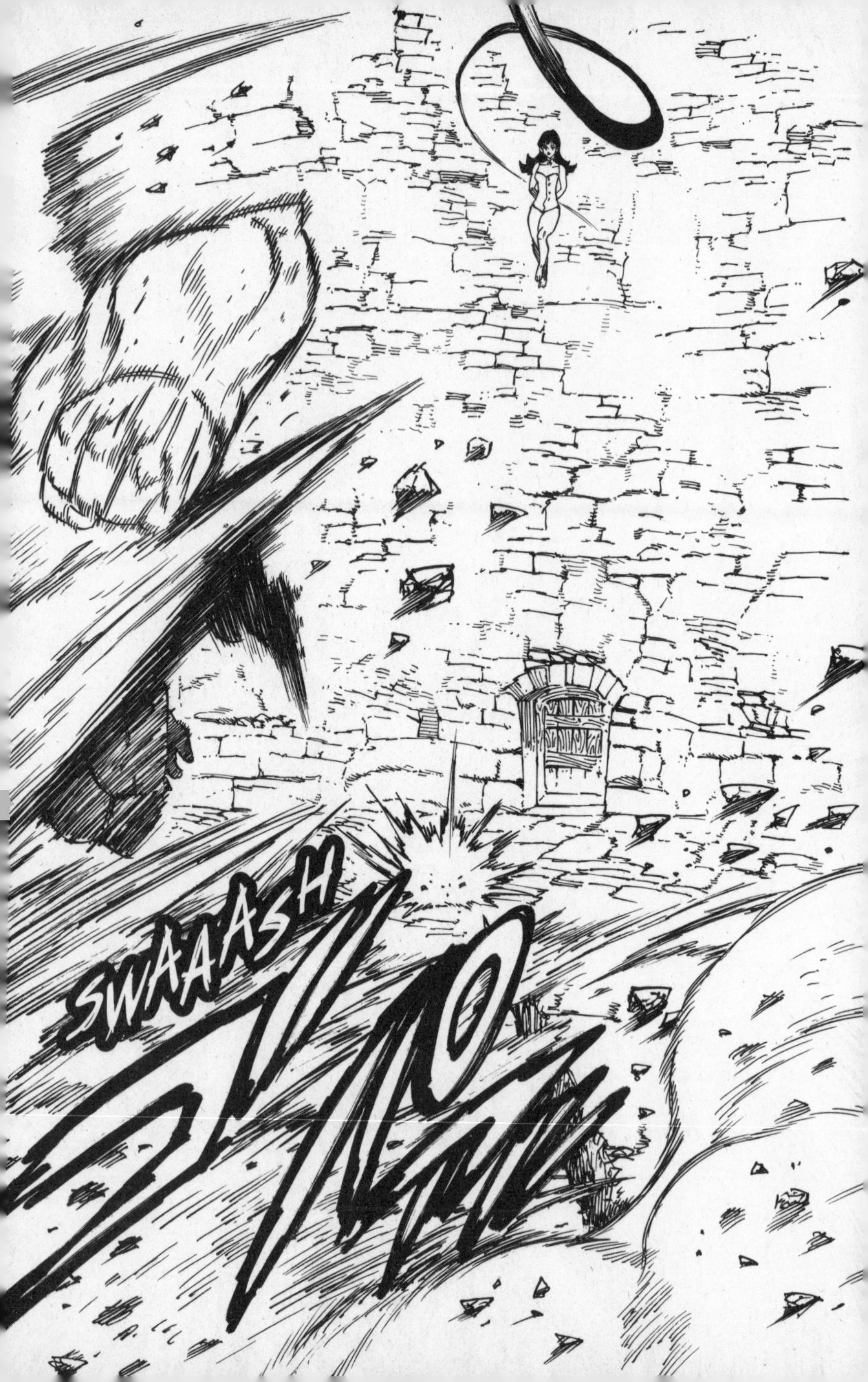
SWAAASH

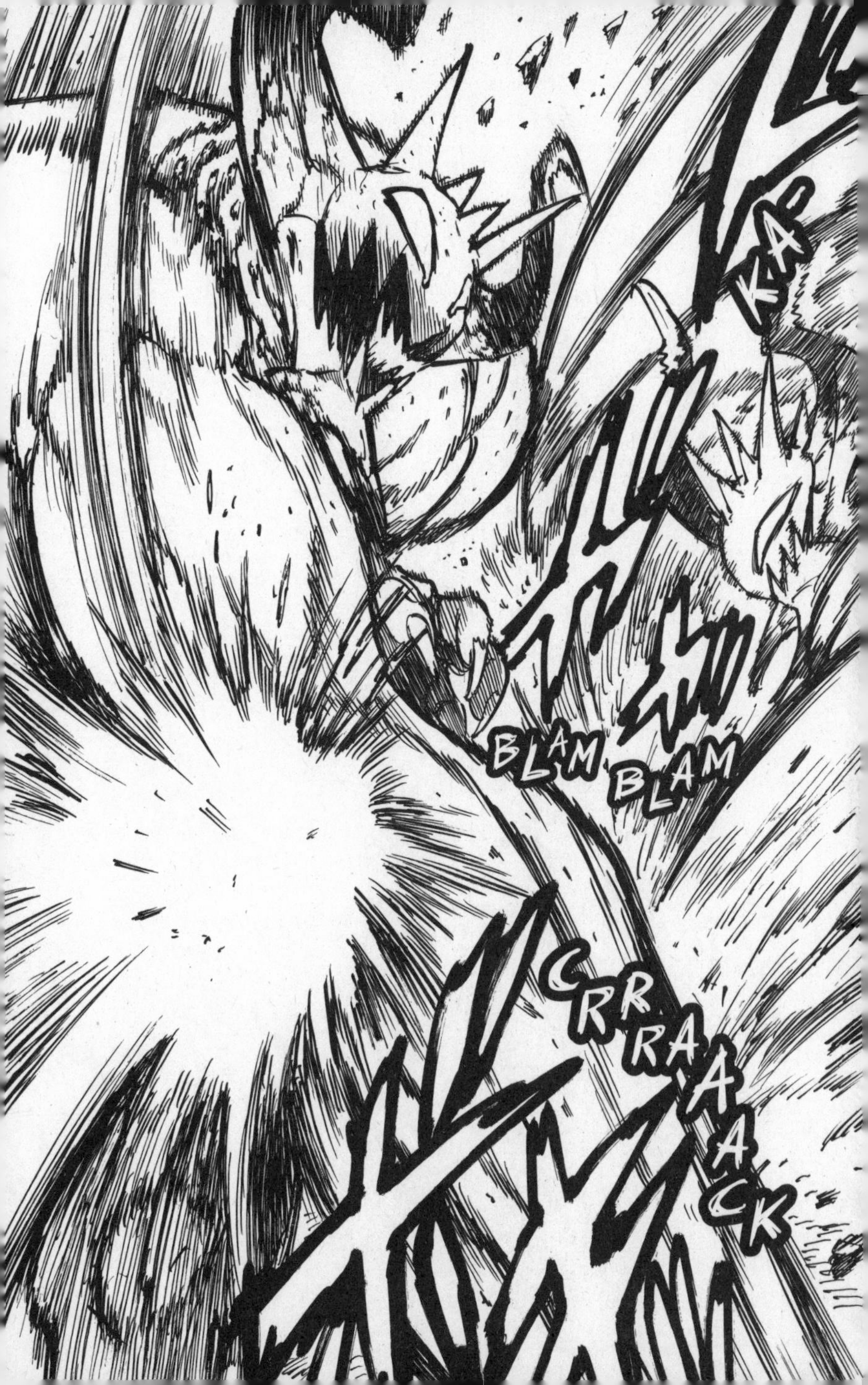
KA
BLAM BLAM
CRRRAAACK

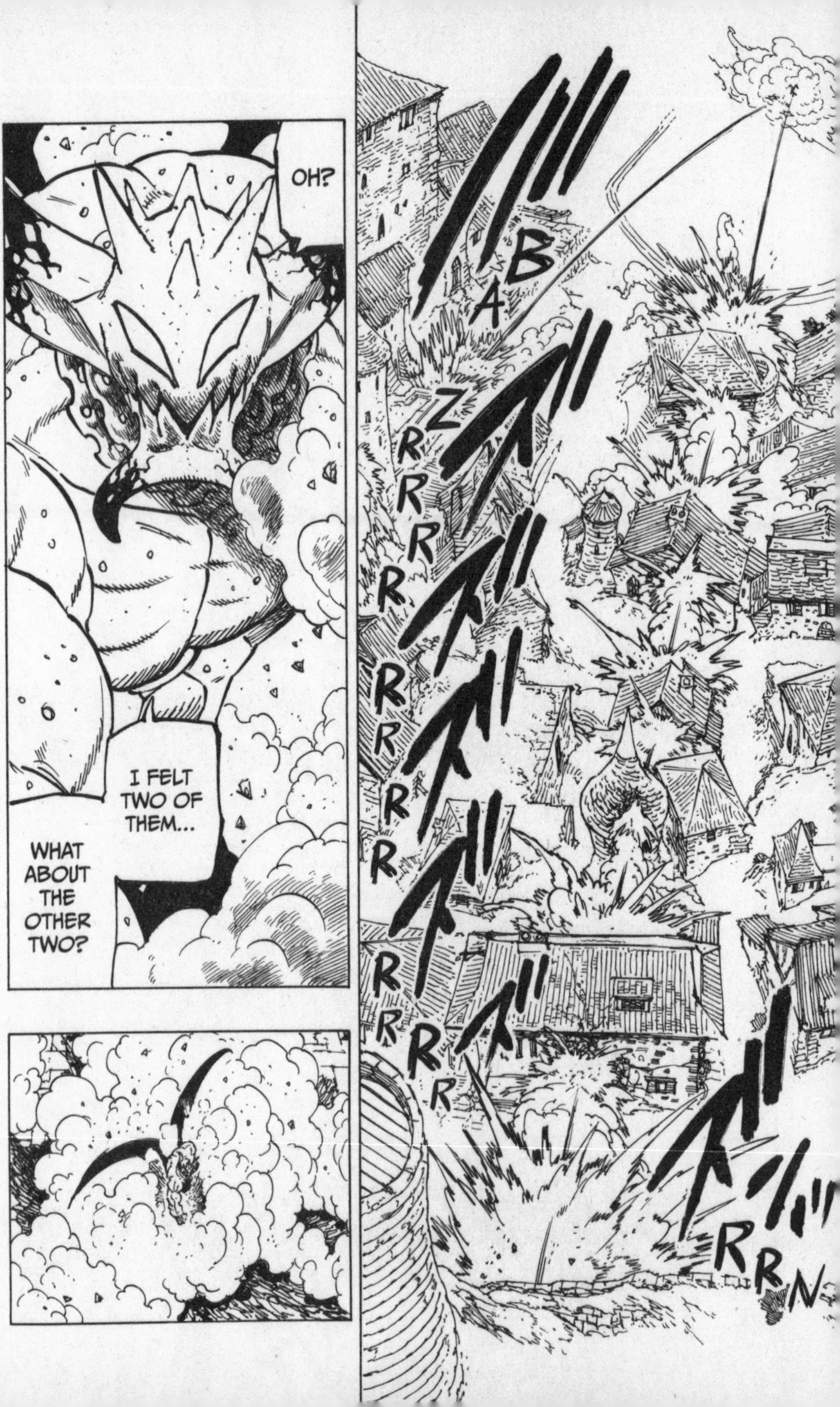
BAZRRRRRRRRRRRRR
RRRN
OH?
I FELT TWO OF THEM...
WHAT ABOUT THE OTHER TWO?

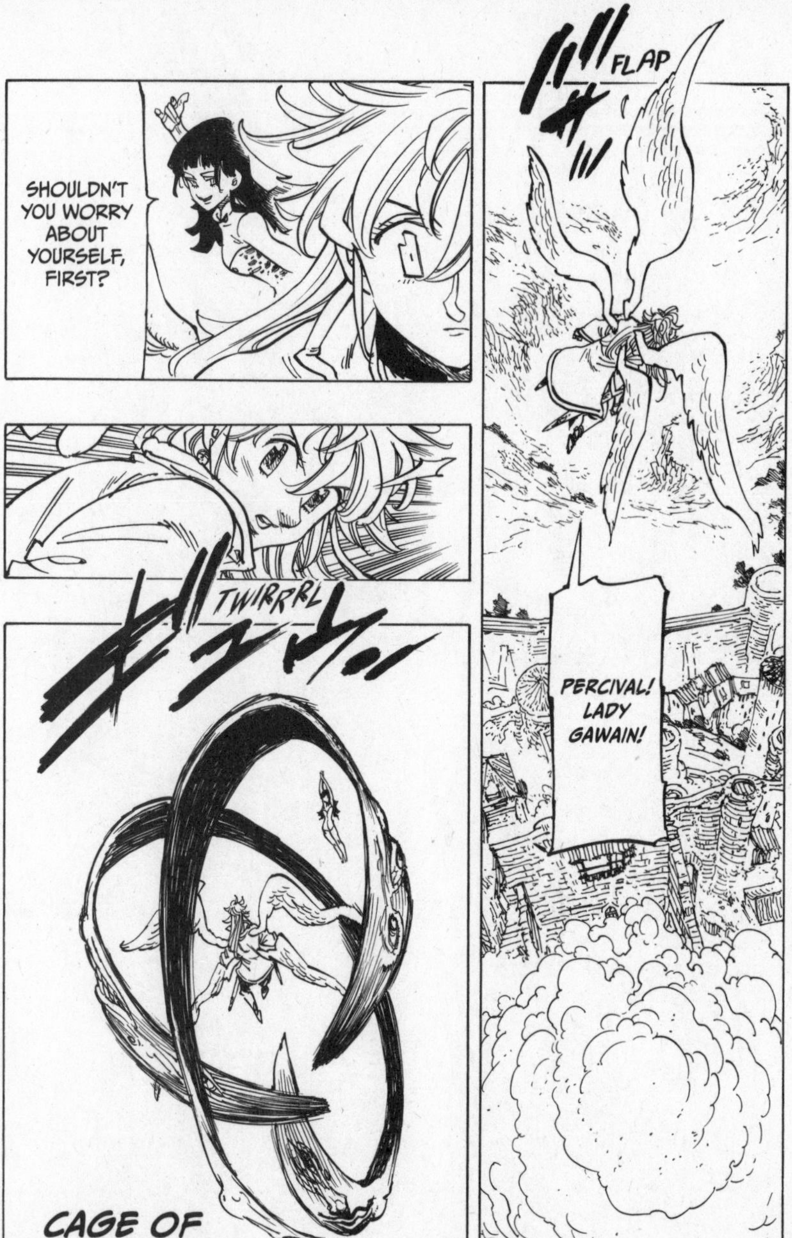
FLAP
PERCIVAL! LADY GAWAIN!
SHOULDN'T YOU WORRY ABOUT YOURSELF, FIRST?
TWIRRRL
CAGE OF DARKNESS!

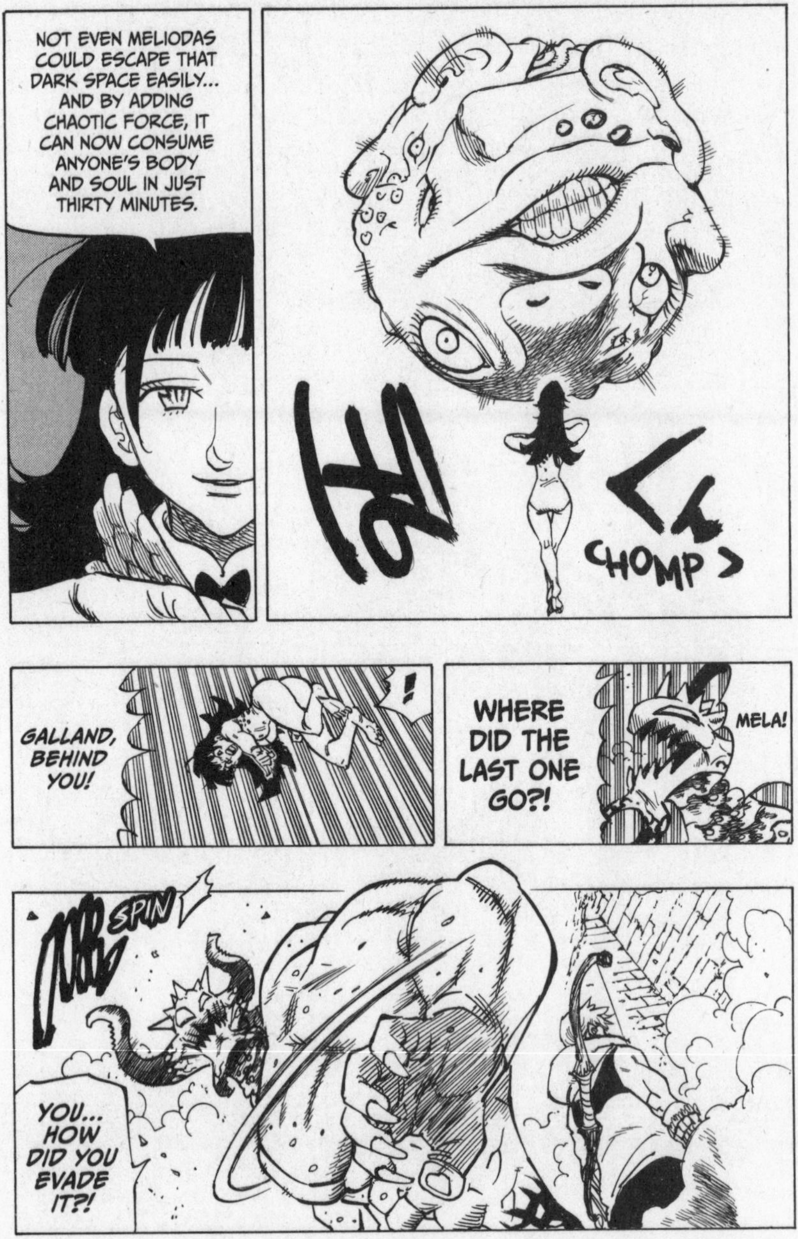
CHOMP
NOT EVEN MELIODAS COULD ESCAPE THAT DARK SPACE EASILY... AND BY ADDING CHAOTIC FORCE, IT CAN NOW CONSUME ANYONE'S BODY AND SOUL IN JUST THIRTY MINUTES.
MELA!
WHERE DID THE LAST ONE GO?!
!
GALLAND, BEHIND YOU!
SPIN
YOU... HOW DID YOU EVADE IT?!

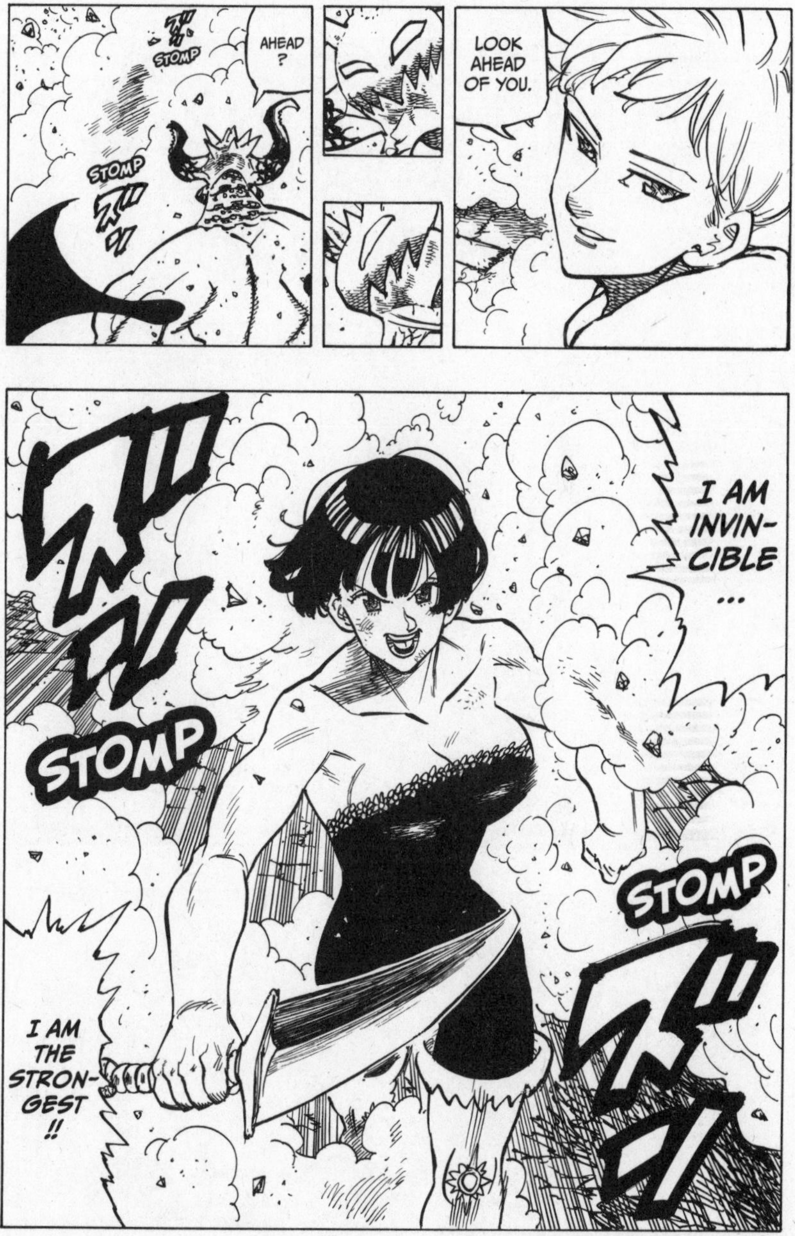
LOOK AHEAD OF YOU.
AHEAD ?
STOMP
STOMP
I AM INVINCIBLE ...
STOMP
STOMP
I AM THE STRONGEST !!

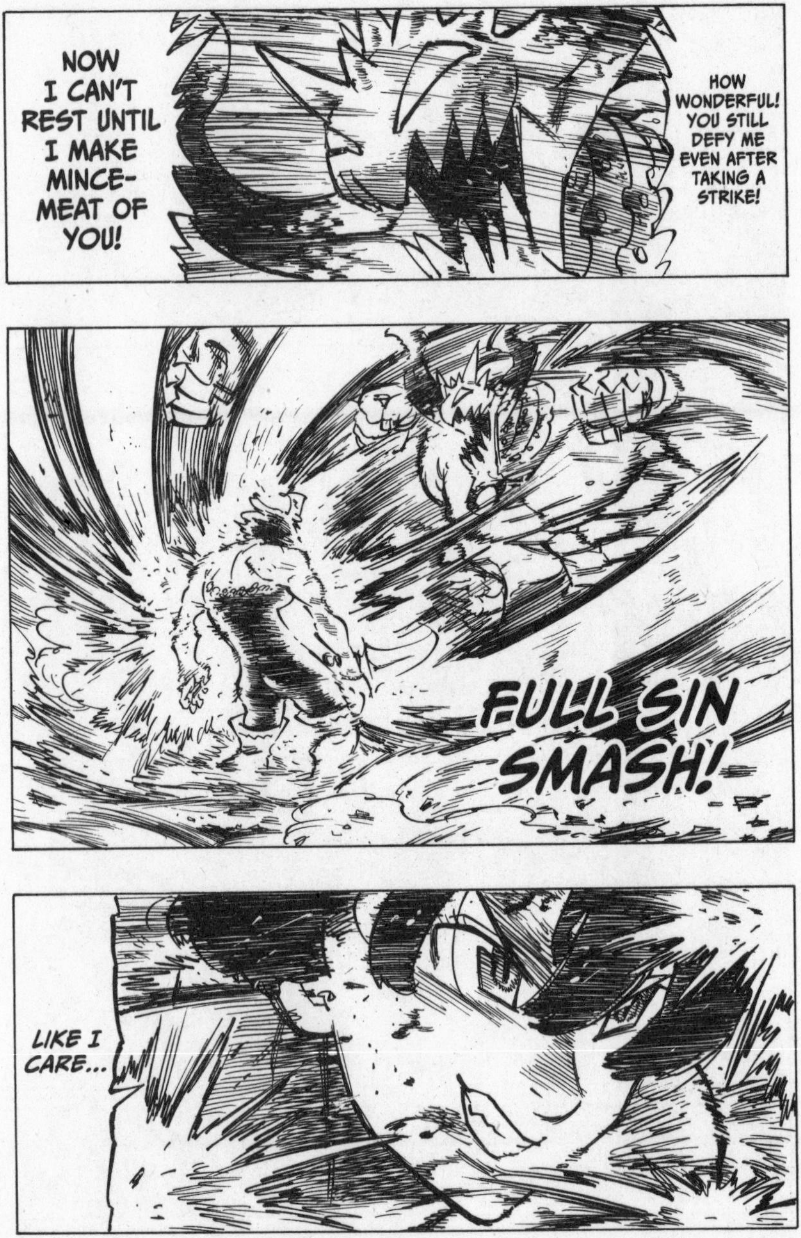
HOW WONDERFUL! YOU STILL DEFY ME EVEN AFTER TAKING A STRIKE!
NOW I CAN'T REST UNTIL I MAKE MINCE-MEAT OF YOU!
FULL SIN SMASH!
LIKE I CARE...

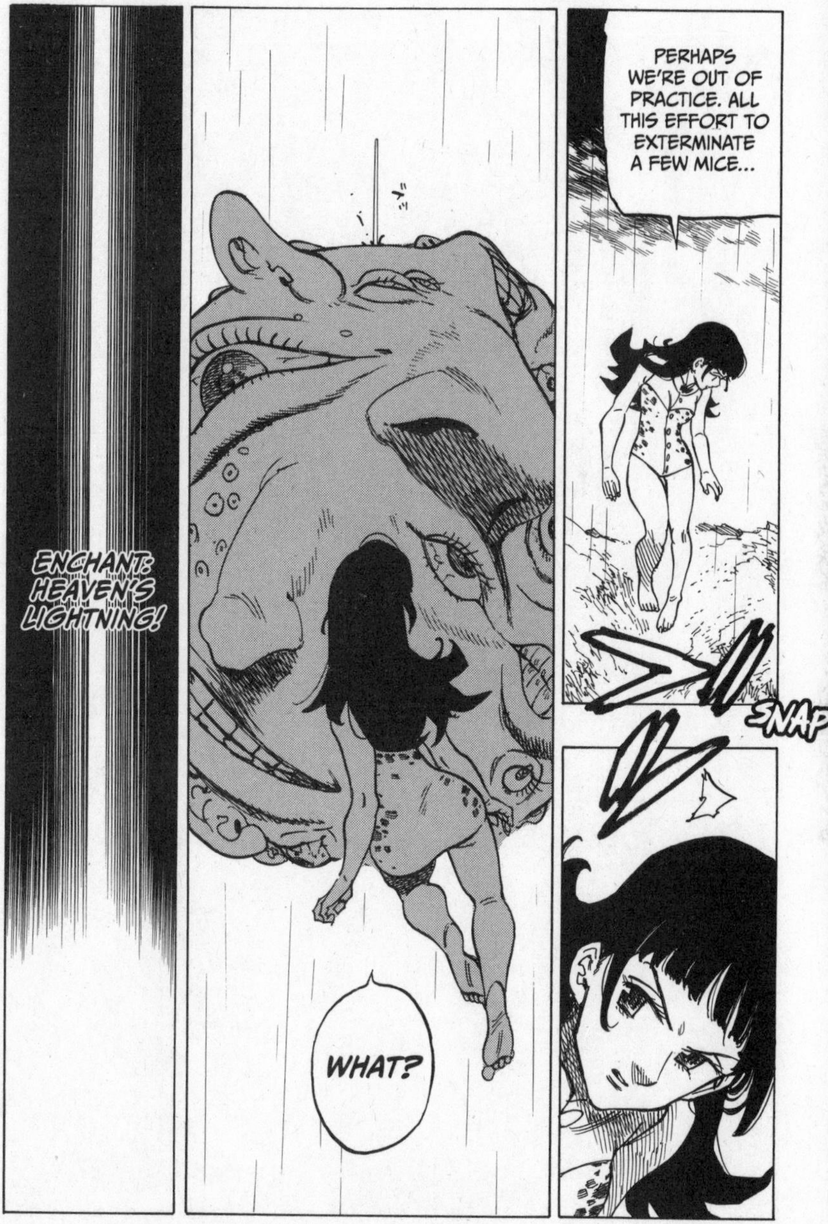
PERHAPS WE'RE OUT OF PRACTICE. ALL THIS EFFORT TO EXTERMINATE A FEW MICE...
SNAP
WHAT?
ENCHANT: HEAVEN'S LIGHTNING!

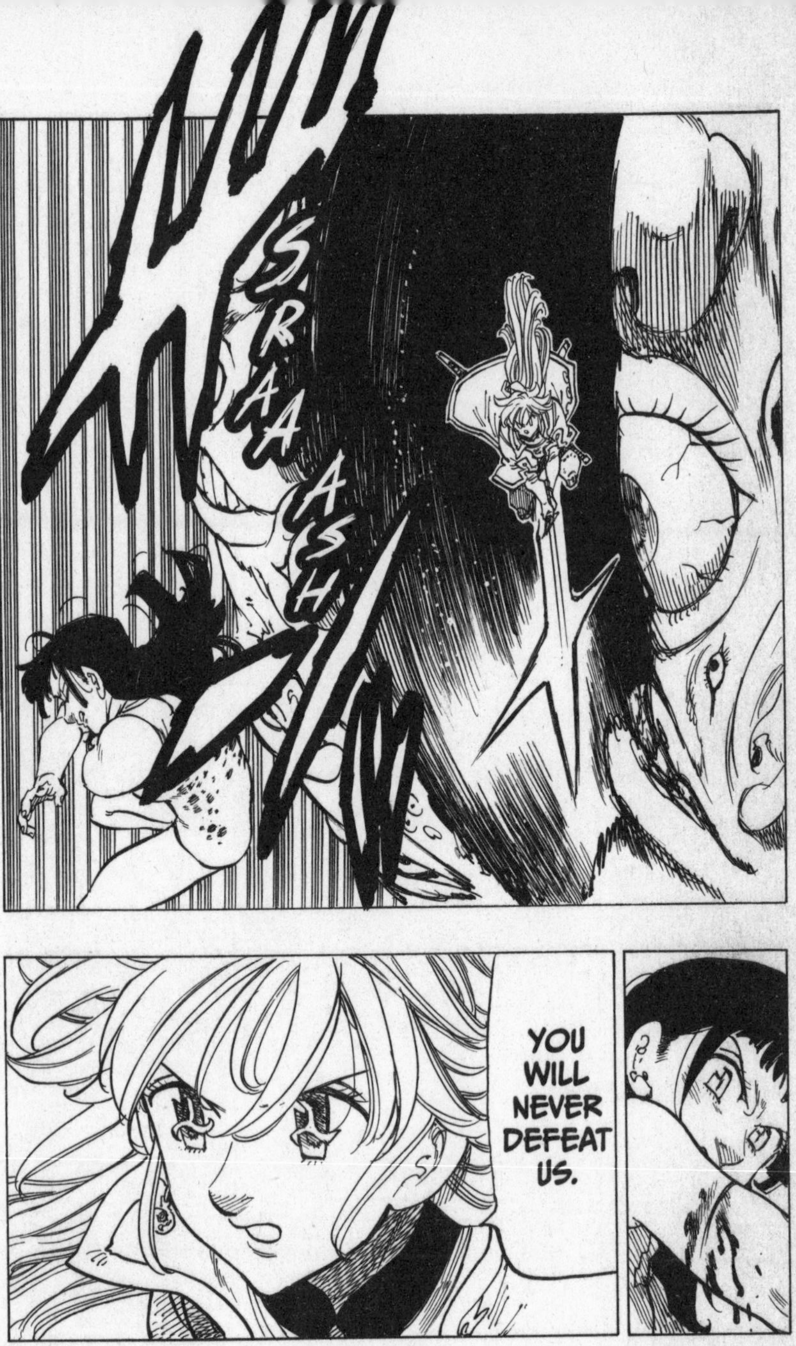
SRAAASH
YOU WILL NEVER DEFEAT US.

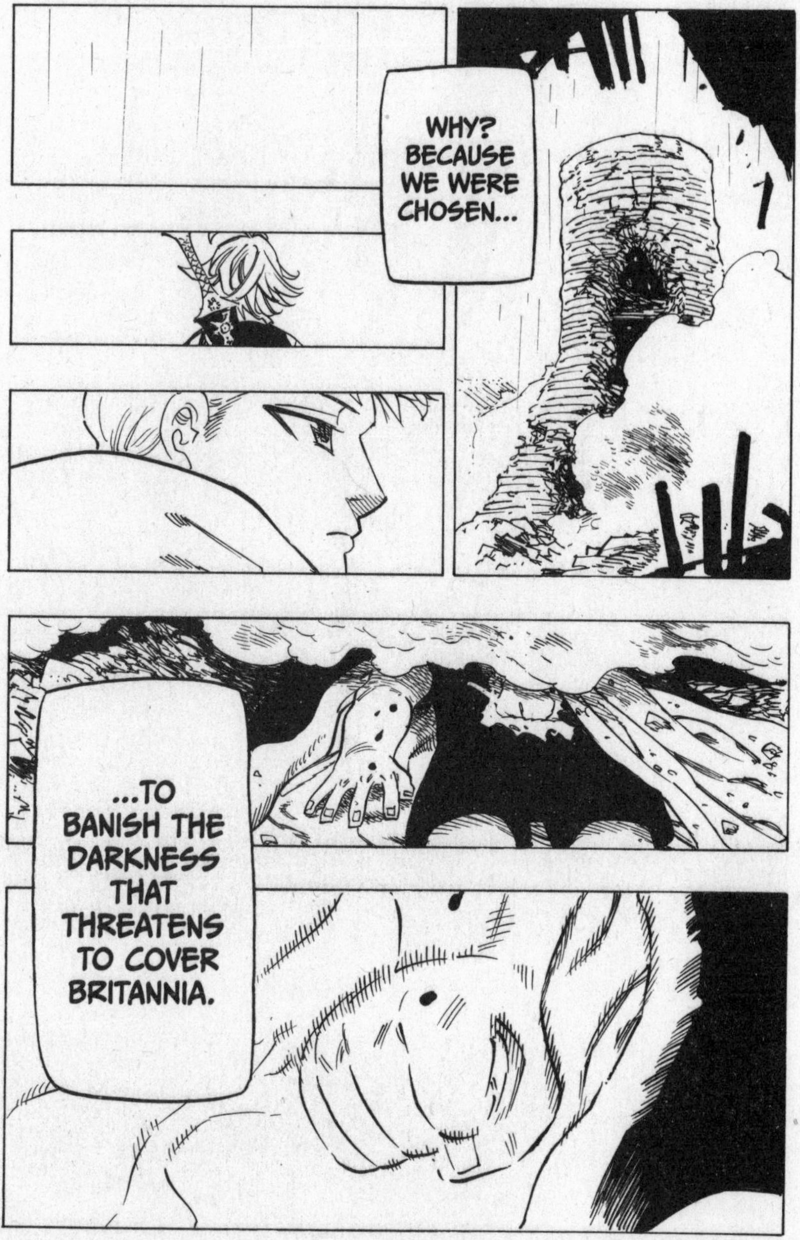
WHY? BECAUSE WE WERE CHOSEN...
...TO BANISH THE DARKNESS THAT THREATENS TO COVER BRITANNIA.

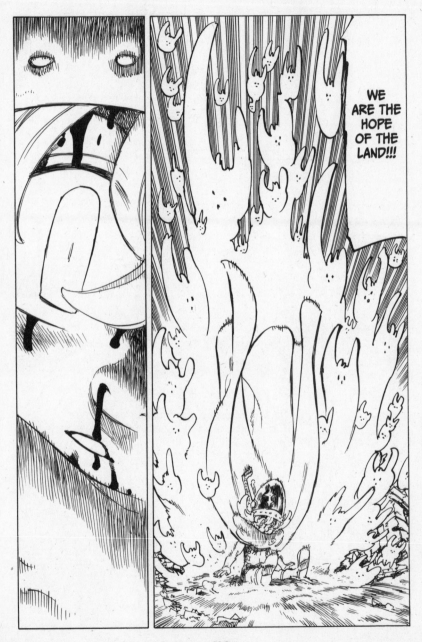

WE
ARE THE
HOPE
OF THE
LAND!!!

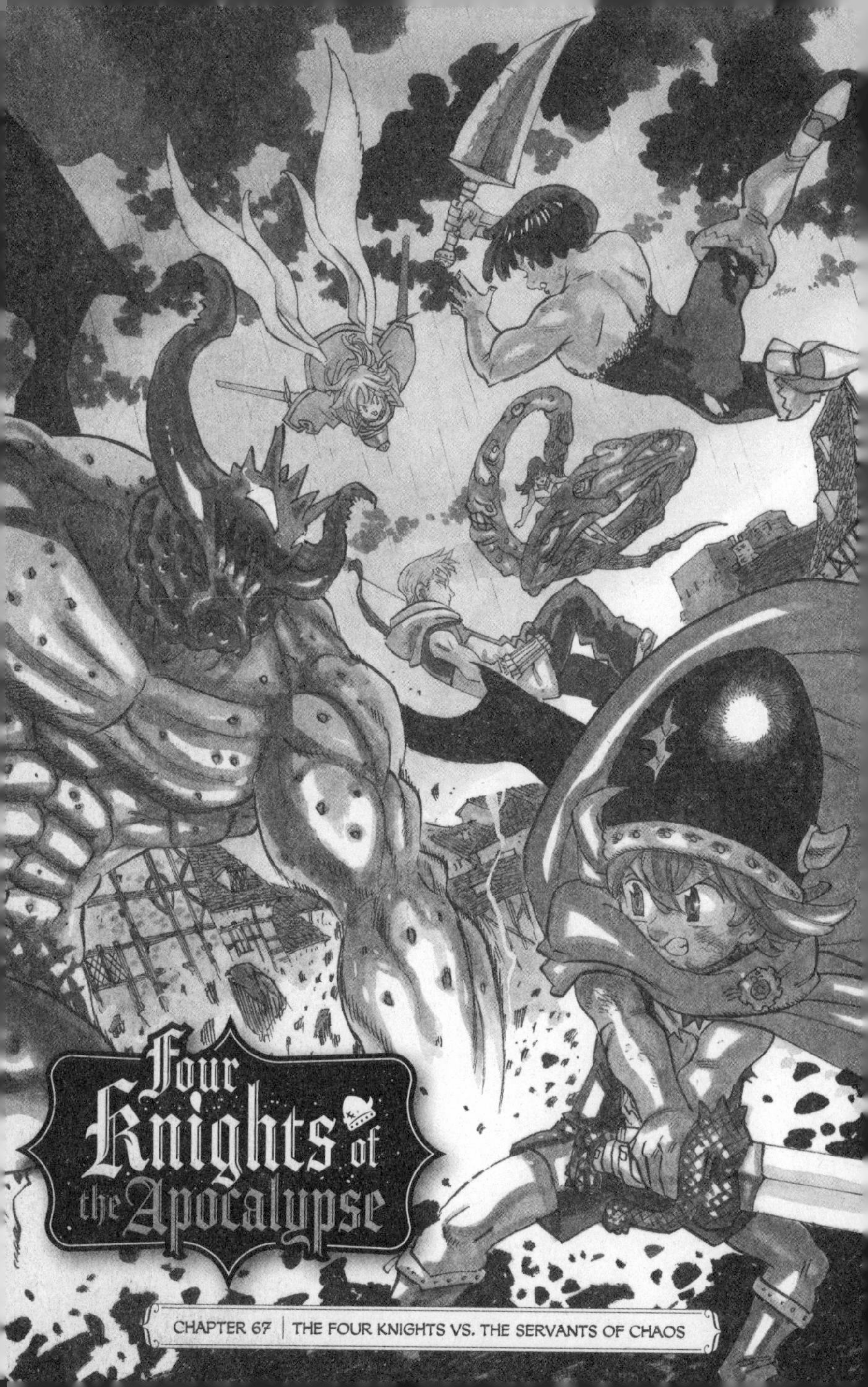
Four Knights of the Apocalypse
CHAPTER 67 | THE FOUR KNIGHTS VS. THE SERVANTS OF CHAOS

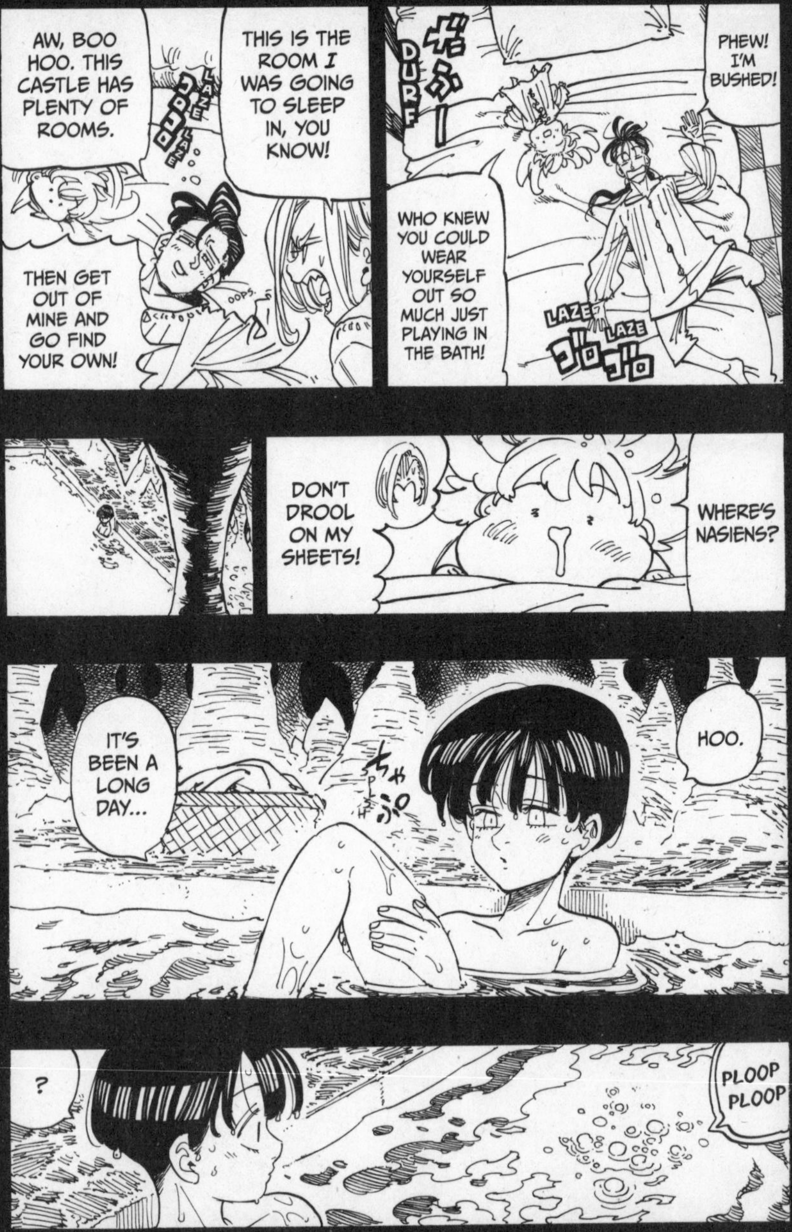
PHEW! I'M BUSHED!
DURF
WHO KNEW YOU COULD WEAR YOURSELF OUT SO MUCH JUST PLAYING IN THE BATH!
LAZE LAZE
THIS IS THE ROOM I WAS GOING TO SLEEP IN, YOU KNOW!
AW, BOO HOO. THIS CASTLE HAS PLENTY OF ROOMS.
LAZE LAZE
THEN GET OUT OF MINE AND GO FIND YOUR OWN!
OOPS.
WHERE'S NASIENS?
DON'T DROOL ON MY SHEETS!
HOO.
IT'S BEEN A LONG DAY...
PLOOP PLOOP
?

CONT'D ON P. 189

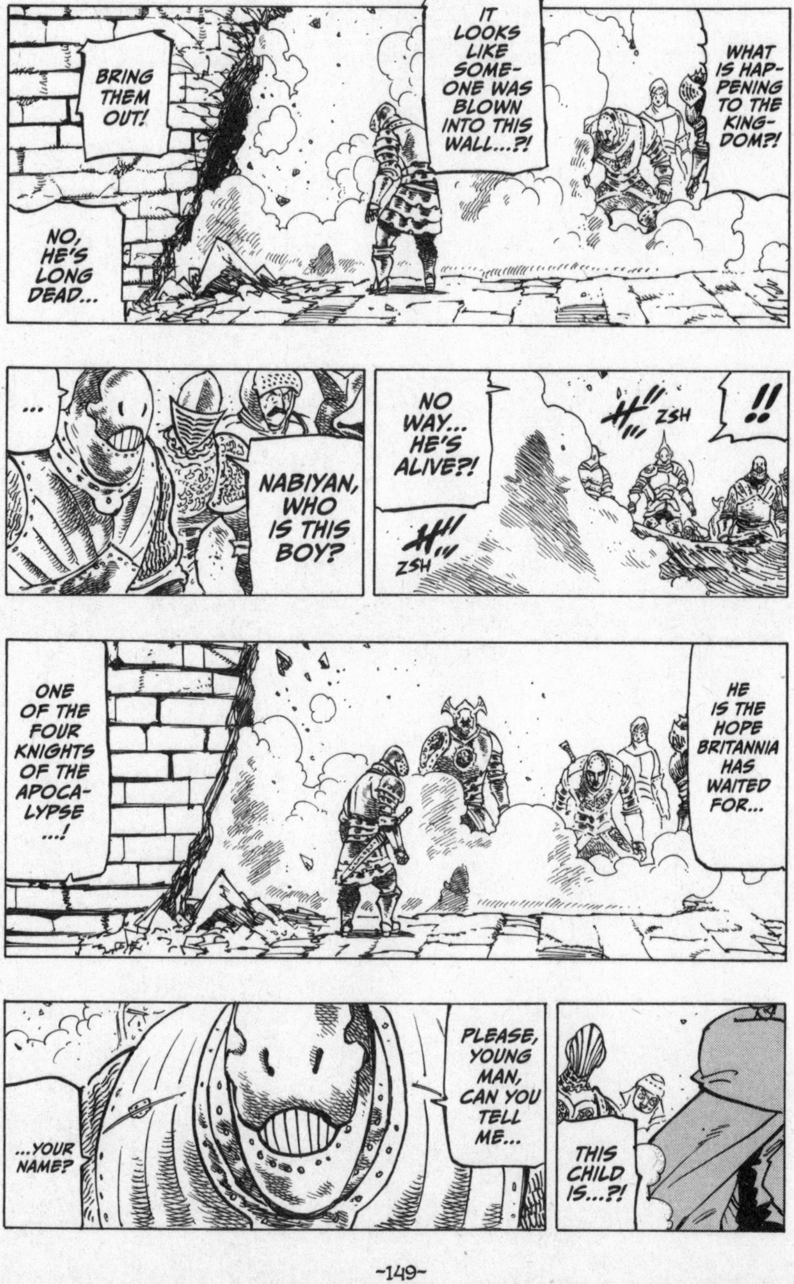
WHAT IS HAPPENING TO THE KINGDOM?!
IT LOOKS LIKE SOMEONE WAS BLOWN INTO THIS WALL...?!
BRING THEM OUT!
NO, HE'S LONG DEAD...
!!
ZSH
NO WAY... HE'S ALIVE?!
ZSH
NABIYAN, WHO IS THIS BOY?
...
HE IS THE HOPE BRITANNIA HAS WAITED FOR...
ONE OF THE FOUR KNIGHTS OF THE APOCALYPSE ...!
THIS CHILD IS...?!
PLEASE, YOUNG MAN, CAN YOU TELL ME...
...YOUR NAME?

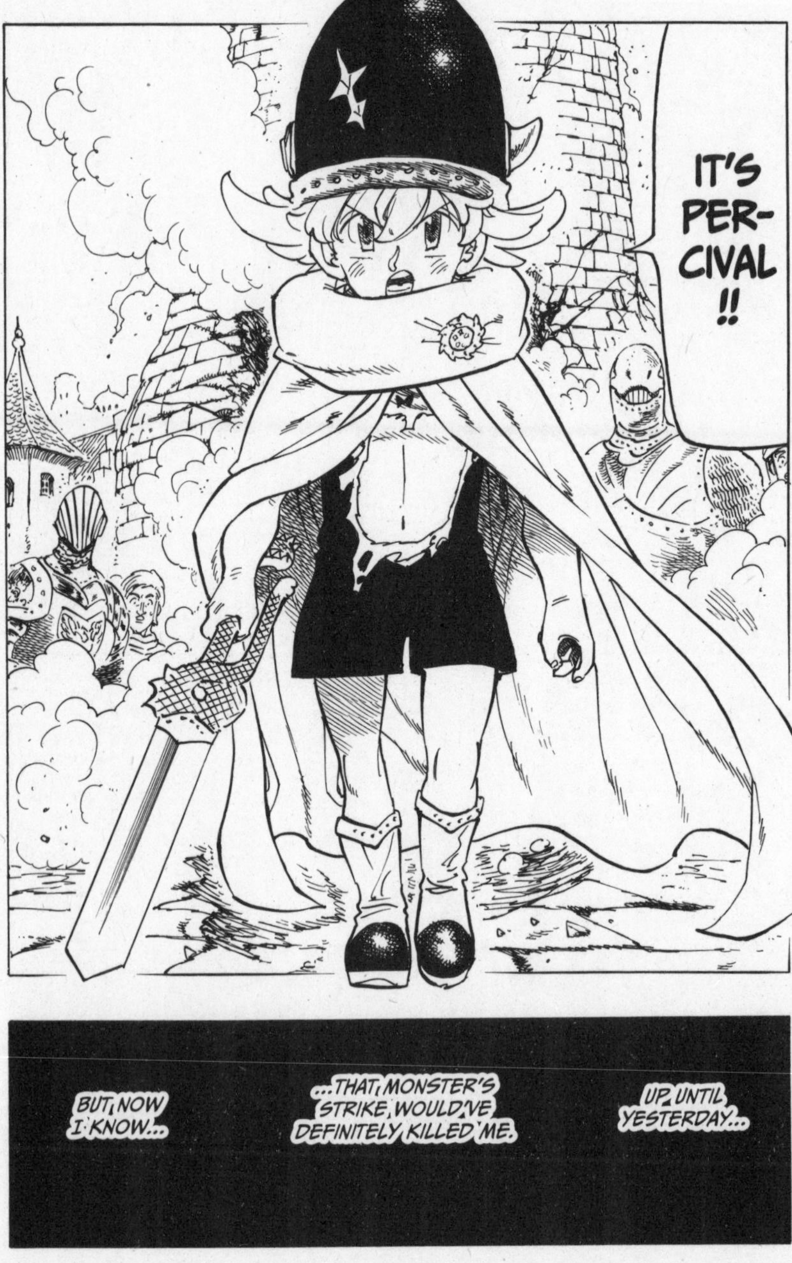
IT'S PER-CIVAL!!
UP UNTIL YESTERDAY...
...THAT MONSTER'S STRIKE WOULD'VE DEFINITELY KILLED ME.
BUT NOW I KNOW...

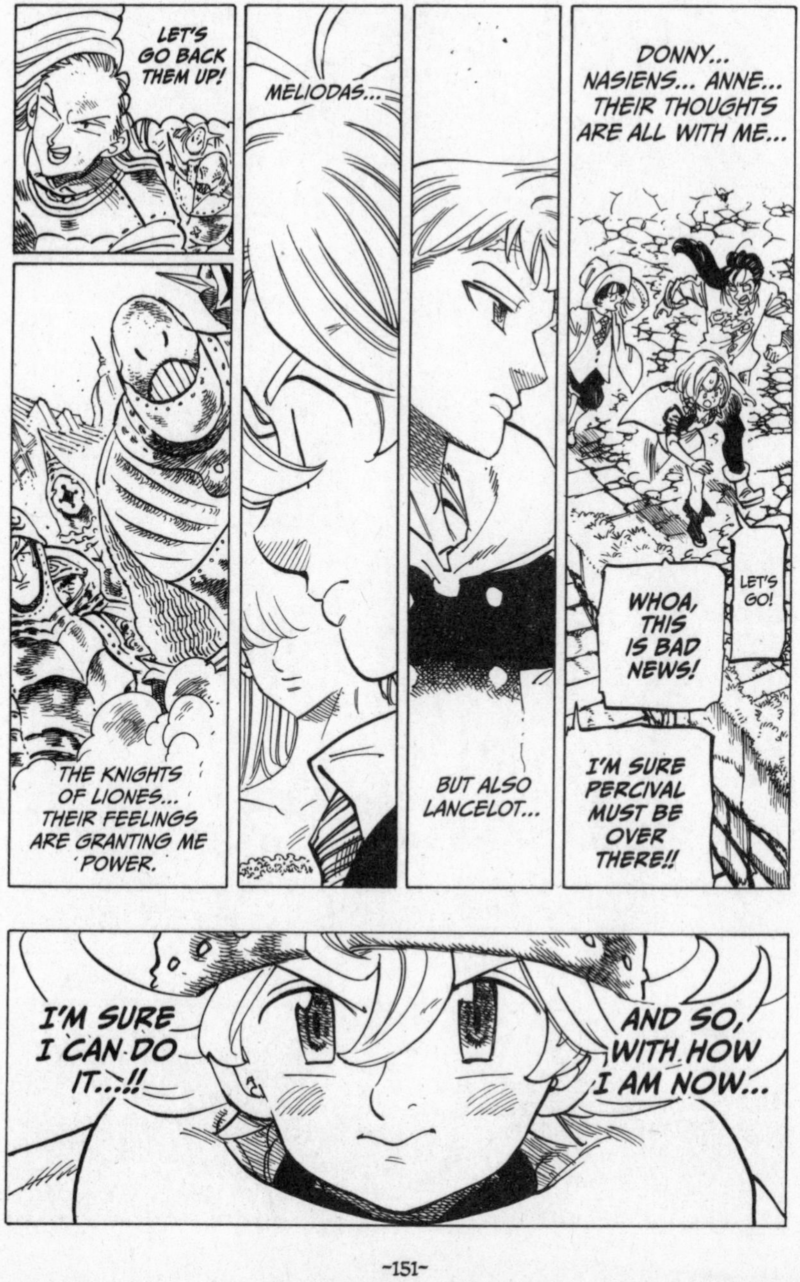
DONNY... NASIENS... ANNE... THEIR THOUGHTS ARE ALL WITH ME...
LET'S GO!
WHOA, THIS IS BAD NEWS!
I'M SURE PERCIVAL MUST BE OVER THERE!!
BUT ALSO LANCELOT...
MELIODAS...
LET'S GO BACK THEM UP!
THE KNIGHTS OF LIONES... THEIR FEELINGS ARE GRANTING ME POWER.
AND SO, WITH HOW I AM NOW...
I'M SURE I CAN DO IT...!!

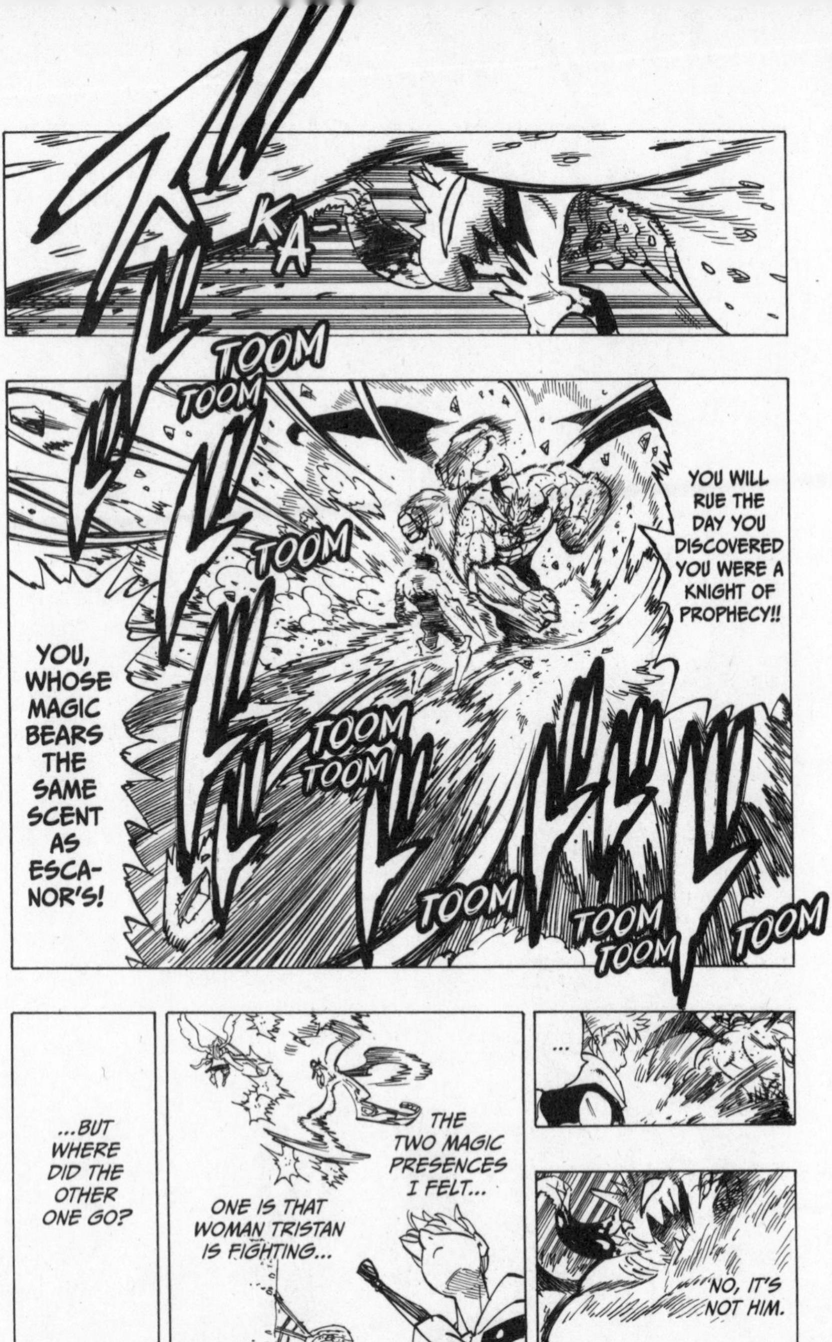
KA
TOOM
TOOM
TOOM
YOU WILL RUE THE DAY YOU DISCOVERED YOU WERE A KNIGHT OF PROPHECY!!
YOU, WHOSE MAGIC BEARS THE SAME SCENT AS ESCA-NOR'S!
TOOM
TOOM
TOOM
TOOM
TOOM
TOOM
...
NO, IT'S NOT HIM.
THE TWO MAGIC PRESENCES I FELT...
ONE IS THAT WOMAN TRISTAN IS FIGHTING...
...BUT WHERE DID THE OTHER ONE GO?

SLASH

IT'S ALWAYS
"ESCANOR"
THIS,
"ESCANOR"
THAT WITH
YOU...

SHUT
UP!!

MY
NAME IS
GAWAIN!

I'LL
CARVE
IT INTO
YOUR
SOUL
WITH MY
BLADE!

THUNN

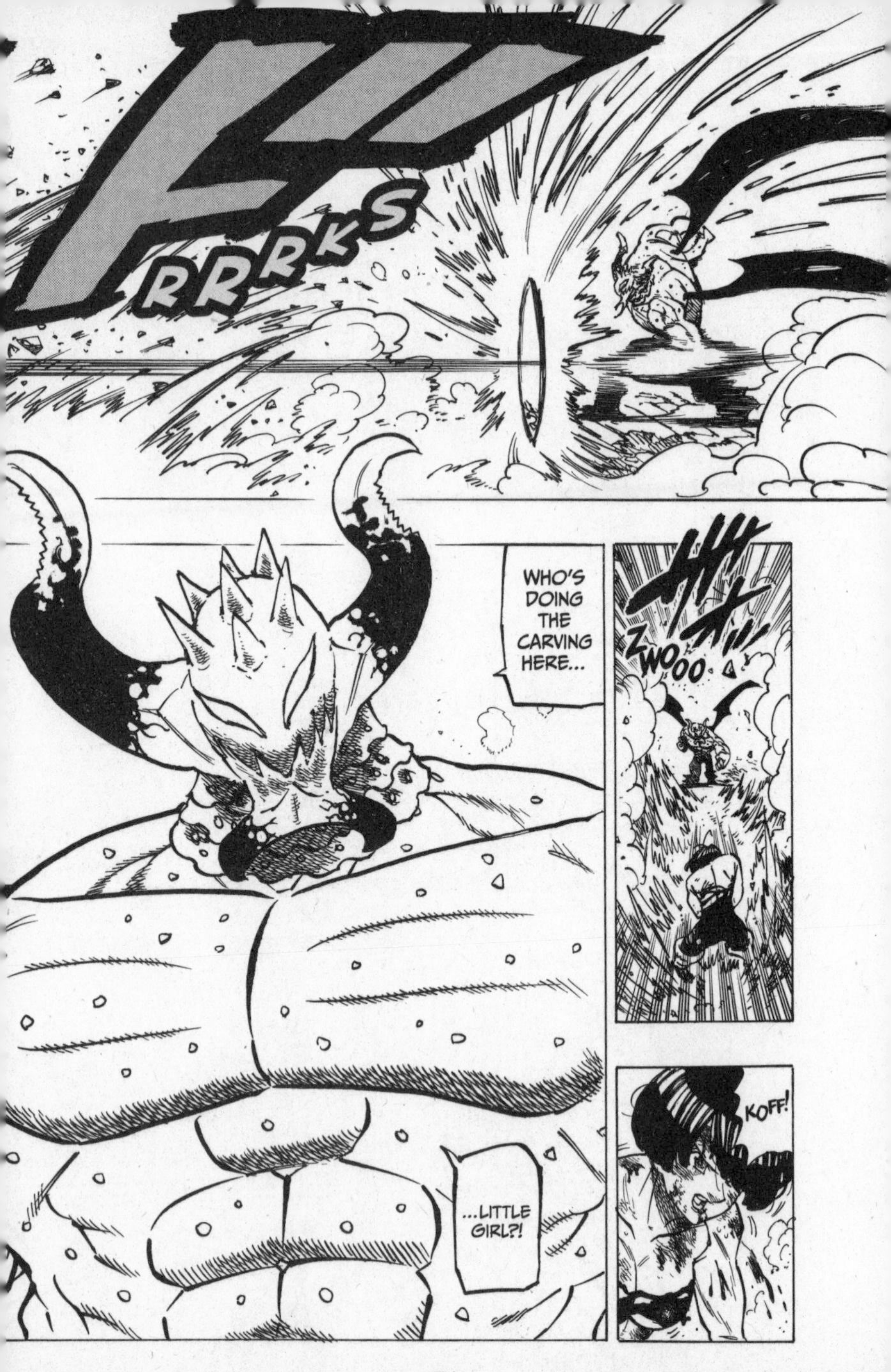
FRRRKS
ZWOOO
KOFF!
WHO'S DOING THE CARVING HERE...
...LITTLE GIRL?!

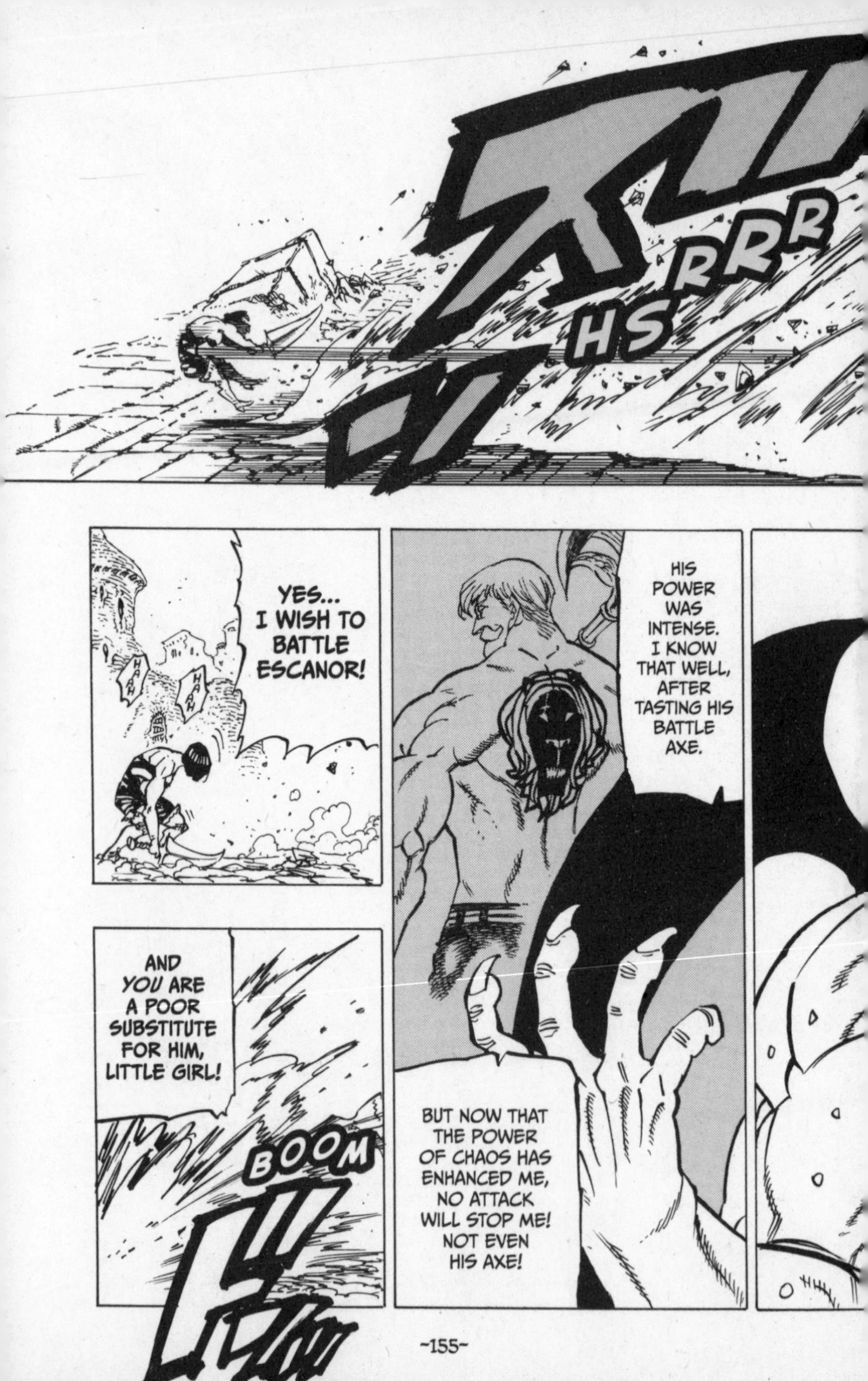
HSRRRR
HIS POWER WAS INTENSE. I KNOW THAT WELL, AFTER TASTING HIS BATTLE AXE.
BUT NOW THAT THE POWER OF CHAOS HAS ENHANCED ME, NO ATTACK WILL STOP ME! NOT EVEN HIS AXE!
YES... I WISH TO BATTLE ESCANOR!
HAAH
HAAH
AND *YOU* ARE A POOR SUBSTITUTE FOR HIM, LITTLE GIRL!
BOOM

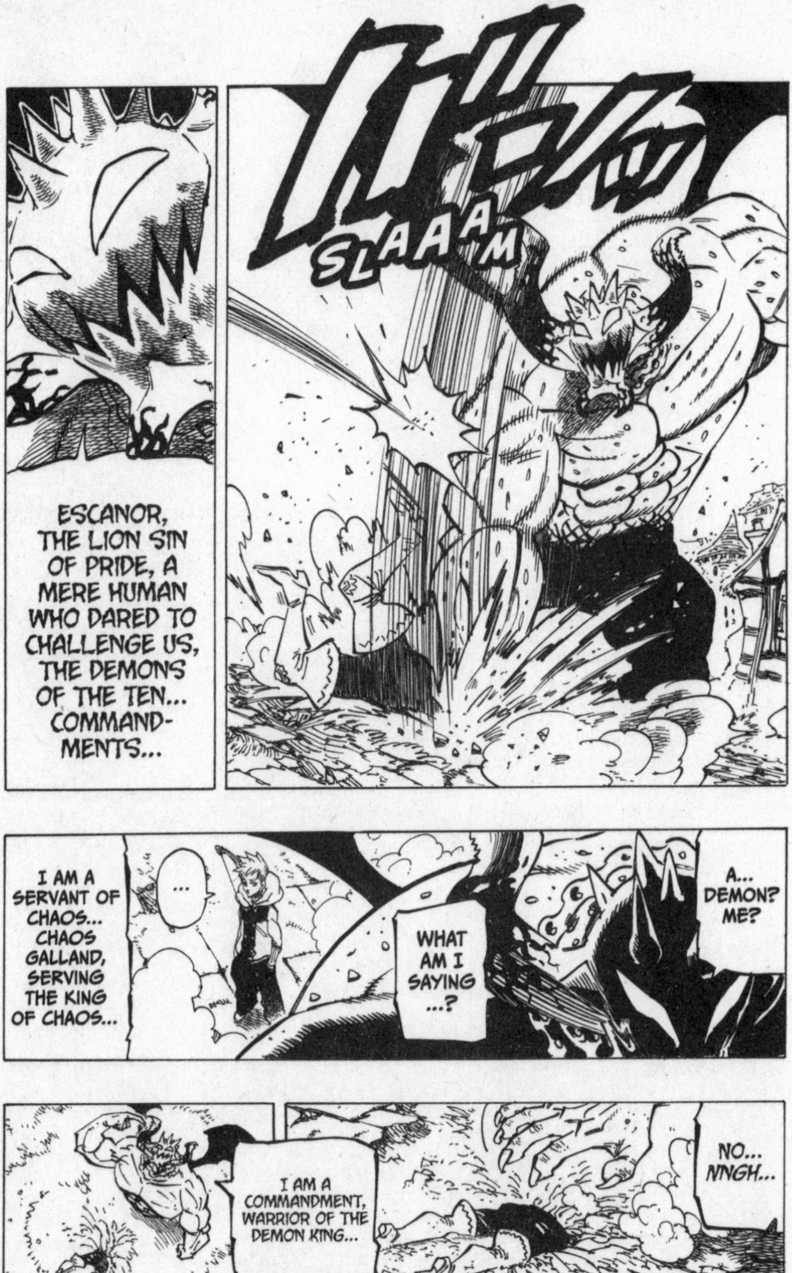
SLAAAM
ESCANOR, THE LION SIN OF PRIDE, A MERE HUMAN WHO DARED TO CHALLENGE US, THE DEMONS OF THE TEN... COMMAND-MENTS...
A... DEMON? ME?
WHAT AM I SAYING ...?
...
I AM A SERVANT OF CHAOS... CHAOS GALLAND, SERVING THE KING OF CHAOS...
NO... NNGH...
I AM A COMMANDMENT, WARRIOR OF THE DEMON KING...

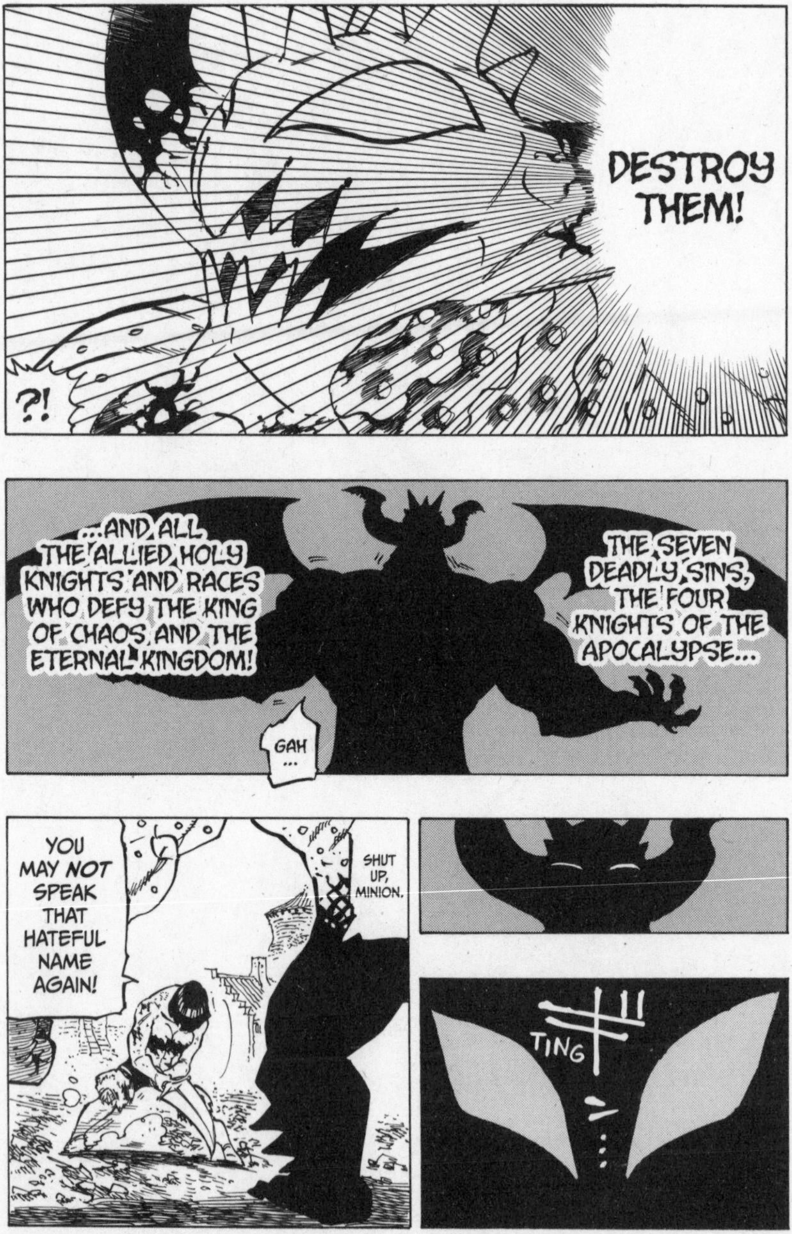
DESTROY THEM!
?!
THE SEVEN DEADLY SINS, THE FOUR KNIGHTS OF THE APOCALYPSE...
...AND ALL THE ALLIED HOLY KNIGHTS AND RACES WHO DEFY THE KING OF CHAOS AND THE ETERNAL KINGDOM!
GAH ...
TING
SHUT UP, MINION.
YOU MAY *NOT* SPEAK THAT HATEFUL NAME AGAIN!

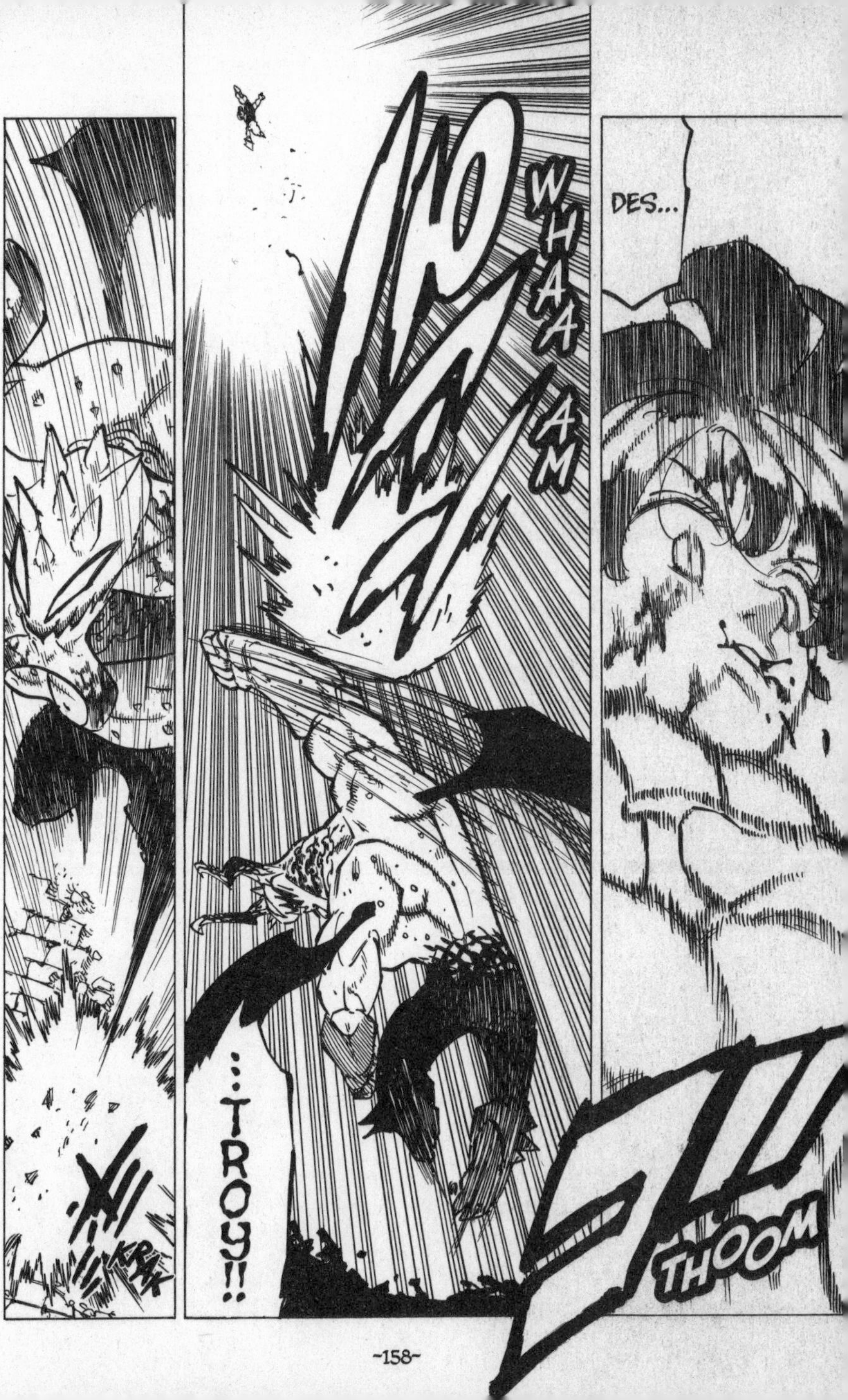
DES...
THOOM
WHAAAM
...TROY!!
KRAK

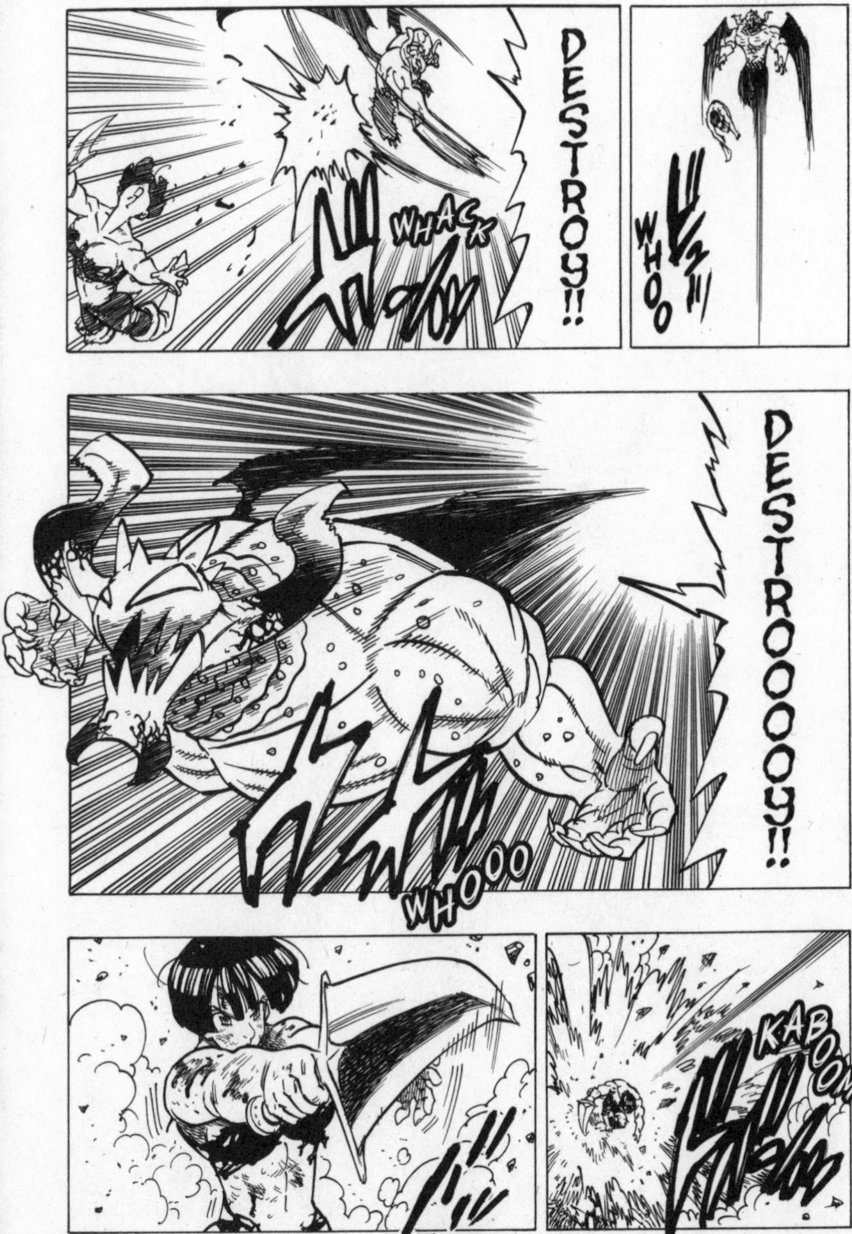
WHOO
DESTROY!!
WHACK
DESTROOOOOY!!
WHOOO
KABOOM
ZING

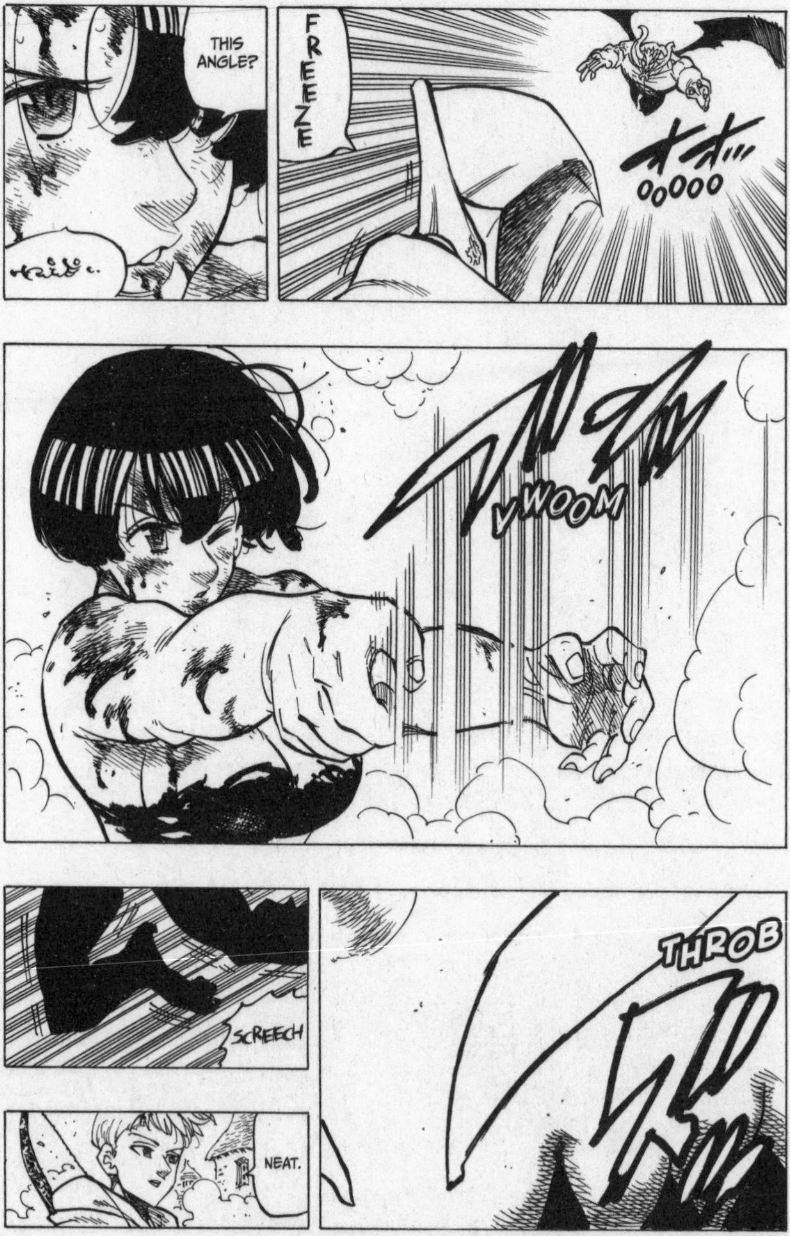
FREEZE
OOOOO
THIS ANGLE?
VWOOM
THROB
SCREECH
NEAT.

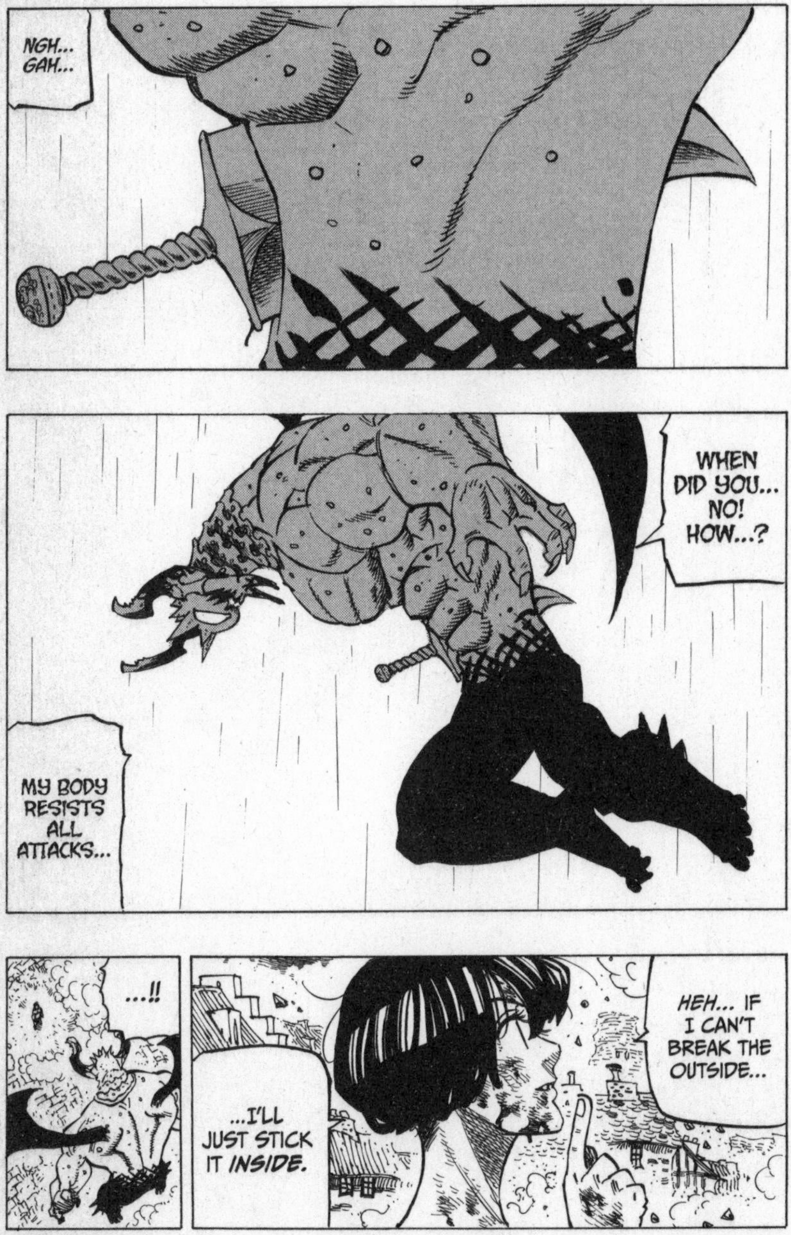
NGH... GAH...
WHEN DID YOU... NO! HOW...?
MY BODY RESISTS ALL ATTACKS...
HEH... IF I CAN'T BREAK THE OUTSIDE...
...I'LL JUST STICK IT *INSIDE.*
...!!

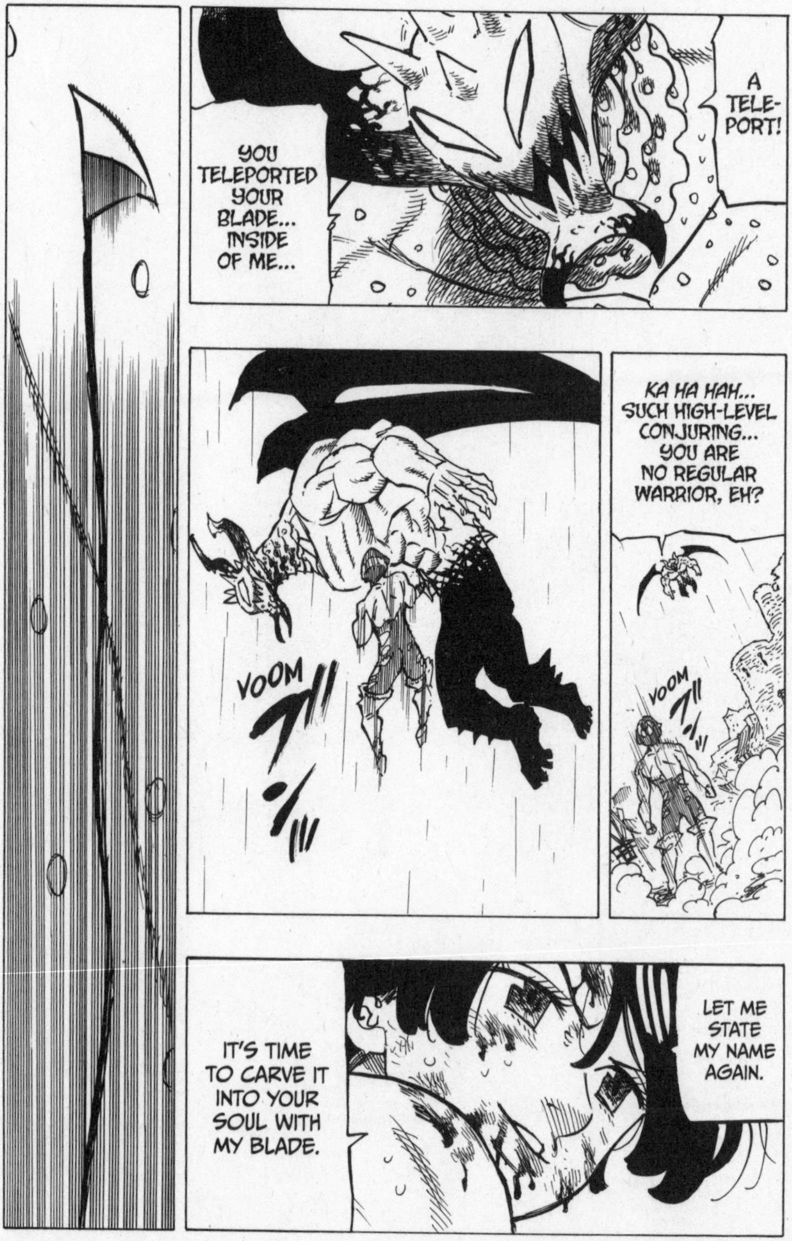
A TELEPORT!
YOU TELEPORTED YOUR BLADE... INSIDE OF ME...
KA HA HAH... SUCH HIGH-LEVEL CONJURING... YOU ARE NO REGULAR WARRIOR, EH?
VOOM
VOOM
LET ME STATE MY NAME AGAIN.
IT'S TIME TO CARVE IT INTO YOUR SOUL WITH MY BLADE.

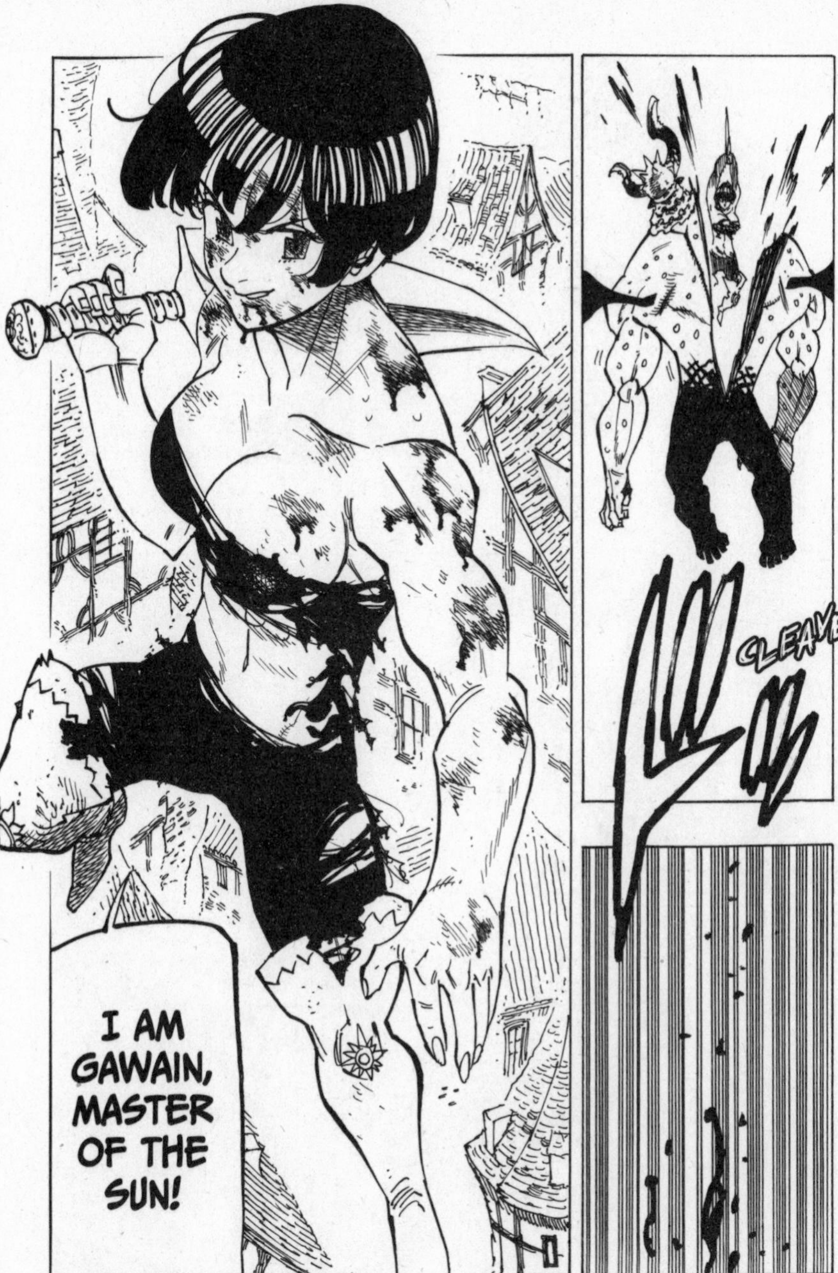
CLEAVE
I AM GAWAIN, MASTER OF THE SUN!

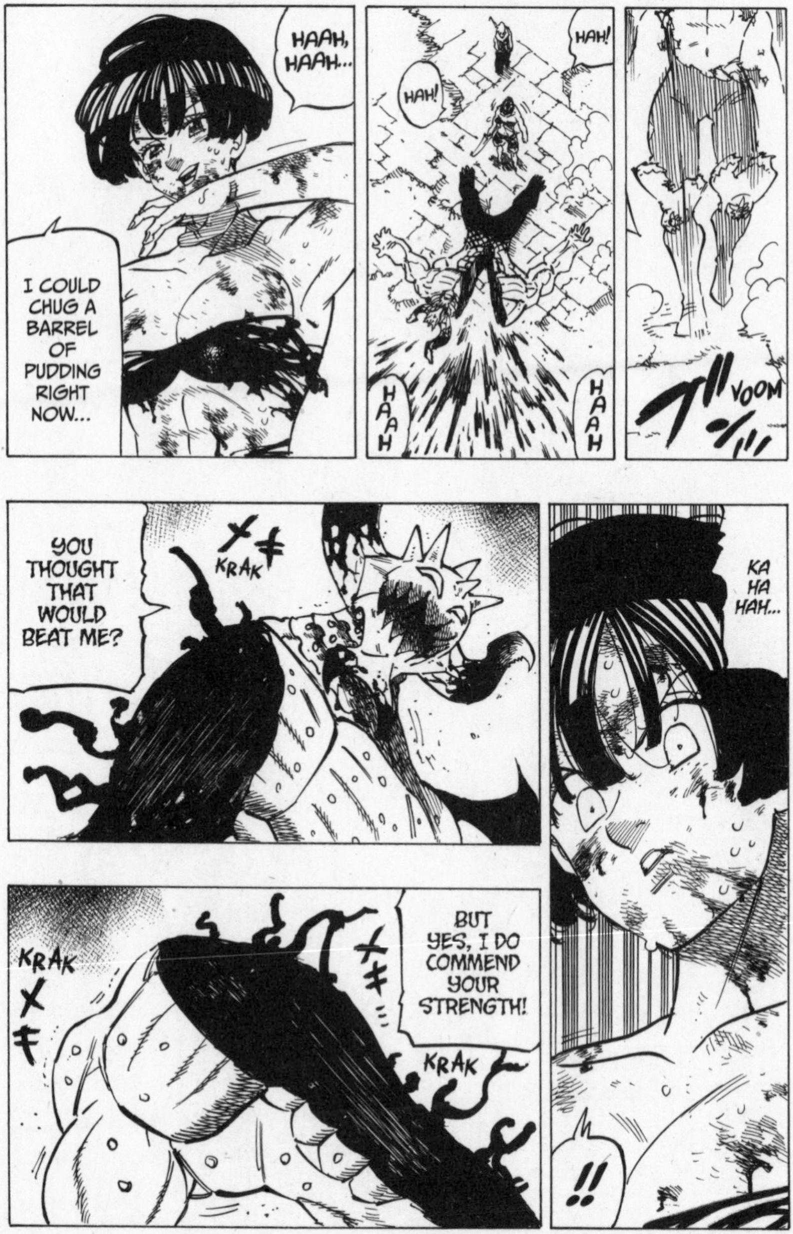
VOOM
HAH!
HAH!
HAAAH
HAAAH
HAAAH, HAAAH...
I COULD CHUG A BARREL OF PUDDING RIGHT NOW...
KA HA HAH...
!!
KRAK
YOU THOUGHT THAT WOULD BEAT ME?
BUT YES, I DO COMMEND YOUR STRENGTH!
KRAK
KRAK

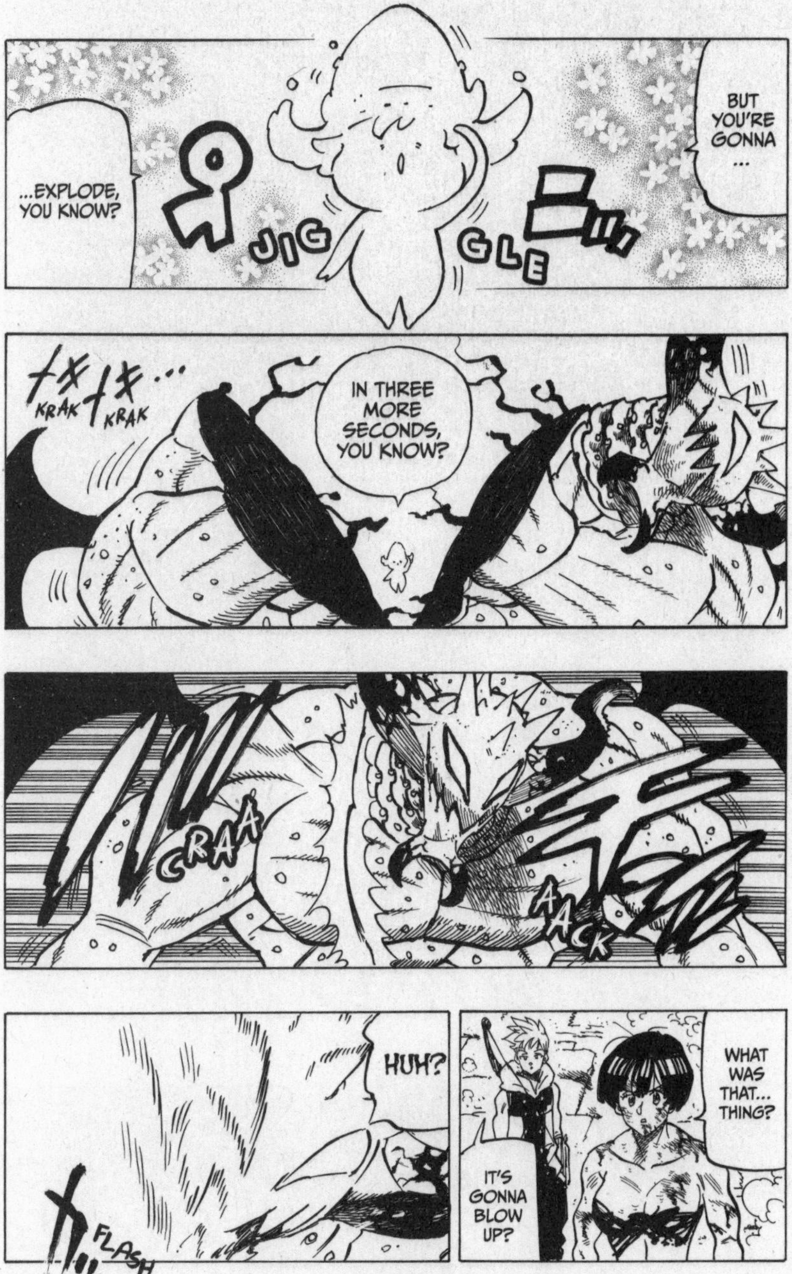

BUT YOU'RE GONNA ...
JIGGLE
...EXPLODE, YOU KNOW?
KRAK KRAK...
IN THREE MORE SECONDS, YOU KNOW?
CRAA
AACK
WHAT WAS THAT... THING?
IT'S GONNA BLOW UP?
HUH?
FLASH

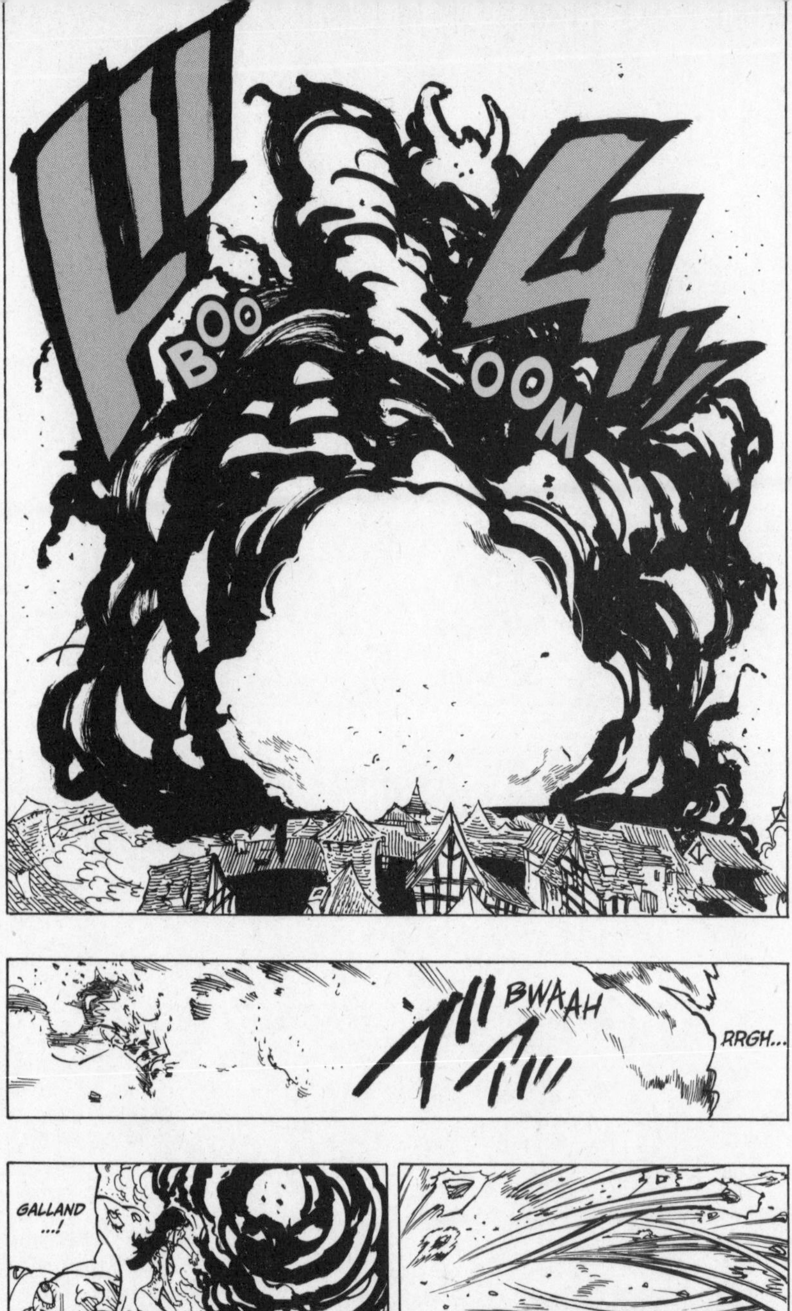
BOOOOM
RRGH...
BWAAH
GALLAND ...!

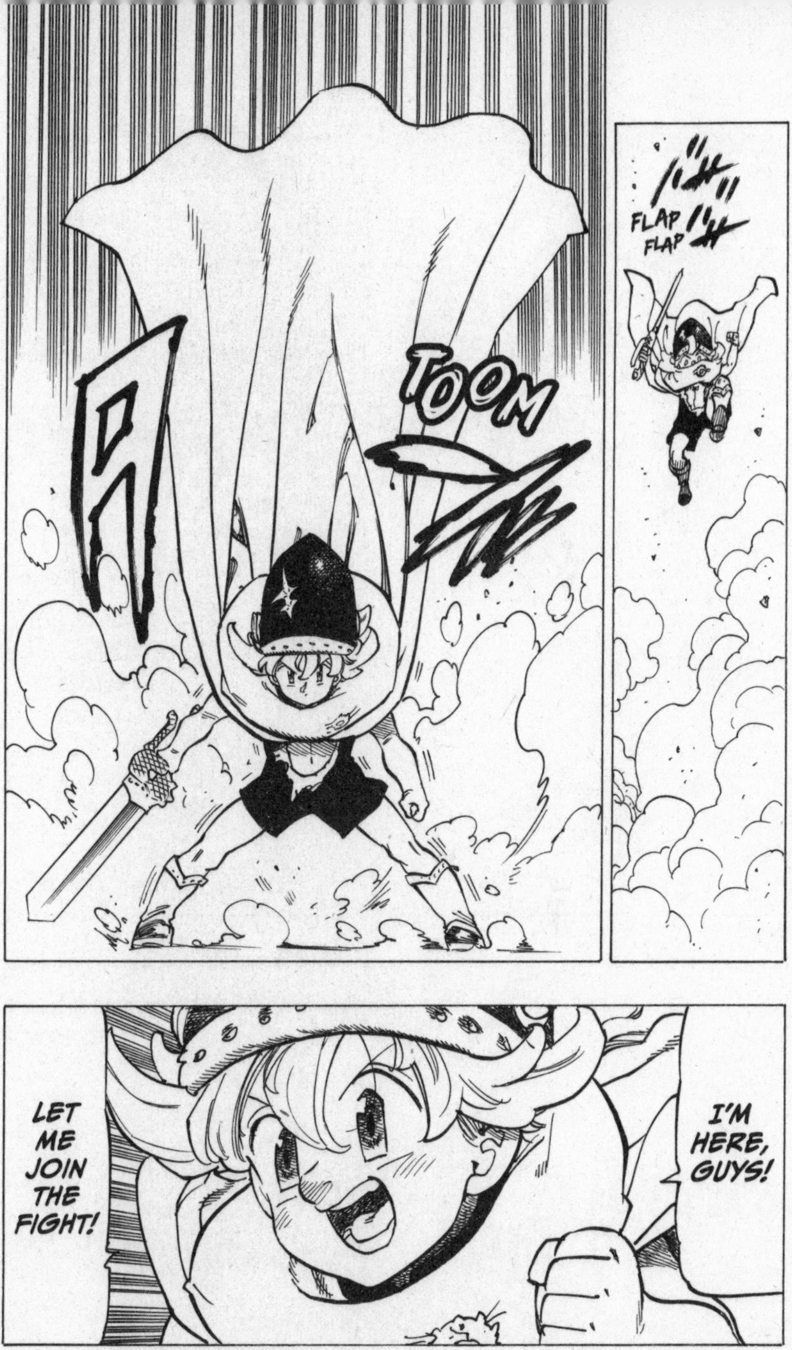
FLAP FLAP
TOOM
I'M HERE, GUYS!
LET ME JOIN THE FIGHT!

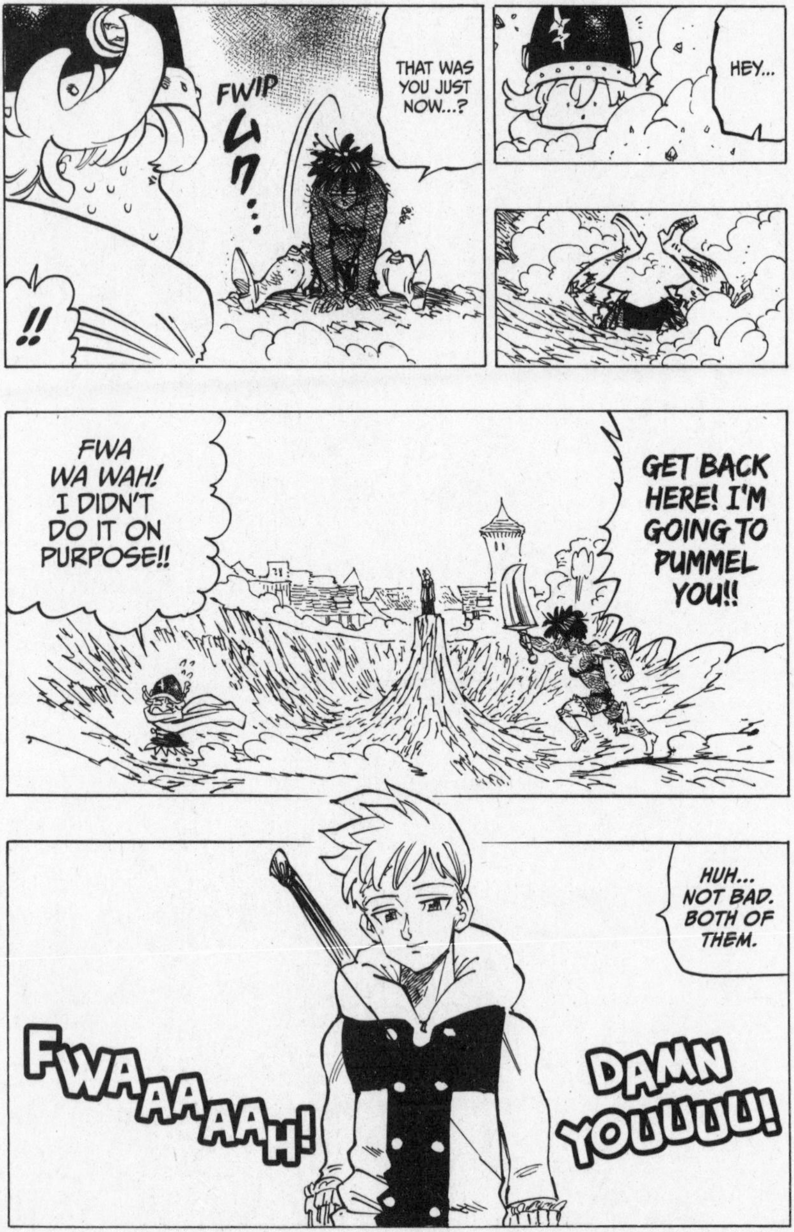
HEY...
THAT WAS YOU JUST NOW...?
FWIP ムク...
!!
GET BACK HERE! I'M GOING TO PUMMEL YOU!!
FWA WA WAH! I DIDN'T DO IT ON PURPOSE!!
HUH... NOT BAD. BOTH OF THEM.
DAMN YOUUUU!
FWAAAAAH!

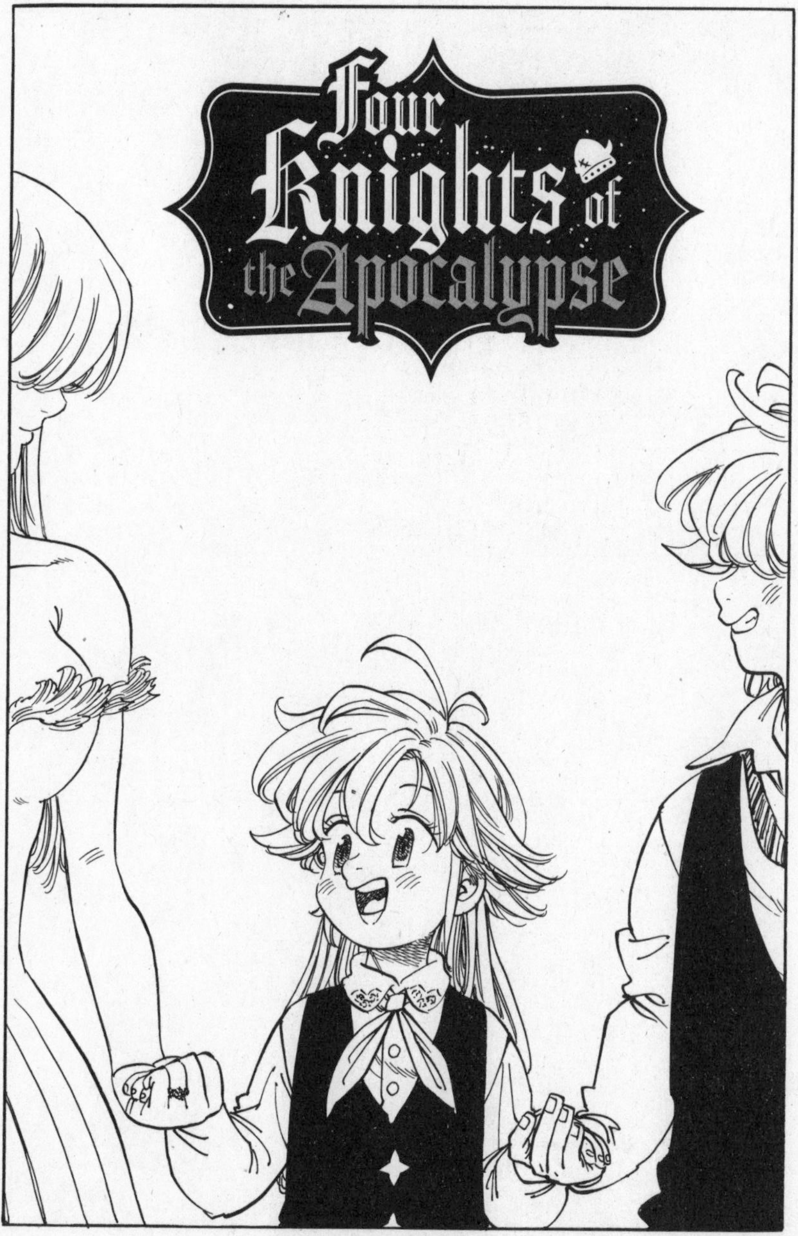
Four Knights of the Apocalypse

CHAPTER 68: THE NEPHILIM

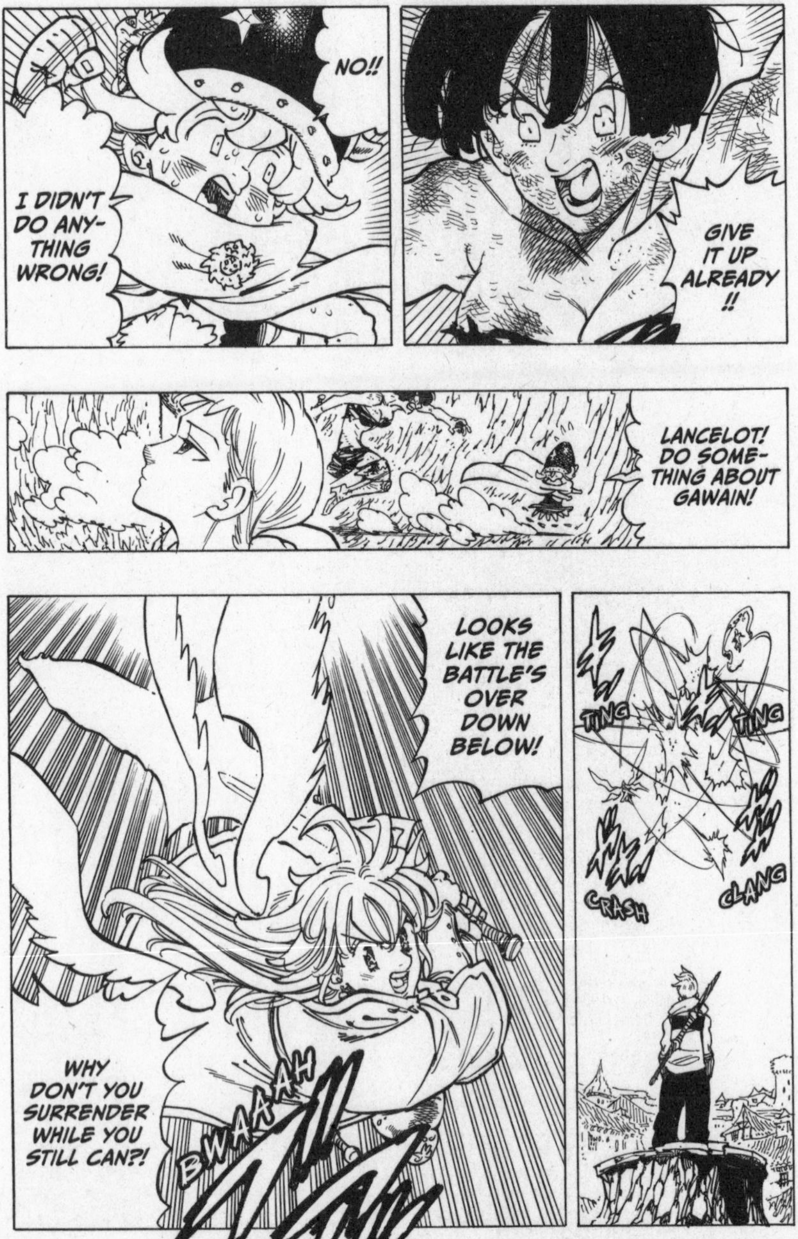
GIVE IT UP ALREADY!!
NO!!
I DIDN'T DO ANY-THING WRONG!
LANCELOT! DO SOME-THING ABOUT GAWAIN!
TING
TING
CRASH
CLANG
LOOKS LIKE THE BATTLE'S OVER DOWN BELOW!
WHY DON'T YOU SURRENDER WHILE YOU STILL CAN?!
BWAAAH

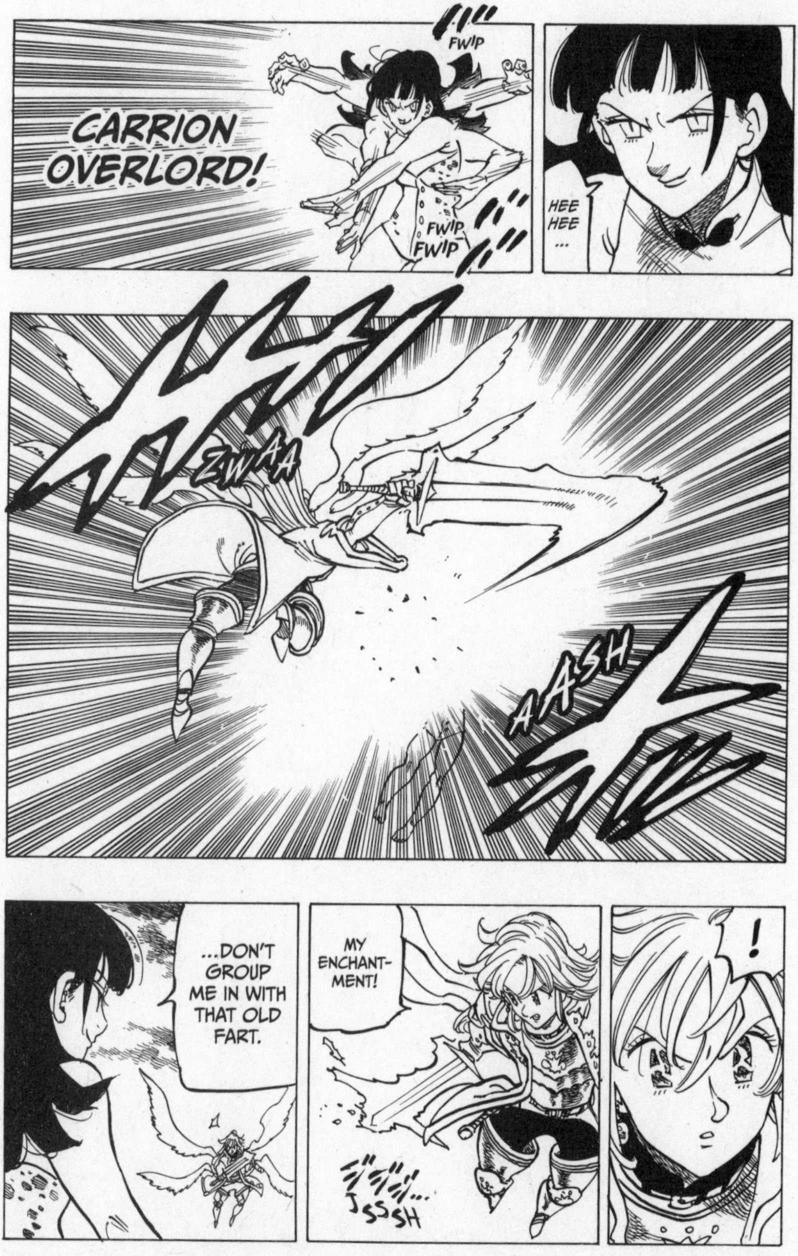
HEE HEE ...
FWIP
CARRION OVERLORD!
FWIP FWIP
ZWAA
AASH
!
MY ENCHANT-MENT!
JSSSH
...DON'T GROUP ME IN WITH THAT OLD FART.

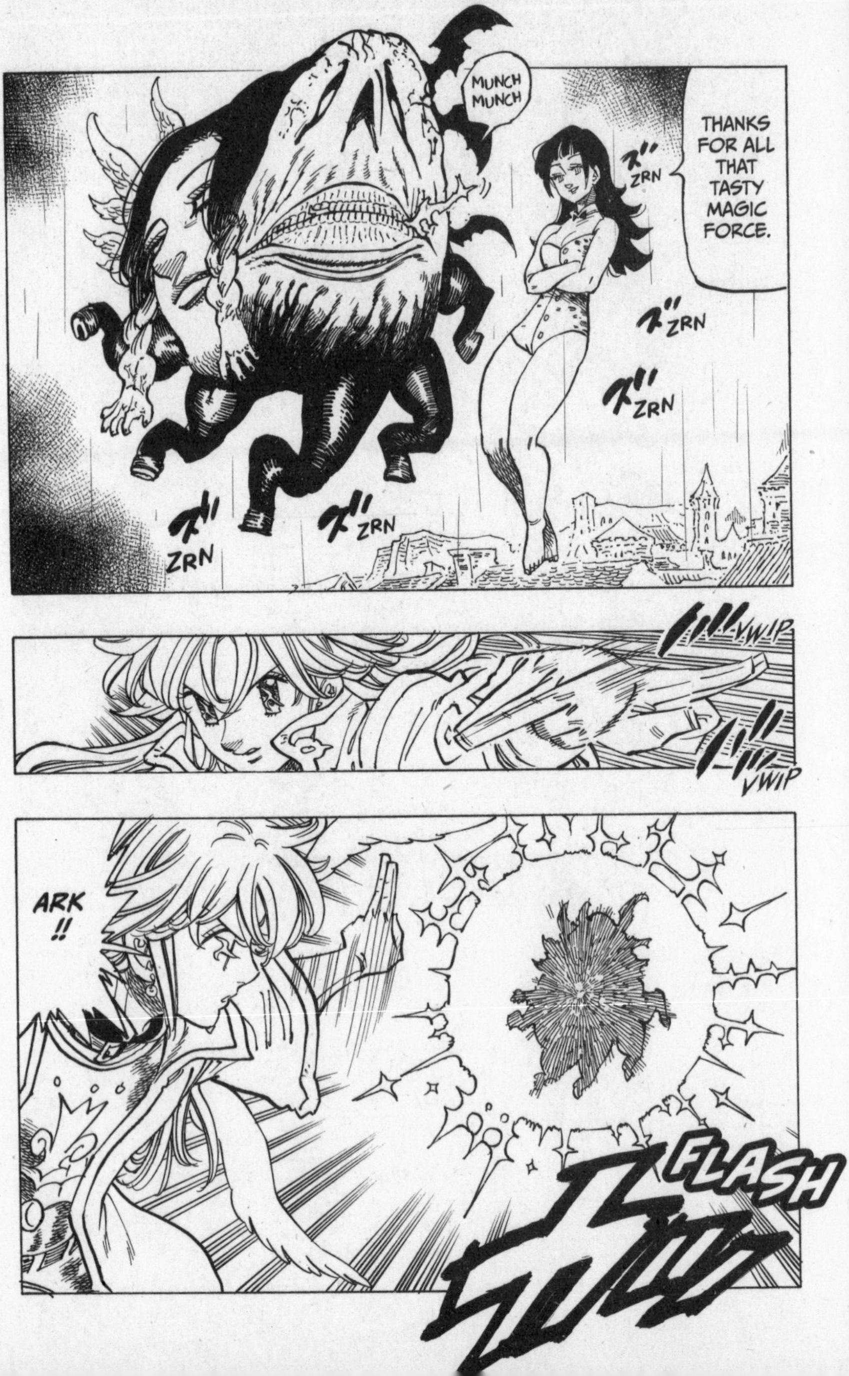
THANKS FOR ALL THAT TASTY MAGIC FORCE.
ZRN
MUNCH MUNCH
ZRN
ZRN
ZRN
ZRN
VWIP
VWIP
FLASH
ARK !!

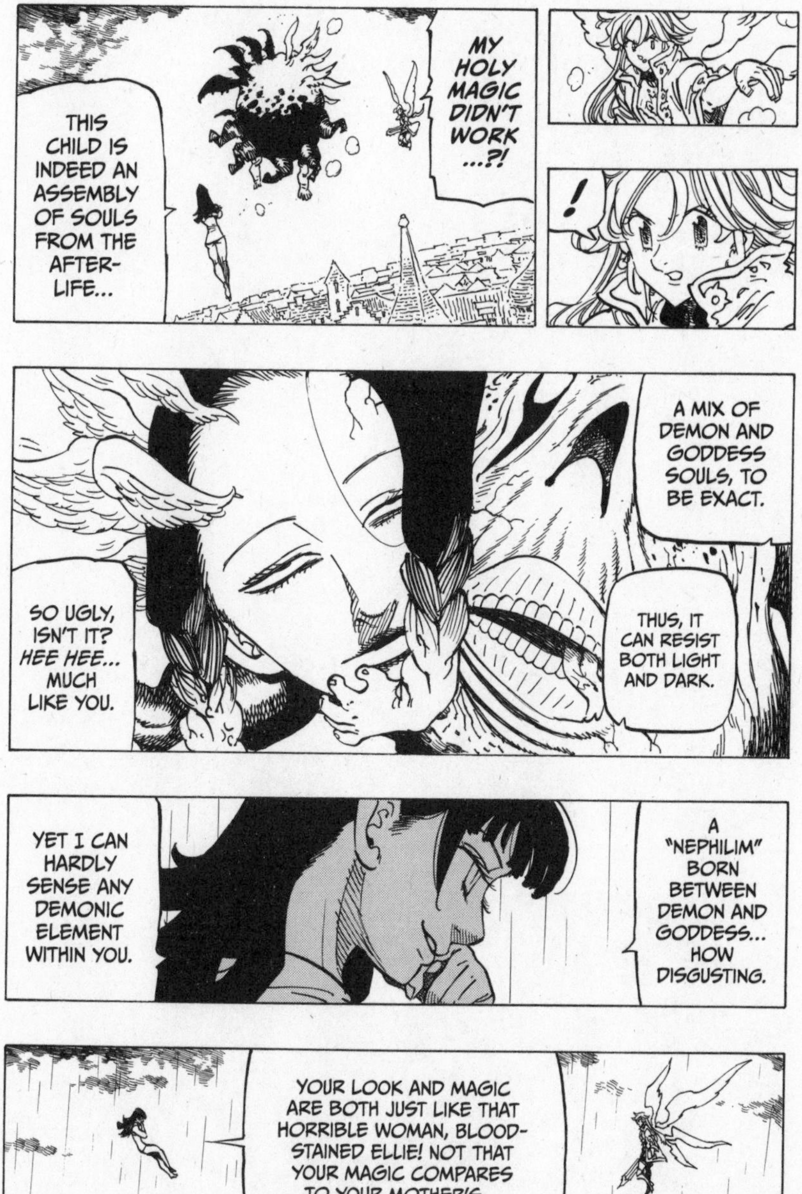
!
MY HOLY MAGIC DIDN'T WORK ...?!
THIS CHILD IS INDEED AN ASSEMBLY OF SOULS FROM THE AFTER-LIFE...
A MIX OF DEMON AND GODDESS SOULS, TO BE EXACT.
THUS, IT CAN RESIST BOTH LIGHT AND DARK.
SO UGLY, ISN'T IT? *HEE HEE...* MUCH LIKE YOU.
A "NEPHILIM" BORN BETWEEN DEMON AND GODDESS... HOW DISGUSTING.
YET I CAN HARDLY SENSE ANY DEMONIC ELEMENT WITHIN YOU.
YOUR LOOK AND MAGIC ARE BOTH JUST LIKE THAT HORRIBLE WOMAN, BLOOD-STAINED ELLIE! NOT THAT YOUR MAGIC COMPARES TO YOUR MOTHER'S...

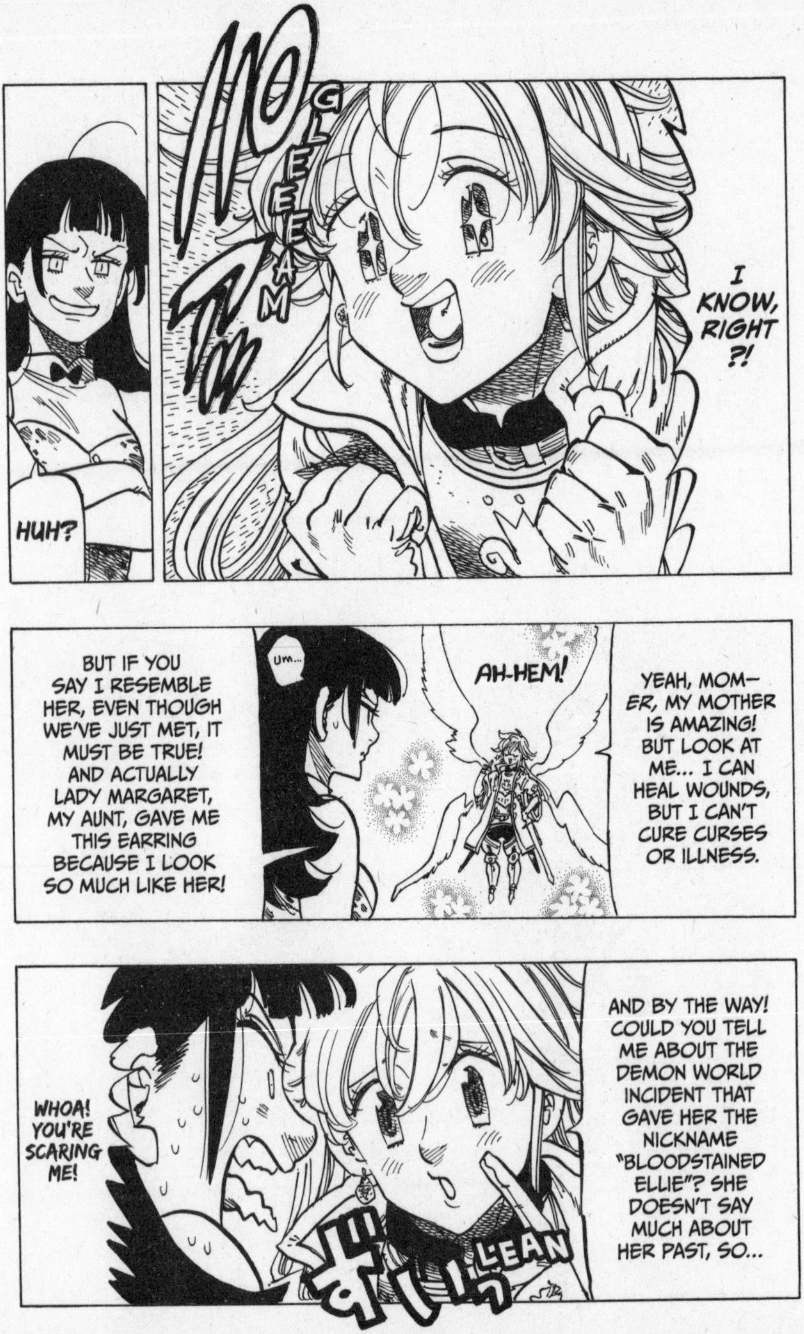
GLEEEAM
I KNOW, RIGHT?!
HUH?
YEAH, MOM— ER, MY MOTHER IS AMAZING! BUT LOOK AT ME... I CAN HEAL WOUNDS, BUT I CAN'T CURE CURSES OR ILLNESS.
AH-HEM!
UM...
BUT IF YOU SAY I RESEMBLE HER, EVEN THOUGH WE'VE JUST MET, IT MUST BE TRUE! AND ACTUALLY LADY MARGARET, MY AUNT, GAVE ME THIS EARRING BECAUSE I LOOK SO MUCH LIKE HER!
AND BY THE WAY! COULD YOU TELL ME ABOUT THE DEMON WORLD INCIDENT THAT GAVE HER THE NICKNAME "BLOODSTAINED ELLIE"? SHE DOESN'T SAY MUCH ABOUT HER PAST, SO...
LEAN
WHOA! YOU'RE SCARING ME!

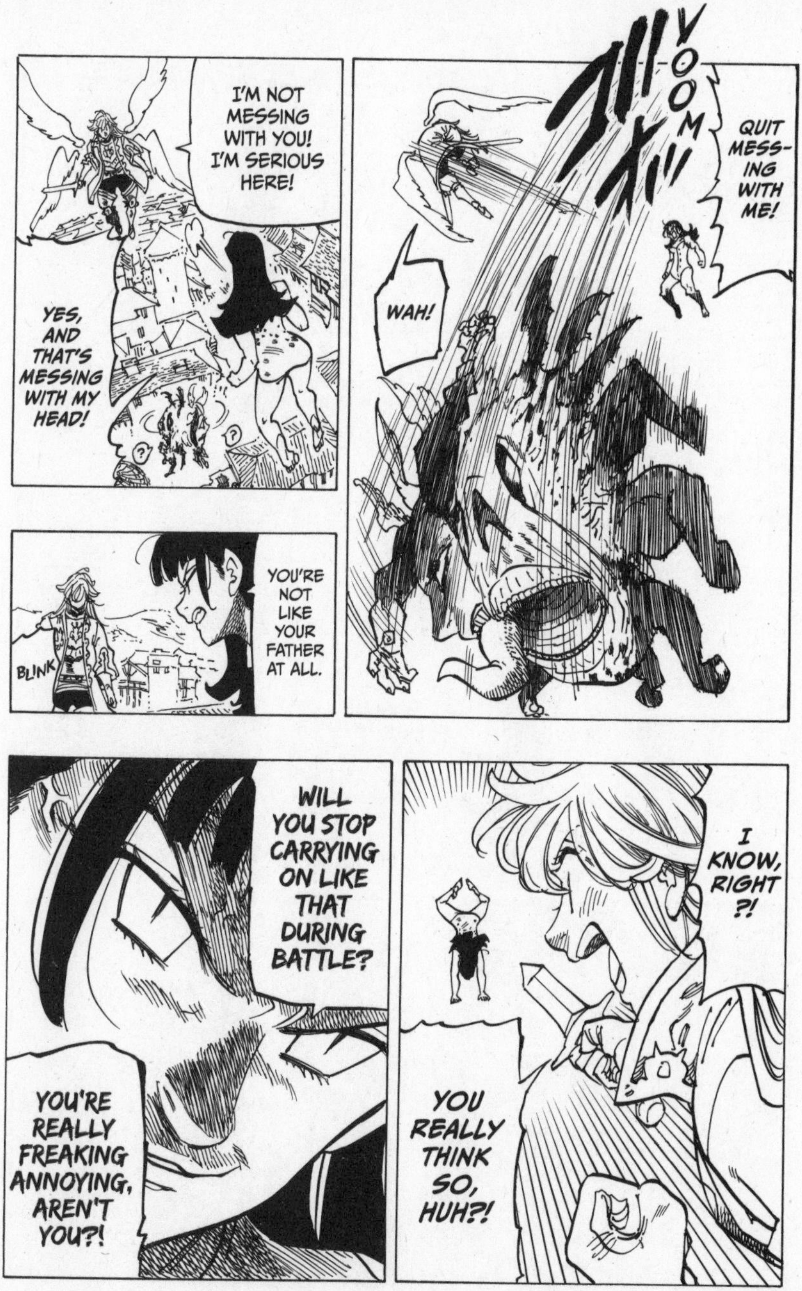
VOOM
QUIT MESSING WITH ME!
WAH!
I'M NOT MESSING WITH YOU! I'M SERIOUS HERE!
YES, AND THAT'S MESSING WITH MY HEAD!
YOU'RE NOT LIKE YOUR FATHER AT ALL.
BLINK
I KNOW, RIGHT?!
YOU REALLY THINK SO, HUH?!
WILL YOU STOP CARRYING ON LIKE THAT DURING BATTLE?
YOU'RE REALLY FREAKING ANNOYING, AREN'T YOU?!

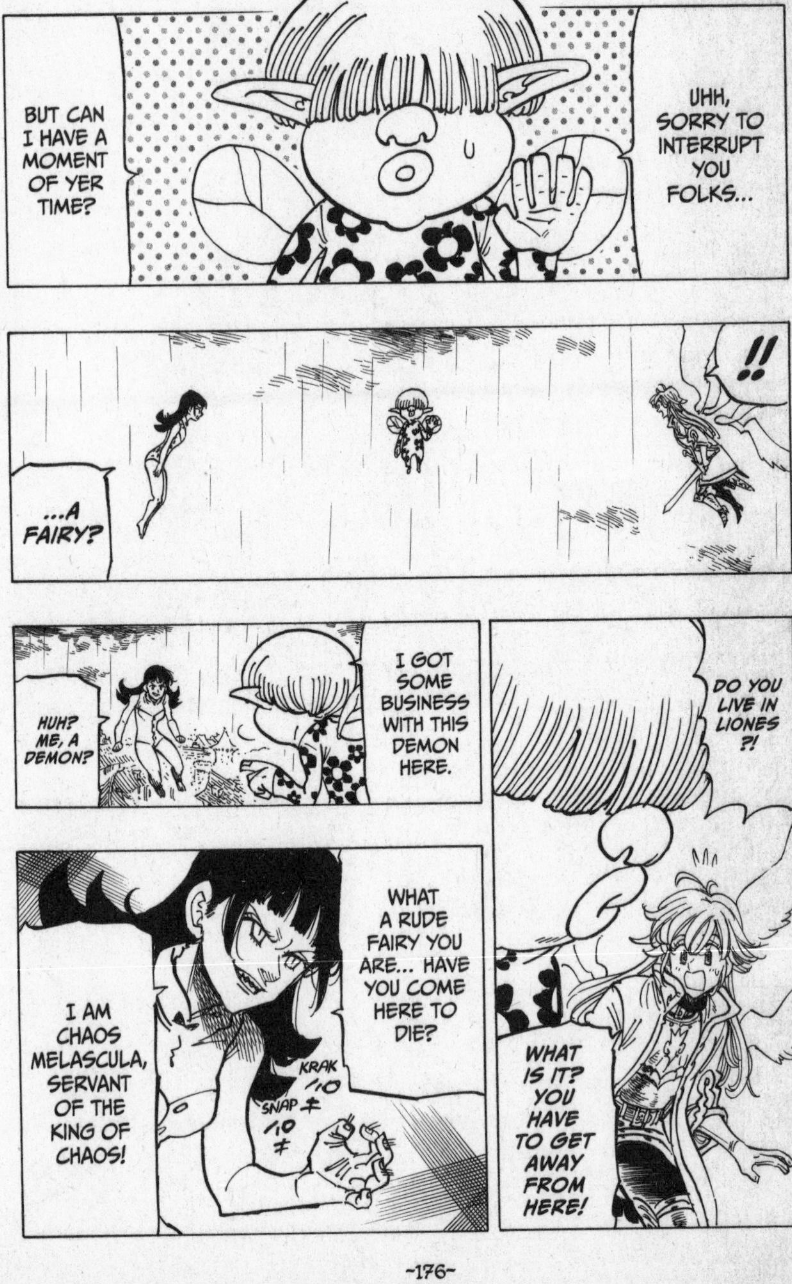
UHH, SORRY TO INTERRUPT YOU FOLKS...
BUT CAN I HAVE A MOMENT OF YER TIME?
!!
...A FAIRY?
DO YOU LIVE IN LIONES ?!
WHAT IS IT? YOU HAVE TO GET AWAY FROM HERE!
I GOT SOME BUSINESS WITH THIS DEMON HERE.
HUH? ME, A DEMON?
WHAT A RUDE FAIRY YOU ARE... HAVE YOU COME HERE TO DIE?
KRAK
SNAP
I AM CHAOS MELASCULA, SERVANT OF THE KING OF CHAOS!

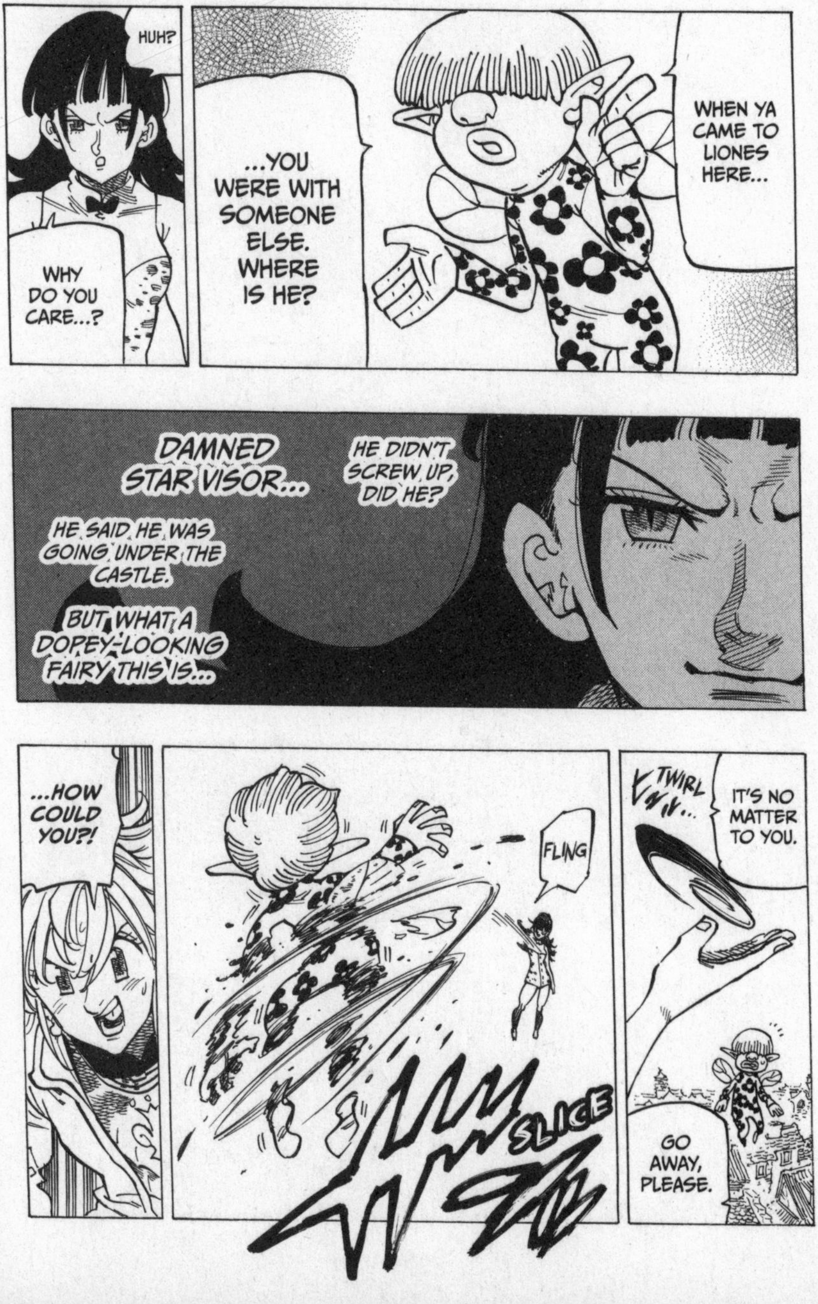
WHEN YA CAME TO LIONES HERE...
...YOU WERE WITH SOMEONE ELSE. WHERE IS HE?
HUH?
WHY DO YOU CARE...?
HE DIDN'T SCREW UP, DID HE?
DAMNED STAR VISOR...
HE SAID HE WAS GOING UNDER THE CASTLE.
BUT WHAT A DOPEY-LOOKING FAIRY THIS IS...
TWIRL
IT'S NO MATTER TO YOU.
GO AWAY, PLEASE.
FLING
SLICE
...HOW COULD YOU?!

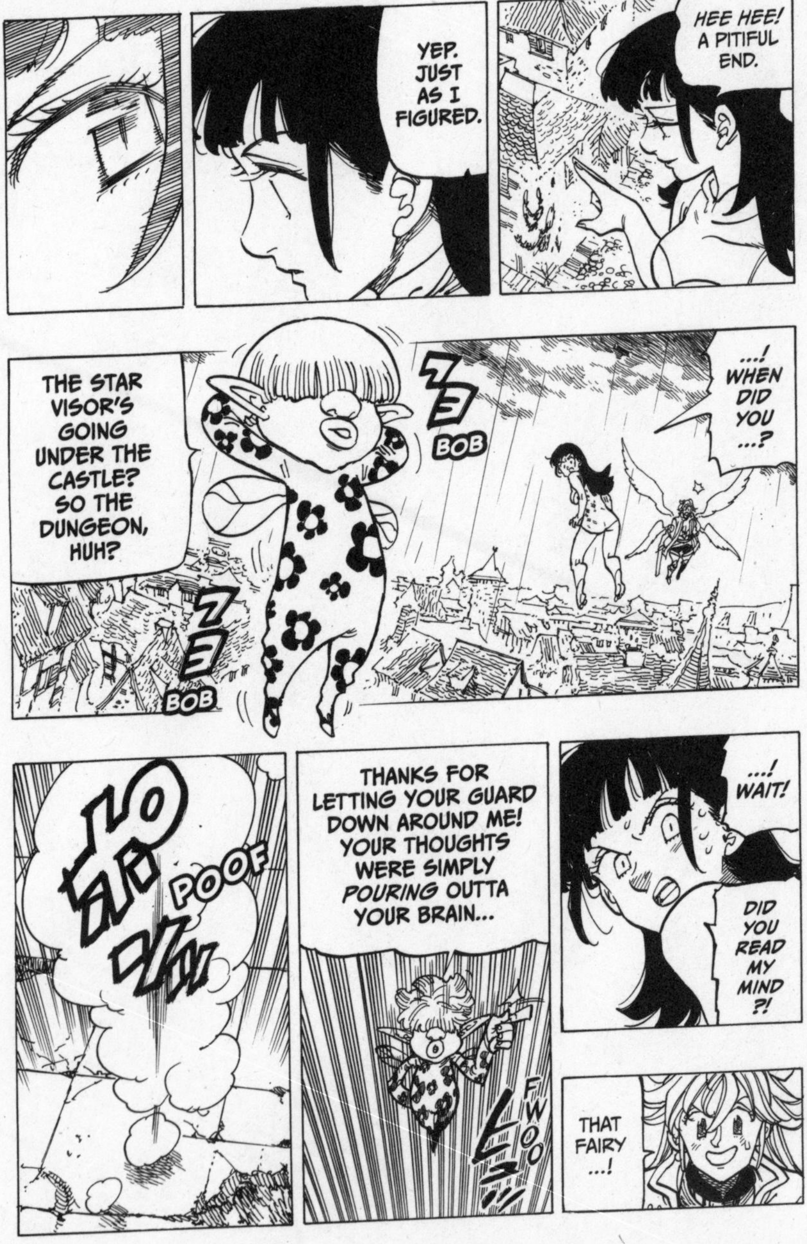
HEE HEE! A PITIFUL END.
YEP. JUST AS I FIGURED.
...! WHEN DID YOU ...?
BOB
BOB
THE STAR VISOR'S GOING UNDER THE CASTLE? SO THE DUNGEON, HUH?
...! WAIT!
DID YOU READ MY MIND ?!
THAT FAIRY ...!
THANKS FOR LETTING YOUR GUARD DOWN AROUND ME! YOUR THOUGHTS WERE SIMPLY *POURING* OUTTA YOUR BRAIN...
FWOO
POOF

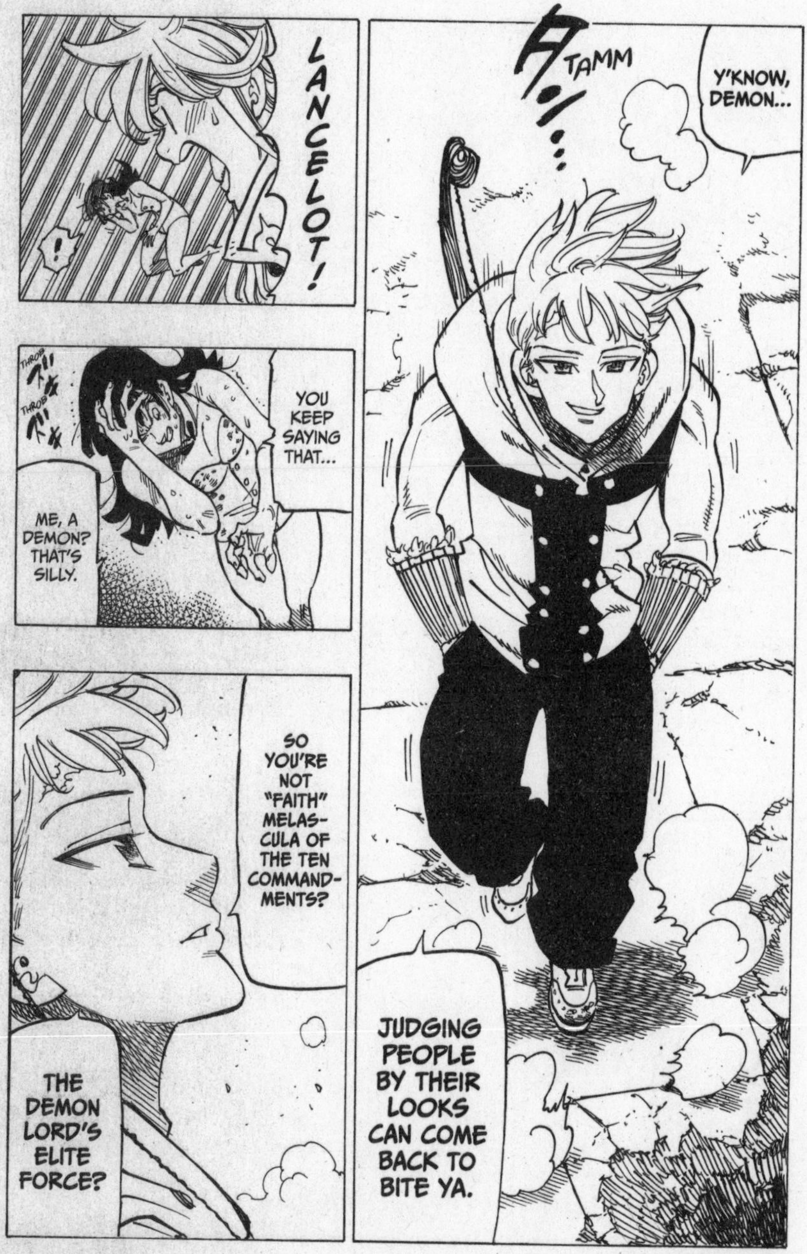
TAMM
Y'KNOW, DEMON...
JUDGING PEOPLE BY THEIR LOOKS CAN COME BACK TO BITE YA.
LANCELOT!
!
THROB
THROB
YOU KEEP SAYING THAT...
ME, A DEMON? THAT'S SILLY.
SO YOU'RE NOT "FAITH" MELASCULA OF THE TEN COMMANDMENTS?
THE DEMON LORD'S ELITE FORCE?

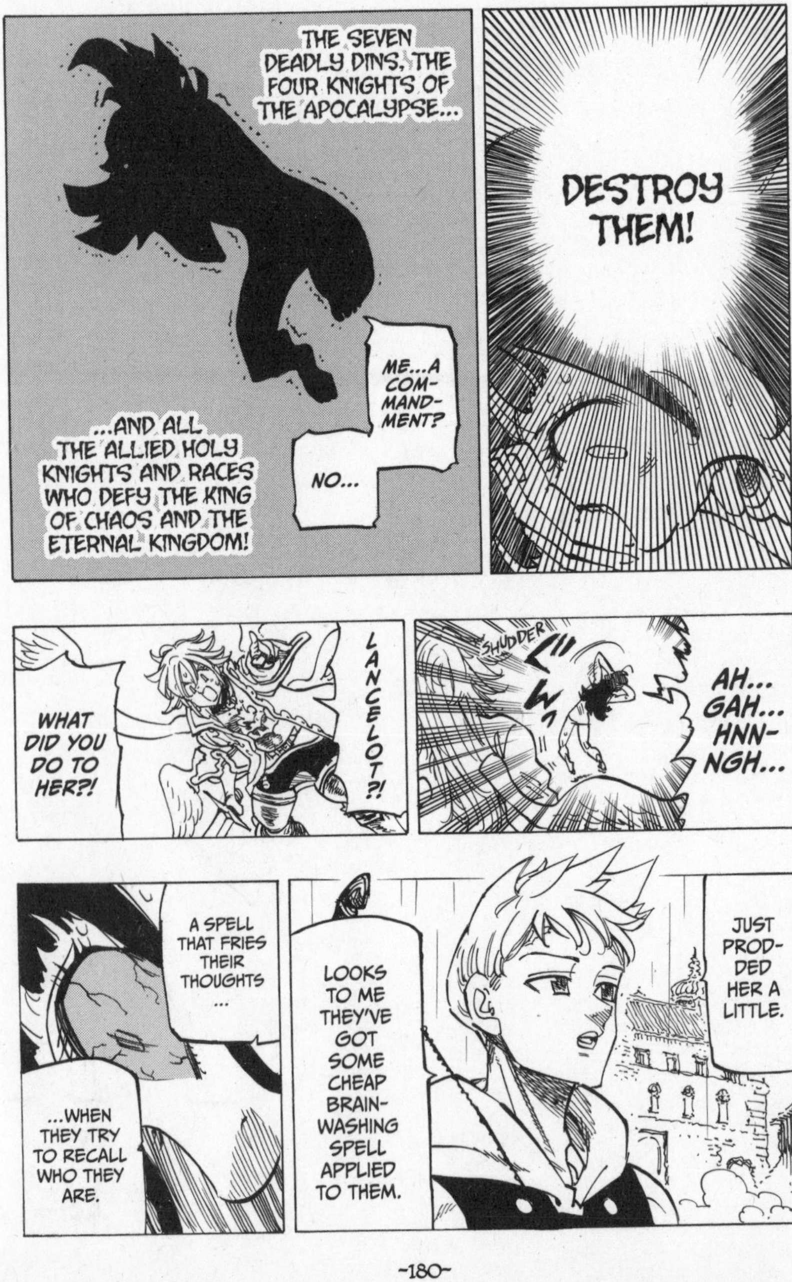
DESTROY THEM!
THE SEVEN DEADLY DINS, THE FOUR KNIGHTS OF THE APOCALYPSE...
ME...A COMMANDMENT?
NO...
...AND ALL THE ALLIED HOLY KNIGHTS AND RACES WHO DEFY THE KING OF CHAOS AND THE ETERNAL KINGDOM!
SHUDDER
AH... GAH... HNN-NGH...
LANCELOT?!
WHAT DID YOU DO TO HER?!
JUST PRODDED HER A LITTLE.
LOOKS TO ME THEY'VE GOT SOME CHEAP BRAINWASHING SPELL APPLIED TO THEM.
A SPELL THAT FRIES THEIR THOUGHTS...
...WHEN THEY TRY TO RECALL WHO THEY ARE.

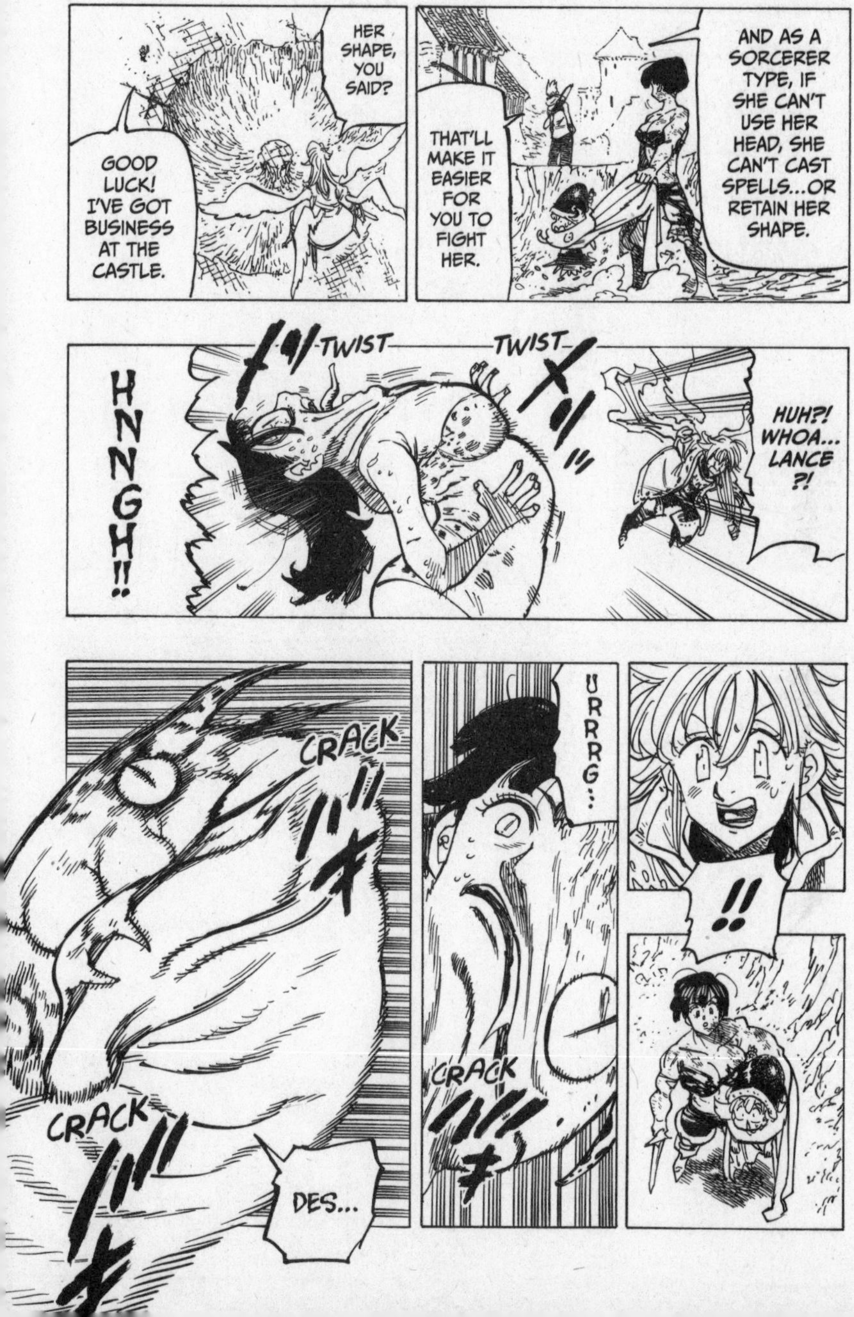
AND AS A SORCERER TYPE, IF SHE CAN'T USE HER HEAD, SHE CAN'T CAST SPELLS...OR RETAIN HER SHAPE.
THAT'LL MAKE IT EASIER FOR YOU TO FIGHT HER.
HER SHAPE, YOU SAID?
GOOD LUCK! I'VE GOT BUSINESS AT THE CASTLE.
HUH?! WHOA... LANCE?!
TWIST
TWIST
HNNGH!!
!!
URRRG...
CRACK
CRACK
CRACK
DES...

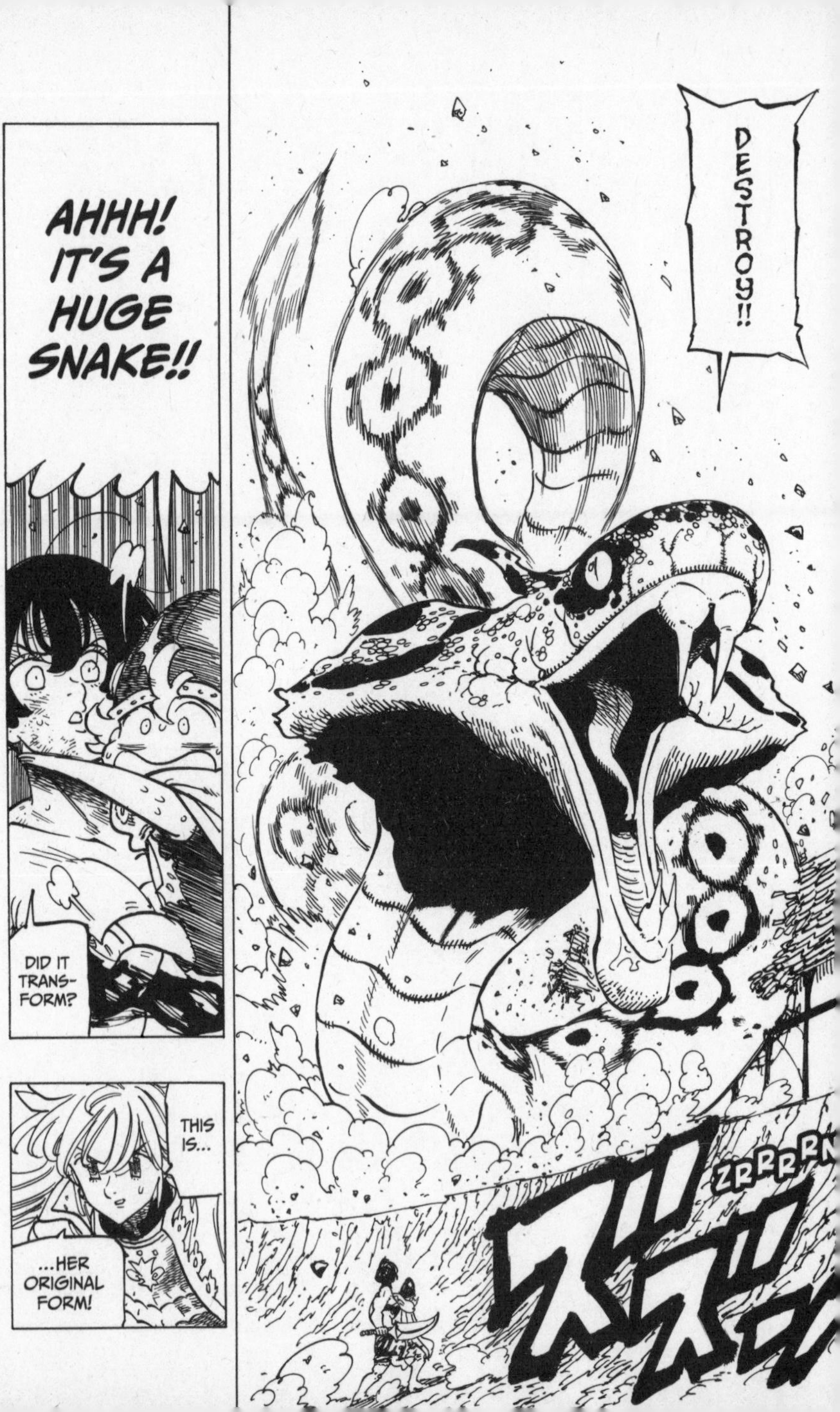
DESTROY!!
ZRRRRN
AHHH! IT'S A HUGE SNAKE!!
DID IT TRANS-FORM?
THIS IS...
...HER ORIGINAL FORM!

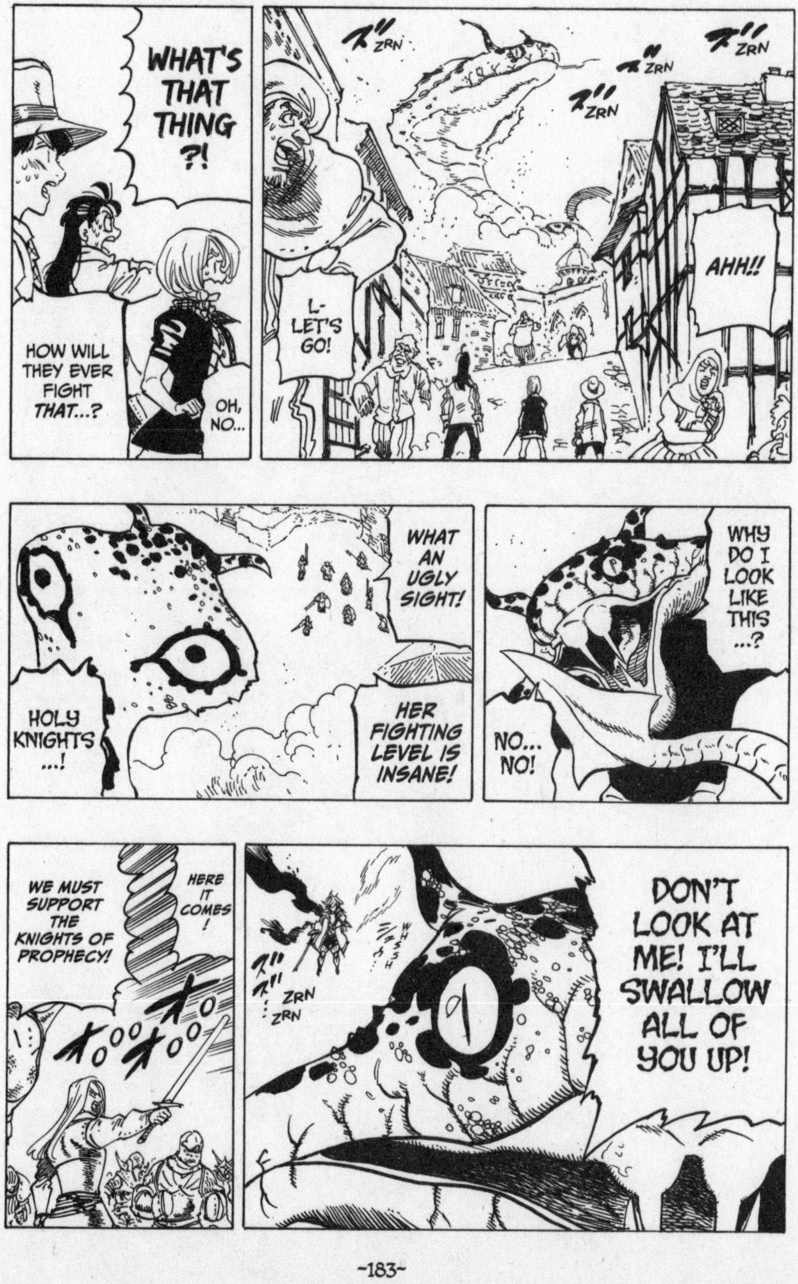

ZRN
ZRN
ZRN
ZRN
AHH!!
L- LET'S GO!
WHAT'S THAT THING?!
OH, NO...
HOW WILL THEY EVER FIGHT THAT...?
WHY DO I LOOK LIKE THIS ...?
NO... NO!
WHAT AN UGLY SIGHT!
HER FIGHTING LEVEL IS INSANE!
HOLY KNIGHTS ...!
DON'T LOOK AT ME! I'LL SWALLOW ALL OF YOU UP!
WHSSH
ZRN
ZRN
HERE IT COMES!
WE MUST SUPPORT THE KNIGHTS OF PROPHECY!

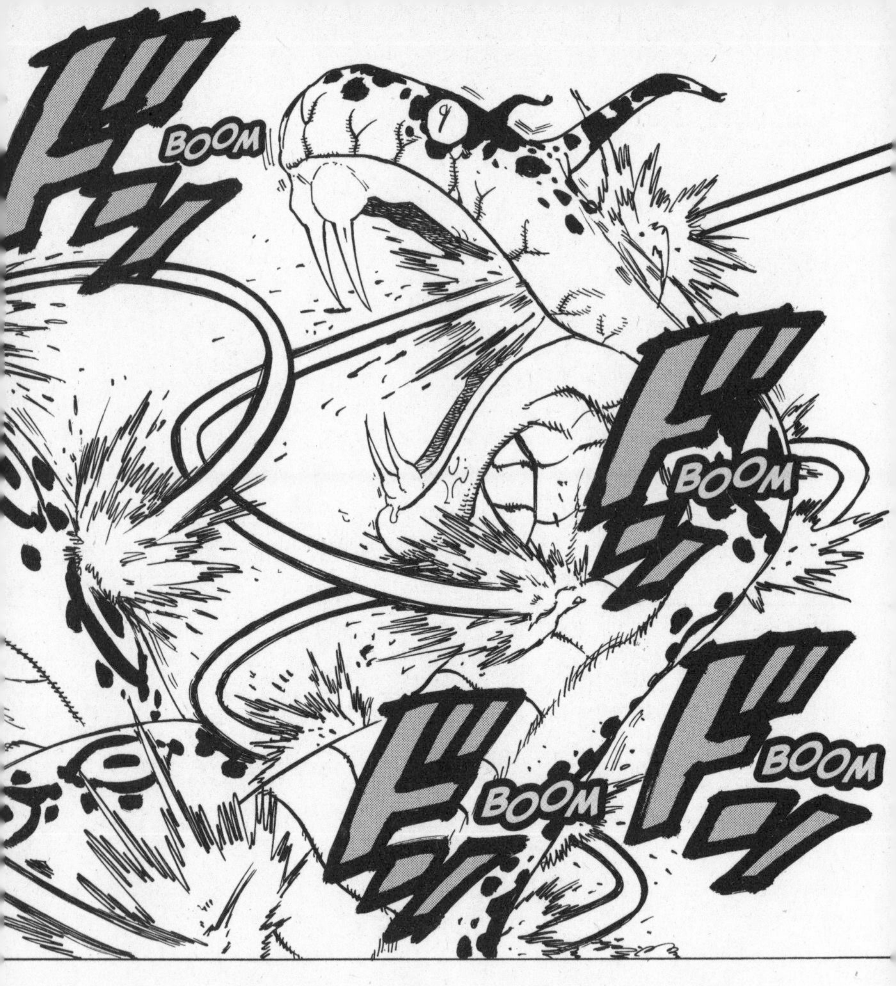
ドッ
BOOM
ドッ
BOOM
ドッ
BOOM
ドッ
BOOM
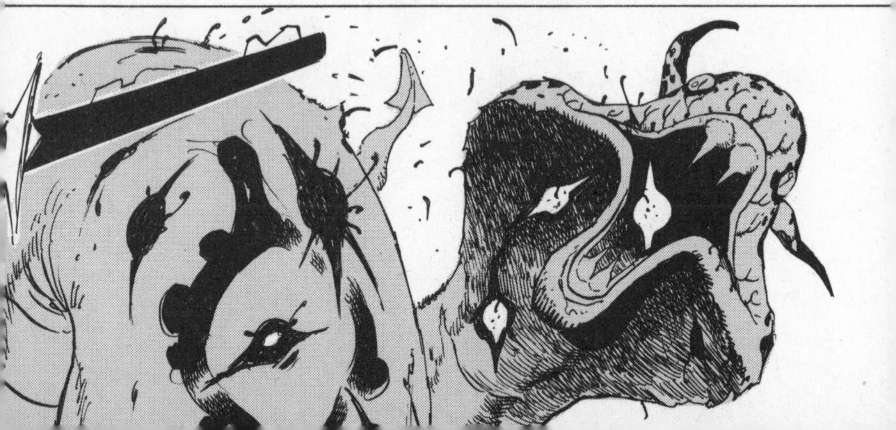

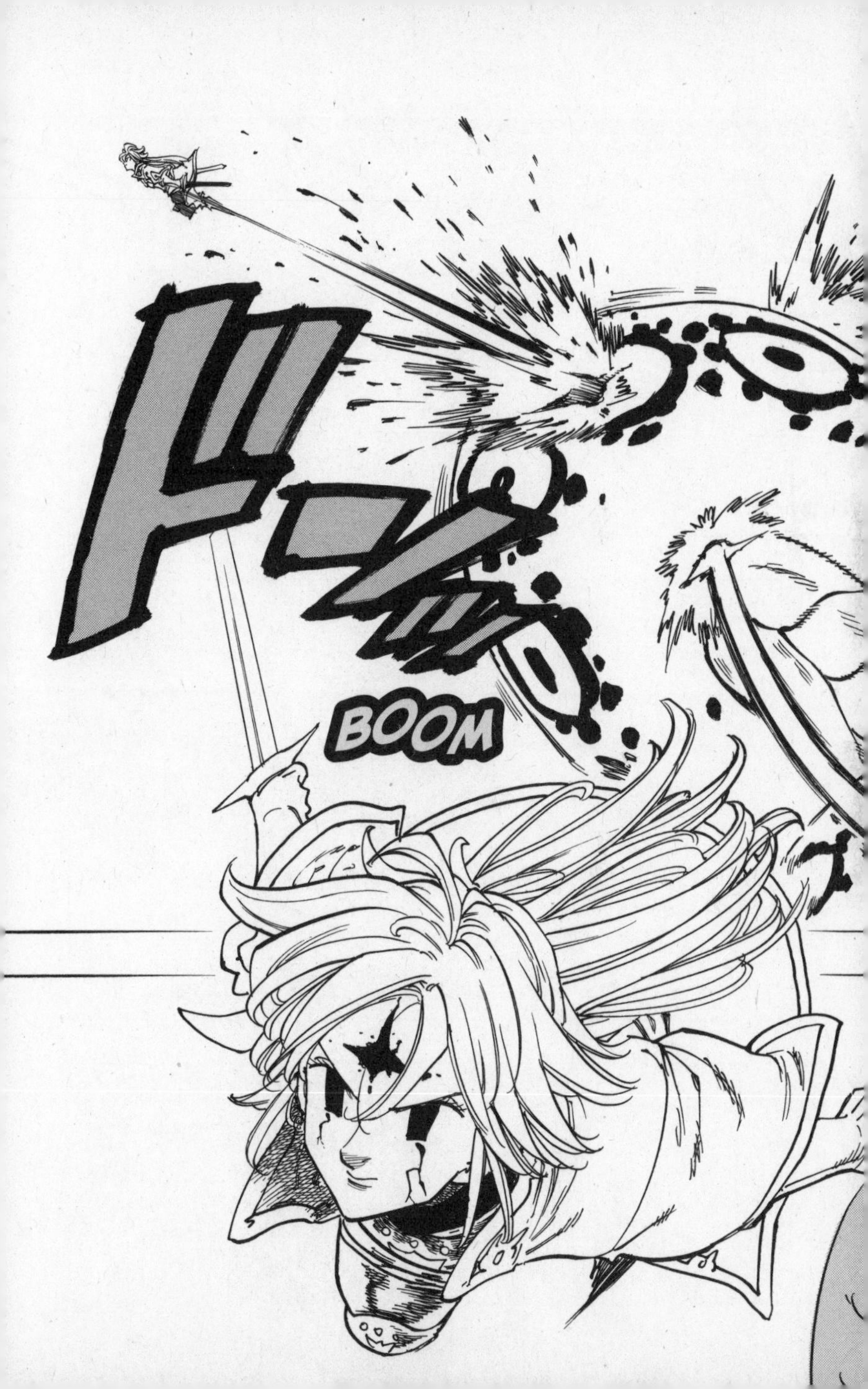
ドーン
BOOM

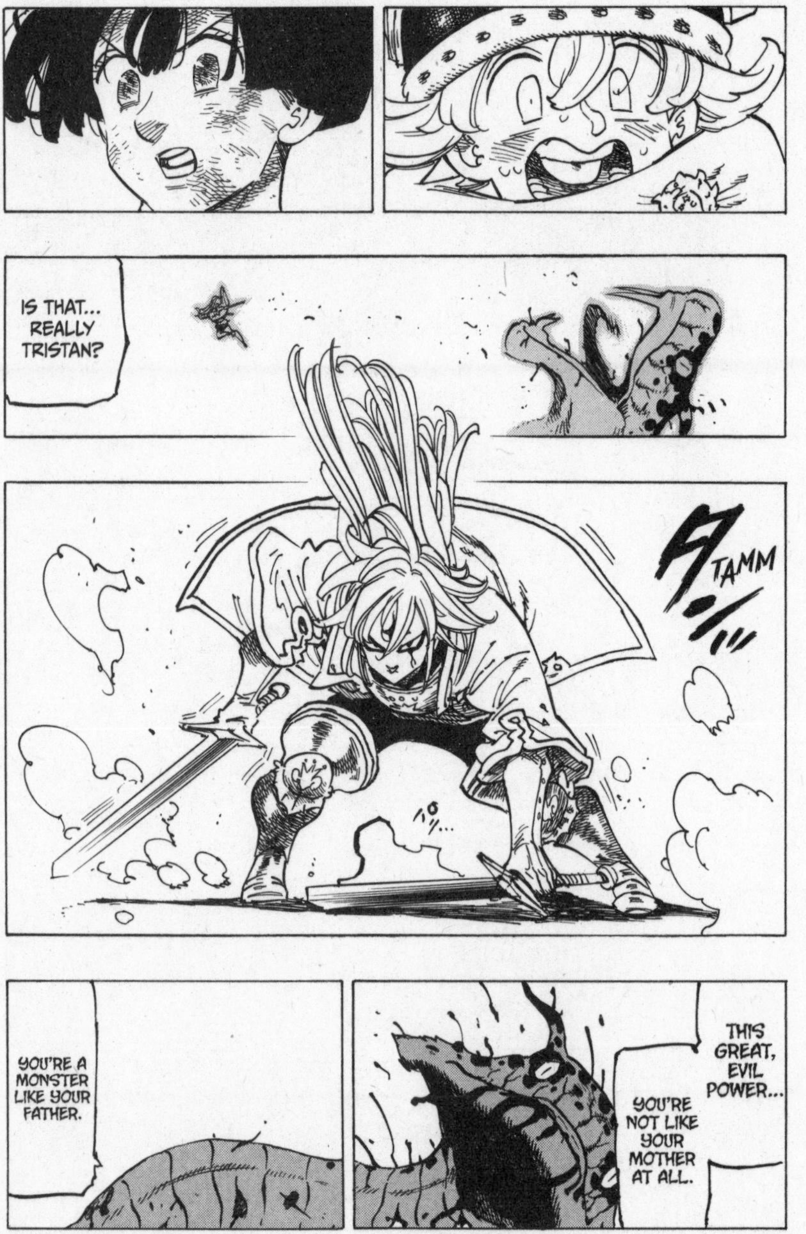

IS THAT... REALLY TRISTAN?
STAMM
THIS GREAT, EVIL POWER...
YOU'RE NOT LIKE YOUR MOTHER AT ALL.
YOU'RE A MONSTER LIKE YOUR FATHER.

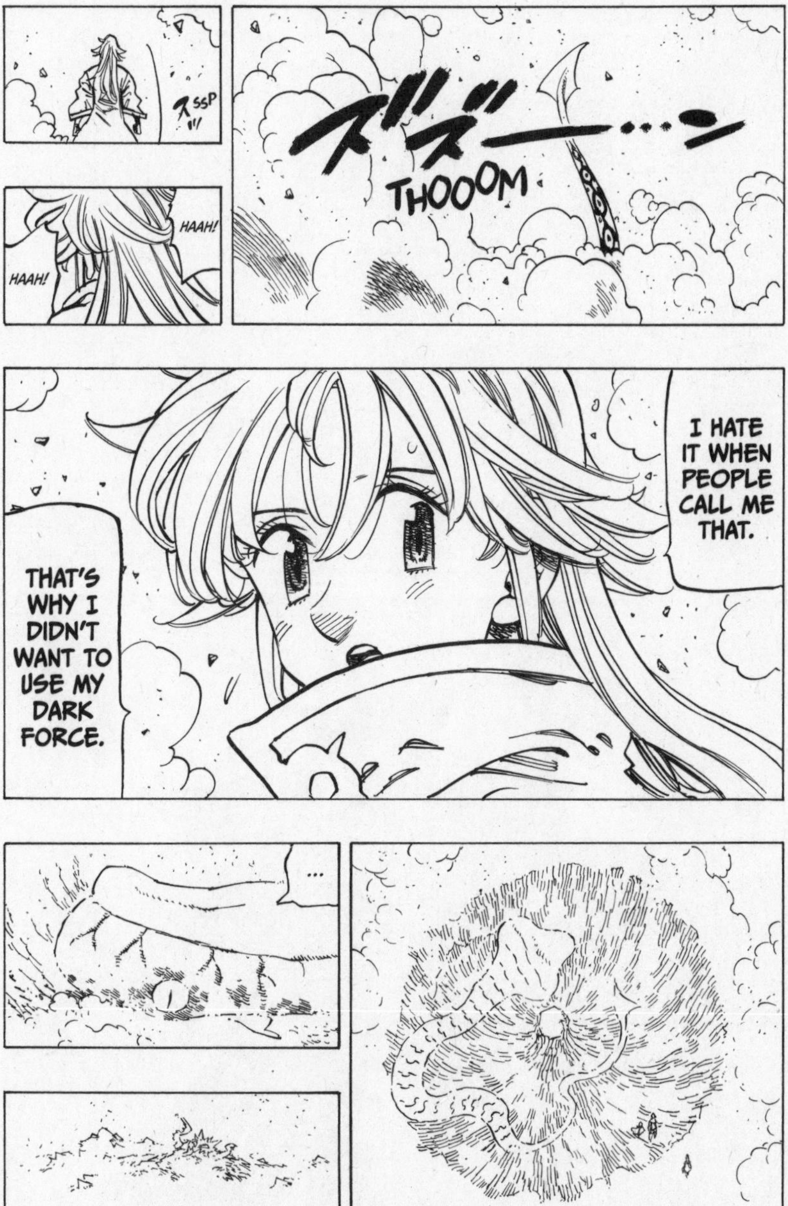
ズズー…ン
THOOOM
スッ
SSP
HAAH!
HAAH!
I HATE IT WHEN PEOPLE CALL ME THAT.
THAT'S WHY I DIDN'T WANT TO USE MY DARK FORCE.
...

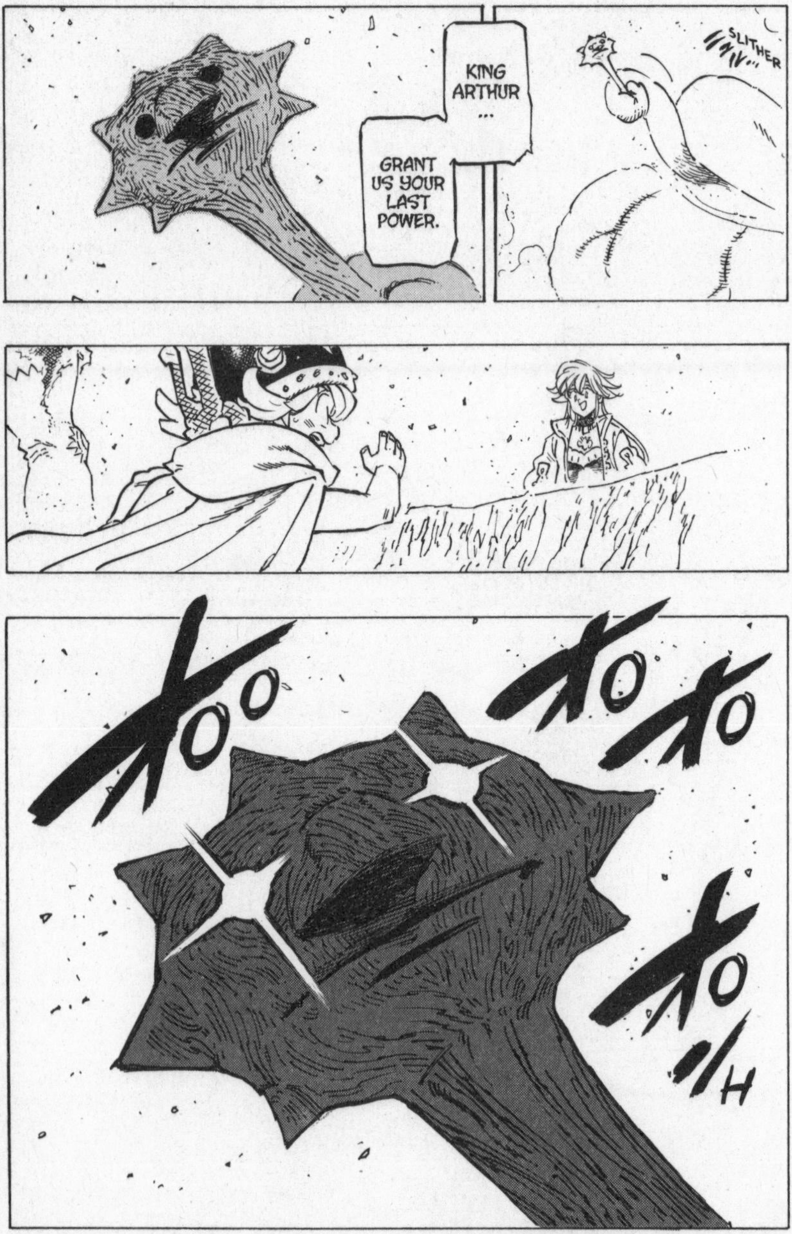
SLITHER
KING ARTHUR ...
GRANT US YOUR LAST POWER.
KOO KO KO KOH

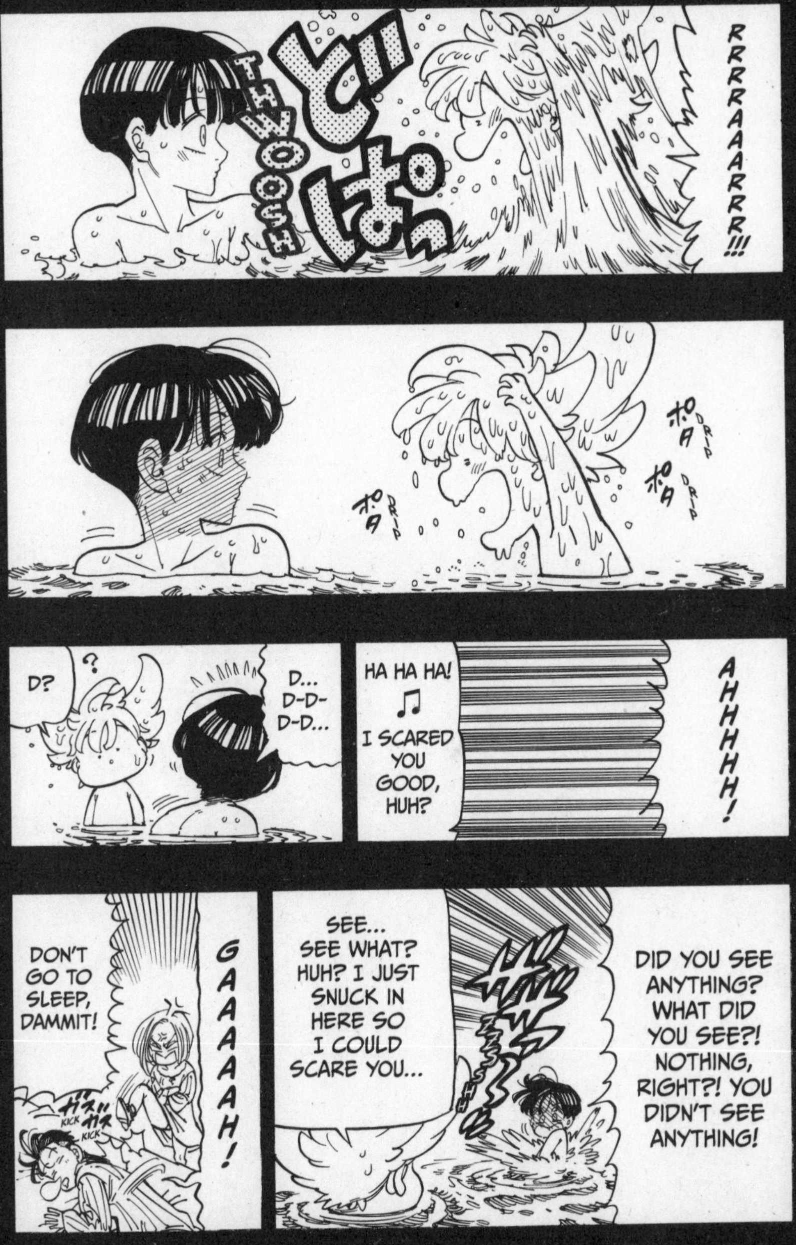
RRRRAAARRR!!!
どぱっ
THWOOSH
ポタ
DRIP
ポタ
DRIP
ポタ
DRIP
AHHHHHH!
HA HA HA! ♫ I SCARED YOU GOOD, HUH?
D... D-D-D-D...
D?
DID YOU SEE ANYTHING? WHAT DID YOU SEE?! NOTHING, RIGHT?! YOU DIDN'T SEE ANYTHING!
SEE... SEE WHAT? HUH? I JUST SNUCK IN HERE SO I COULD SCARE YOU...
GAAAAAAH!
DON'T GO TO SLEEP, DAMMIT!
KICK
KICK

END

AND THE KNIGHTS OF CHAOS!!

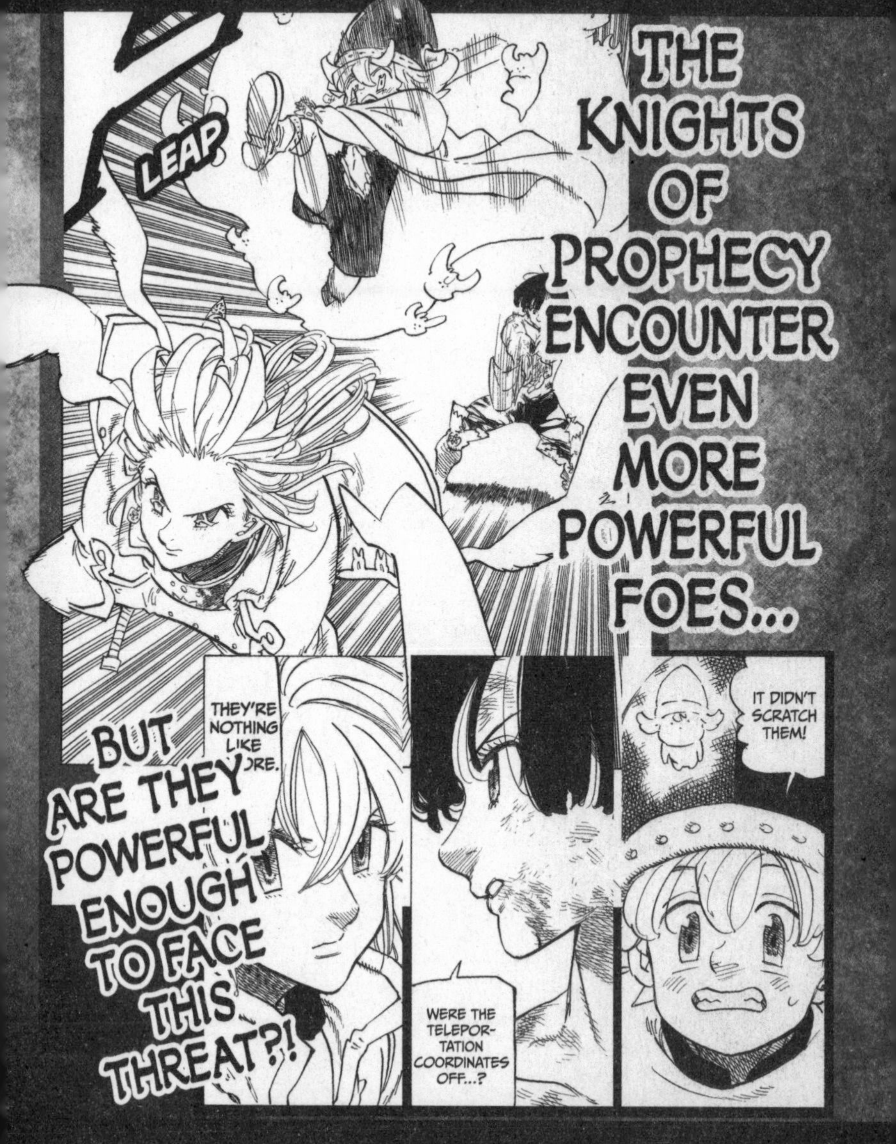
THE KNIGHTS OF PROPHECY ENCOUNTER EVEN MORE POWERFUL FOES...
LEAP
IT DIDN'T SCRATCH THEM!
WERE THE TELEPORTATION COORDINATES OFF...?
THEY'RE NOTHING LIKE
BUT ARE THEY POWERFUL ENOUGH TO FACE THIS THREAT?!

THERE'S NO ESCAPING THIS BATTLE...